GOLD TRADING BOOT CAMP

GOLD TRADING
BOOT CAMP

HOW TO MASTER THE BASICS AND BECOME
A SUCCESSFUL COMMODITIES INVESTOR

GREGORY T. WELDON

BICENTENNIAL
1807
WILEY
2007
BICENTENNIAL

John Wiley & Sons, Inc.

Published by John Wiley & Sons, Inc., Hoboken, New Jersey.
Published simultaneously in Canada.

Wiley Bicentennial Logo: Richard J. Pacifico.

For general information on our other products and services or for technical support,
please contact our Customer Care Department within the United States at
(800) 762-2974, outside the United States at (317) 572-3993 or fax (317) 572-4002.

Wiley also publishes its books in a variety of electronic formats. Some content that
appears in print may not be available in electronic books. For more information about
Wiley products, visit our web site at www.wiley.com.

Library of Congress Cataloging-in-Publication Data:

Weldon, Gregory T., 1960–
    Gold trading boot camp : how to master the basics and become a successful
commodities investor / Gregory T. Weldon.
        p.   cm.
    Includes bibliographical references and index.
    ISBN-13 978-0-471-72800-9 (cloth)
    1. Gold. 2. Gold—Purchasing. 3. Commodity exchanges. 4. Gold—United
States. 5. Gold—Purchasing—United States. 6. Commodity exchanges—United
States. I. Title.
    HG293.W45 2007
    332.64′42410973—dc22

                                                                    2006034740

Printed in the United States of America.

10   9   8   7   6   5   4   3

CONTENTS

Part Seven   Defining and Managing Risk

Part Eight   Putting It All Together

FOREWORD

Commodity trading is never easy. It's not meant to be, but it can be fun and it certainly can be profitable when done well. But even the most experienced investors cannot keep up with the changing markets as often and as well as they'd like because the very nature of the commodities market is to be confusing far more often than not. But amidst that seeming confusion, order can be found.

It does not matter if you are trading gold, soybeans, or bonds, a successful speculator has to keep an eye on what is happening in many markets around the world. At the same time, the speculator must be alert and mindful of his or her individual position in the marketplace.

I have been an observer/participant in the commodities world for more than 30 years. During that time, either as a hedger, floor trader, foreign exchange dealer, bond trader, or individual speculator, I've had far more than my share of dramatic ups and downs in the commodities markets.

It is in this light that I encourage traders everywhere to read Greg Weldon's book. This book offers an intimate and insightful account of a professional trader from his first days as a novice walking onto the floor of the Commodities Exchange Center through the present, where he sits at home in New Jersey surrounded by sophisticated technology that provides him with ready access to data about markets in all corners of the world.

Not everyone will have the intellectual or psychological wherewithal to be a trader, but there's still a good deal to be learned from *Gold Trading Boot Camp*. Whether you're trading your own account, using a professional advisor, or simply wondering whether you have the courage to trade on your own, this book offers an accessible, reasonable, and usable approach to the commodities market. *Gold Trading Boot Camp* provides an overview to the world of commodities and how this world changes, and will change in the future, for investors. Further, Greg explains his approach to the markets, teaching those who read his book the things he relies up that can tell him where the markets may go—and when. Greg explains technical analysis; he explains trend identification; he explains momentum trading—how to understand the relationship between the U.S. economy, global markets, and more.

As I said, commodities trading is not easy, and it most certainly is not for everyone. That's why Greg's no-nonsense, disciplined approach makes sense. We must learn to trade like mercenaries, trading not on the bull side or the bear side, but on the right side, as Jesse Livermore once said. You have to learn to fight and invest on the winning side and be able to change sides immediately when one side has gained the upper hand. This is what Greg's book will help you to do. I encourage every trader—old or new—to read this book and learn its lessons.

DENNIS GARTMAN
President of Gartman Letter

ACKNOWLEDGMENTS

I'd like to thank my parents for their tough-yet-caring love, and for providing me with everything and anything a son could ever wish for. Thank you for giving me the best chance possible to succeed, in business, and in life.

I would particularly like to thank my dad for his never-ending support, loyalty, advice, constructive criticism, and praise. If not for his unconditional love, this book would have never been started, let alone completed. My dad gave, and gave, and gave, and he keeps on giving, without ever asking for anything in return. Thank you. I love you, and I dedicate this book to you.

I want to thank my mother for her love and her courage in the face of grave illness. Her attitude has been inspirational to many of us, more than she will ever know.

I want to thank the gang at Stanley B. Bell and Company: (the late) Stanley Bell, Craig Bell, Don Tierney, and Eugene Pastore, along with my buddy Mike Devaney, for their selflessness and willingness to teach, tutor, and mentor me during my early years on the trading floor of the COMEX.

I want to thank the guys at Moore Capital Management: Bob De-Franco, James Kelley, Chris Pia, and Zack Bacon, in particular, for their support, loyalty, and willingness to share of themselves in helping me develop as a trader and macro-thinker.

I want to thank the crew at Commodities Corporation: Sandra D'Italia, Kathy Filliponi, Chris Rose, Sandra Kaul, Jim Liu, Will Allen, and especially Randy Rose, for their hard work, willingness to share their knowledge, and their friendship.

I want to thank the people at Prudential Securities—John Fallon, Cindy Pavia, Louis Lukac, Fernando Santos, Kathy Jones, Ray Keenan, and Joe "Mason" Madigan—for their loyal support and the time spent assisting me during my evolution as a trader and research provider.

I'd like to say thanks to the personalities at CNBC Television: Consuelo Mack, Ted David, Ron Insana, and Liz Clayman, along with all of the associate producers who have given me the opportunity to share my opinions and insights with the investment public.

I want to thank Scott Ramsey and Michael Strupp of Denali Asset Management, along with (the late) Bill Darby, Greg Parks, and Howie Levine, for their friendship and loyal support.

I want to thank James Grant and Dennis Gartman for their selflessness and their enthusiastic willingness to mentor me in the research business, throughout the past 10 years.

I want to thank Martin Lysaght and Bill O'Herron for playing the role of confidante, for their constant and continuous feedback, critique, and valuable input during the production of this book, and throughout my career . . . and for being the best friends a guy could ever want to have by his side.

I want to thank my "life friends": Mike "Ollie" Oliver, Bob "Bobby-G" Gorham, Bill "Willy" Stein, Craig Pruett, Regina Caggia, Lauren Brofazi, Mike Ferrara, Mike Greco, Adam Kaufman, Steve Sferra, Paul Vames, Dave Conway, Steve Wainwright, John "Johnny Balls" Ferrallo, Gene Pastore, Frank and Kathleen Cohane, Frank and Cheryl Oliver, Sue Oliver, Jim Liu, Clifford and Kristy Moricelli, Marie and (the late) Bob Gernhart, Susan Lee Caruso, (the late) Jim Hughes (the late) Rob Duich (the late) Lee Cordon, my high school basketball coach Mike O'Brien, and of course my two brothers, Brian and Doug . . . along with all those that I failed to mention.

I would like to thank my editor at John Wiley & Sons, Debra Englander. Debra's persistence, dedication, and, most of all, her unbelievable patience, made this incredibly difficult task quite a bit more enjoyable. I am not the easiest person to work with and Debra's unbelievable patience was critical in keeping me motivated, allowing me to finish this project.

I want to thank Judith Gernhart for her unconditional love, support, friendship, and never-ending belief in me, without which this book would never have been started, nor completed. I am eternally grateful to know you. I cherish the time we spent together and the love we shared, and always will.

I want to thank Eileen Cassidy, for her intensity, her passion, and her love. I appreciate all the time you spent assisting me with the editing of this book. Thank you for all the feedback and hard work. You are simply the best career coach I have ever had the pleasure of working with. I am so happy to have met you (for which I am indebted to "Queenie" Bea), and I look forward to being with you for the fulfillment of your birthday wish!

And I would like to thank newly found "life" friends-family, Jack and Joyce Cassidy, John and Tamara Cassidy, Bob and Maureen Bea, Kathleen Cassidy, Andy and Maryalice Goldsmith, Patrick Cassidy, Christopher Fedroff and all the kids (you too, little "Cassidy") . . . laughter and love make a perfect combination.

Last but not least, I want to thank my two children, Taylor and Victoria, for their unconditional love. You are the joy of my life, and watching you grow up has been the best part of the journey. I also dedicate this book to you.

GREGORY T. WELDON

GOLD TRADING
BOOT CAMP

PART ONE

Evolution of a Trader

Trial by Fire

I was walking onto the floor of the Commodities Exchange Center (CEC), formerly within the World Trade Center in New York City. It was 1984; the gold market had just gone through its most bullish price move in history and was in the midst of its postbubble collapse. I felt the same buzz that I used to have when I played basketball in college. The trading floor reminded me of a basketball court—it had that same electric energy coursing through the air. And, I was drawn to it from a place deep within my body.

Given the events of that dreadful day in September 2001, I hesitate even to mention the Twin Towers. But it is important to understand the significance of those buildings. The World Trade Center (WTC) was a testament to the development of global trade after the gold standard was abolished and also was evidence of the burgeoning wealth just beginning to be created in the downtown canyons and exchanges.

The gleaming Twin Towers embodied the proud-to-be-an-American feeling that permeated the country in 1984. There was a groundswell of new confidence that started at the bottom, worked its way up the ladder of wealth, and emanated from the fiscal and foreign policies implemented by Ronald Reagan. President Reagan had also restored a sense of pride in the average U.S. citizen, following the disastrous confidence hit during the Carter administration. Moreover, Paul Volcker, chairman of the Federal Reserve System, had played hardball with monetary policy during the go-go-inflation period. The era was capped by the Hunt brothers' attempt to squeeze the silver market and the run in gold bullion prices to new all-time highs above $800. For gold, it had been a decade-long bull market that began when Richard Nixon removed the shackles from the U.S. dollar.

By 1984, we had already hit the second downslope in the postinflation period, as confidence was rising, prices and interest rates finally were falling, and the U.S. stock market was beginning to make some noise. While unknown at the time, the stirrings in the equity arena, flat for the better part of a decade, reflected the early phases of an evolution that would dominate the financial landscape up to the 1987 crash (and well beyond, through today).

The CEC was like a temple constructed to honor the financial gods. Huge price boards covered three of the four walls that ran more than a hundred yards on each side, with listings of dozens of commodities from potatoes to orange juice, from cotton to sugar, from platinum to heating oil and, of course, gold, silver, and copper. Under each commodity, a number of months were listed, and to the side of each month, there was a series of numbers. Those numbers represented the last trade, the first previous trade, the second previous trade, the third previous trade, the opening range, the high of the day, the low of the day, and yesterday's change.

Imagine those enormous walls covered with constantly changing numbers, flipping a thousand times faster than the train schedule at Penn Station, with people frantically jousting just to secure a space to stand. It was easily the most energetic place I had ever encountered. As I walked across the floor, I observed what can only be described as mayhem: men and women screaming at other men and women, people screaming into phones and at each other on phones, people sprinting across the floor oblivious to the bodies that went flying in nearly every direction. Arms were flailing, fists pumping, faces snarling, mouths drooling, foreheads sweating, and then there was more screaming. I did not at all understand what was happening, but I knew I had found the place I wanted to be. . . .

"Fifty bid for five" . . . "FIFTY BID FOR FIVE DAMMIT."

"Hey, am I filled or what, what are you doing in there, C'MON DAMMIT, AM I FILLED, it's trading at ten, C'MON."

"Tony, HEY Tony, TONY, HEYYYYY TOOOOONY."

"At ten, at ten, at ten, at ten, sold two, at ten, at ten, sold five, sold five, at twenty, at twenty, twenty at twenty. SOLD, twenty at twenty."

"June-Auggie, how . . . June-Auggie, how, hey Jim, where is June-Auggie . . . one bid at thirty???"

"My stop is violated, hey, did you execute my stop?" . . .

It was a free-for-all, a bunch of psychopaths screaming at one another in a foreign language that I could not understand. It was not the stodgy, stuck-up, blue-blooded, button-down white-collar environment I had imagined. In fact, wearing a suit jacket and tie made me stand out more than usual. Every nook and cranny in the place was jammed with men and women in various states of distressed-dress—open shirts, wrinkled cotton trader jackets of many colors (particularly pastels), and barely a tie to be seen. Many of the traders were sweating profusely.

Innocently enough, I was there merely to visit a friend of mine for a Manhattan-based Friday afternoon happy hour in celebration of my 24th birthday. My high school buddy Bob (Bobby-G) Gorham worked as a clerk in the gold pit. My exchange escort took me over to that area, where I stood and watched the market close. I was awestruck that such chaos could be monitored and recorded, let alone understood. That my buddy Bob knew what was going on, amid what amounted to absolute confusion, was most impressive to me. This meant that perhaps the madness made sense.

The markets closed, the screaming stopped sans the occasional trader yelling at a clerk regardless of onlookers, and Bob told me to wait while he reconciled the late-day transactions. I stood to the side trying to look inconspicuous, which since I am 6 feet 10 inches tall, is not easy to do. Sure enough, a man approached me and asked me how tall I was. I replied politely, and the soft-spoken 60 (something)-year-old gentleman, who seemed completely out of place—almost too comfortable and casual given the chaos that dominated just minutes ago—engaged me in a conversation about basketball. My new friend related his tale of collegiate hoops mastery at New York University during the 1940s when NYU was big-time city-college hoops. I shared an anecdote or two from my own big-time Division One travels with Colgate University. We spent a pleasant few minutes sharing experiences. Little did I know the impact that this seemingly casual conversation was about to have on my life.

I noticed that Bobby-G had finished his paperwork, and as he strode over to me, I introduced myself to my new friend, and excused myself at the same time. Preparing to leave for our night out, Bob turned to me and asked me what I thought. I stared him down directly in the eye, and replied that I wanted a job on the floor. When he finished laughing and saw that I was serious, he quickly spun around pointing in the direction of my new basketball buddy, Stan. Bob whispered to me that

Stan was Stanley B. Bell, Commodity Exchange (COMEX) member, CEC gold-badge holder, and owner of one of the largest brokerage firms on the exchange. In one of those life-defining, grab-the-bull-by-the-horns moments, I walked back over to Stanley B. Bell of Stanley B. Bell and Company and reintroduced myself, stating that I was looking for a job.

Stanley asked me whether I had any relevant experience. I had studied English Literature in college, and had work experience in telecommunications, but admitted that I had no market experience. I then pointed into the middle of the gold "ring" (pit) and told Stan, the ex-college Big Man on Campus, that the ring would become my next "basketball lane" and that I wanted to get in there and start throwing elbows. I told him that I sought to stake out my position and earn my living as an inside player. Stanley loved the analogy. He ate it up to the point where he immediately called out for his son to join us. I quickly learned that Stanley no longer ran the day-to-day operations, and that his son, Craig Bell, was the boss. Before I even saw Craig Bell, I knew he was approaching, just by the way the crowd parted on the trading floor. In physical stature, Craig Bell was smaller than the average man, but in pure presence, Craig Bell was a giant on the exchange floor. He stood next to me, peered straight up at me, looked over at Stanley, and exclaimed, "Who's the Jolly Green Giant?" Stanley told him that I was looking for a job. Without a moment's hesitation, Craig looked at me and told me I was hired. Then he looked back at his father and stated, "I want him right next to me in the ring." Ecstatic, I went so far as to use the phone in the booth of Stanley B. Bell and Company to call my boss at the telecom firm in New Jersey and tell him I was quitting, effectively immediately. I was to start work on the COMEX for Bell, the very next Monday. (For the record, my buddy Bobby-G and I painted the town red that Friday night in May 1984.)

When I arrived early on Monday, the premarket atmosphere on the floor was relatively serene. Clerks milled about passing paper, discussing trades, and noting the opening calls; meanwhile, traders spoke with clients on the phones, spewing out their spin per the expectations for the opening market action based on the changes in gold and silver prices during Asian and European trading.

Naturally, I was lost. But my anxiety lessened when Stanley appeared and took me under his wing, explaining the responsibilities of each member of the team. It was a well-oiled machine that operated with uncanny precision amid the chaos and confusion. The market opened, gyrated, and traded; and of course, I had no idea what was happening, or why. Stanley turned to me and suggested we go to breakfast in the members' dining room, during which time he sold me on trading as a career. I can recall the conversation as vividly today as I did later that same day. I remember Stanley Bell telling me that except for professional athletics or acting, trading was the only career that combined financial opportunities with the competitively cerebral quest to succeed.

After breakfast, we went back down to the trading floor where the activity was ongoing. Stanley turned to me and said, "You've had enough for the first day," and he sent me home.

I returned Tuesday morning, but Stanley Bell was not around (he was semiretired and by that time was only coming to the exchange floor a few hours a week). I was on my own, and no one in the company knew what to do with me until Don Tierney, a gruff and grizzled old sod who barked like a dog but had the heart of a lion, ordered me to the write-up room. This dimly lit dungeon was located one floor below the trading floor. A low ceiling covered the expanse of a luncheonette-styled room, furnished with scarred tables and broken chairs. The write-up room looked more like a bingo parlor in an outdated, anti-quated New Jersey shore town on a Saturday night than like a place where fortunes were reconciled every half hour.

In fact, the write-up room was the neural network that funneled and captured all the upstairs trading floor energy. Every utterance, scream, hand signal, and nod of the head from upstairs was recreated down-stairs, in sequence, to ensure that, indeed, the traders knew what they were doing. The hundreds of clerks in the write-up room provided in-valuable and nonteachable skills in settling out trades and making sure that the chaos resulted in a perfect zero-sum outcome, every day. Some of the write-up room clerks were smart enough to become great traders in their own right but their innate underground skills trapped them in the write-up room. Many of them spent years trying to shed those ca-reer shackles.

I spent about an hour there copying numbers from one sheet of paper to another and handing off papers to runners while being handed new sheets of papers from other runners. Then suddenly, seemingly out of nowhere, a din arose, gradually rising until it had be-come a roar.

The ceiling in the write-up room literally began to shake, calling into question its ability to hold. It sounded and felt as if a stampede had been unleashed on the trading floor and was spilling down the staircase into the write-up room as runners suddenly swarmed. Above all the activity and noise, the phone rang out loud and clear. Deep down, I instantly knew what was about to happen. The clerk across the desk from me screamed, "Craig wants that tall s-o-b upstairs, *now!*"

Ordered back onto the trading floor, I made my way into the middle of the mayhem, not yet knowing that the gold market had just hit an intermediate-term bottom that would stand for several months and was in the process of reversing sharply higher. The next few hours were a blur, as I was put at the *point* spot in the silver ring. At 6 feet 10 inches tall, the mere fact that I could see over everybody—that I could see back into the Bell booth where a wall of phones was ringing off the hook—was a great advantage. I could see the clerks and signal to them where the market was and I could take their orders without them having to find a stand to climb on. Additionally, at my height, with a wingspan exceeding seven feet, I could easily reach down into the pit to hand order tickets back and forth.

As I quickly learned, the point position on the trading floor was much like the point in basketball, where a point guard handles the ball, distributes it, and runs the offense. On the floor, the point handled all the order flow into and out of the ring: on paper, verbally, and via hand signals, distributing the orders to the traders in the pit. In essence, the point handled the ball and ran the offense. And here I was, working the point with only few brief hours of experience in the industry. In short, I had no clue what I was doing.

It was truly a trial by fire.

Fortunately, pressure is a positive catalyst for me. Throw in my athletic-competitive mentality along with the allure provided by the tens of millions of dollars changing hands every minute, and I was hooked. It provided the exact atmosphere in which I thrive.

The point man is responsible for the *order book.* It is literally a book of standing orders, both above and below the market, limits and stops, that the point man holds and distributes to the pit traders as the price levels change and the orders are *touched* (the price on a standing order is reached, thus mandating that the order to buy, or sell metal, be executed).

During my first week, I let a stop order fall into the back of the order book, meaning that it was not executed when it should have been. Craig Bell had to make up the difference, making the client *whole* (pay the difference between the price at which the order was supposed to have been executed, and the price at which it eventually was executed) out of his own pocket because of my oversight. After I had realized my error and brought it to Craig's attention, he filled the order, passed the paper back to the booth, and then turned toward me while standing on the top step of the ring so that he could, almost, look at me eye-to-eye. He proceeded to rip into me, screaming right in my face. This was not overly unusual on the floor, yet it did create rubbernecking. Trading usually would come to a near halt as brokers watched in amusement while someone was ripped apart, or in extreme cases, literally beaten. Craig ripped me in front of the entire exchange, and I took it with little reaction. After all, I had screwed up and cost him almost $10,000.

I'll never forget the fallout. Taking abuse from Craig without cracking under the verbal humiliation gave me status among the other clerks, many of whom I had leapfrogged to steal the point position, even though they had much greater experience and tenure at Bell. The other Bell employees and even employees of the companies in the adjacent booths (it was a tightly knit group, working in close quarters under extreme duress) rallied around me. I had been accepted into the clerks' clique.

After the close of business, Craig Bell came over to me and calmly apologized for being so harsh. I told him I fully understood, and besides, being humiliated in front of my peers was nothing new to me, since basketball coaches, particularly my high school coach, had given me far worse dressing-downs. I told him he was a pussycat compared with them. He laughed and shook my hand, and I walked away feeling I had earned his respect. I held the point position at Bell for the next two years.

Within a week, I had arrived. The only problem was that it was still my first week and I had no clue about what was going on around me. But gradually, I realized that I could sense or feel, instinctively, when the activity in the market began to change, when dominant momentum reversed, or vice versa. I wanted a way to quantify the feeling.

At this point, I became fascinated by the point-and-figure charts (PFCs) that a couple of local traders kept by hand while trading in the pits (for a description of point-and-figure charting, see Part Four, Chapter 16).

The PFCs derive their activity from price reversals of a predetermined size. You might use one cent as a point for a PFC in silver; using a three-figure reversal would mean that the chart reflects a change for every reversal of three cents or more, including intradaily swings.

I began keeping my own point-and-figure charts for gold and silver, and later I added currencies and U.S. bonds. Tick by tick, hour by hour, day by day, week by week, for years into the future, I kept those charts. They helped me hone my natural instincts. As the charts got larger, I simply taped more paper side-to-side, and wrapped the sheets around a large piece of cardboard so that I could keep continuous charts in a microformat that was easy to update. I still have those charts, covering years of price action, in my closet.

I still had little clue *why* the markets moved, but I spent my two years on the COMEX learning exactly how order flow is handled. From micro to macro, I came to understand the business from the bottom floor, with a particular sense for the importance of momentum, as defined by the swings on my point-and-figure charts.

I came to realize the sheer power of momentum once it is unleashed and intensified by position dynamics. From a lesson that became the earliest input I had in a risk management thought process, I learned that no one is immune from the potential negative impact of momentum. It was Monday March 18, 1985. Just three weeks earlier, gold had gapped down below $300 and touched a new postbubble bear market low at $284. On Friday March 15, the market rallied and closed at the high for the week, reaching its highest level since it hit $284, and in the middle of the open downside gap from three weeks prior.

Monday morning chatter related to a potential banking crisis that involved Continental in Chicago, and word began to circulate on the floor. The market had been going straight down for months and had accelerated lower once the $335 level had given way in early December 1984. This precipitated the last leg of the bear market that culminated in the gap-down low at $284 in March 1985. In conjunction with the heavy directional move, volatility had been tanking right in line with prices, more than halving after breaking down in mid-1984, and hitting its lowest level since 1972 when gold was trading at $62.90.

Subsequent to that, and having been living large on the wild volatility, active trading, and boom times of the early 1980s, the largest pool of locals, who ran their own clearing firm, called Volume Investors, had become accustomed to a certain high-flying lifestyle. As a result, when volume began to shrink in line with the persistent bearish price action and volatility was in a virtual free fall, locals decided that selling naked call options (selling out-of-the-month calls without a "covering" purchase of the underlying commodity, leaving the option seller "open upside" risk, if the price of the commodity rose above the option's "call level") would provide a steady source of income without risk.

They were right . . . for months.

They were wrong . . . for one day. And, thanks to leverage and an explosion in volatility linked to the breaking banking crisis, when gold rallied nearly $40 that day (a single-day move of nearly 14 percent), Volume Investors was crushed, losing far more in that single day than they had made during months and months of call selling. Volume Investors went bust in one day, and some of the most powerful men on the exchange were reduced to tears. It was a memorable lesson in the sheer power of momentum, and the importance of a calculated risk assessment.

Of course, I decided that it would have been cool to have been on the other side of that trade!

For every fortune lost, a fortune is earned. That, too, is a powerful dynamic.

With my point-and-figure charts as a backbone, I immersed myself in the study of momentum. I would go to the New York City Public Library after work, and go through microfilms of the *Wall Street Journal,* writing out highs and lows on sheet after sheet of paper. Late at night, at home, I would use the calculator to apply various momentum models to the price data, creating a historical database of studies.

I was doing all this by hand, without the benefit of computers, which had yet to be introduced into the industry. Today, price quotes, charts, and customized historical studies can be accomplished with ease. I would never trade the experience for the comfort. Poring through pages and pages of data, making calculations by hand, and keeping point-and-figure charts in real time provided invaluable subconscious input that I would later harness as the "basis" for my methodology.

As my instincts became sharper, I quickly realized that the precious metals markets were losing stature as an efficient vehicle for hedging inflation risk. For one, inflation was on the decline. Second, investors had been burned by the bull market in gold and silver in the early 1980s amid exchange controls, market manipulation, a huge price rally, and subsequent collapse.

Then came the Volume Investors debacle, and many investors and local floor traders had their accounts frozen or vaporized during the firm's liquidity squeeze. Investors had become increasingly skittish about trading the metals markets. But most significantly, the introduction of new financial contracts and the increasing use of currency futures were drawing speculators away from gold and silver.

When the number of Chicago-COMEX silver arbitrage phone lines dwindled and the number of locals calling the Chicago Mercantile Exchange (CME) to place currency trades soared, the message came across to me loud and clear. I decided to transition off the trading floor into the upstairs institutional trading arena where I could expand my scope to include financial futures, particularly with the introduction of foreign fixed-income futures trading in London.

Neophytes and Neanderthals

There was no tunnel leading to the trading floor, as there was at the Commodities Exchange Center.

There was barely even chaos.

Rather, a serene calm prevailed, so still that the hum of the air conditioning was the dominant sound, intermittently interrupted by soft-toned phone ringing.

I had just walked onto the institutional futures trading floor of Lehman Brothers in the newest of New York City's downtown ivory towers, the magnificent World Financial Center. I had taken a job as a trader's assistant for Howard Levine, one of the most successful futures brokers in the industry. He was a quirky but brilliant broker who demanded perfection in the services he provided his clients.

With the introduction of foreign fixed-income futures on the London Financial Futures Exchange (LIFFE), the recently introduced Standard & Poor's 500 Stock Index futures, and the still fairly new and expanding trading in crude oil futures, the mid-to-late 1980s became a heyday for institutional futures brokerage. There were fat commissions, scant competition, and full-blown service operations to support the business. Lehman was a boutique firm that specialized in cutting-edge products offered by cutting edge brokers such as Howard Levine, Stan Jonas, Martin Lysaght, and Louis Bacon.

Although I would be starting all over again, I would begin with a rapid learning curve and would gain my introduction to hard-core macrofundamentals. An institutional broker had to be able to recite chapter and verse about the dominant fundamental influences in a multitude of markets, at any given moment, whenever the phone might ring.

Moreover, Howie Levine was a workhorse when tracking down information—as focused and frank an individual as I have ever met. He demanded that his assistants know everything that was happening in every market, at all times. His drive became my drive, and I dove into a study of the fundamentals of every commodity and financial sector, poring over reams of U.S. Department of Agriculture (USDA) data, reading research reports, and talking to industry insiders on a constant basis.

Further, I read as many books as I could, from J. R. Levien's *Anatomy of a Crash* (New York: Fraser Publishing, 1997); to the classic story of Jesse Livermore, *Reminiscences of a Stock Operator* by Edwin Lefèvre (Hoboken, NJ: John Wiley & Sons, 2005); and even *The Alchemy of Finance* by George Soros (New York: John Wiley & Sons, 1994). Little by little, I was finally putting the pieces together and learning the fundamentals of market movements.

My work with momentum and point-and-figure charts drew some attention from Howie's clients; and with Howie often distracted by the tragic illness of his young son, I found myself increasingly involved with these institutional traders. They began to respect my input, driving me to deeper study of technical analysis. I began reading books on technical analysis, starting with the basic must-reads such as John Murphy's epic *Technical Analysis of the Futures Market* (New York: John Wiley & Sons, 1991), before graduating to one of the most influential books I ever studied, Perry J. Kaufman's *The New Commodity Trading Systems and Methods* (New York: John Wiley & Sons, 1987).

My methodology began to take shape, molded with a top-down fundamental understanding of the dominant macroinfluences as well as a strong underpinning of technical analysis. Moreover, I began studying technical trading systems by creating and testing momentum-based models.

Yet again, a single major event impressed me the most during my tenure as a broker at Lehman: the sequence of events leading up to the first Gulf War. On August 2, 1990, the date of the Iraqi invasion of

Kuwait, a bunch of us had been out to dinner and came back to the office to check the late Asian action when the news hit the wires. Crude oil spiked, after having been pressing new bear move lows just weeks before, with the front month New York Mercantile Exchange (NYMEX) contract almost moving below $15 in June of that year.

By October, it was trading above $40, more than doubling in just nine weeks. Again, I was impressed by the power of momentum, as fortunes were made and lost, in just over two months. But gold barely budged, trading from $380 as of the end of July 1990, to a high of $415 in mid-August, before crumbling all the way back down to $360 by October.

Fundamentally, one might have believed that gold would have rallied more forcefully, given the reflationary push in crude oil and the general support derived from the uncertainty related to war.

But gold failed to hold its early gains. The rise in crude weighed on the global economy, driving interest rates lower as well as driving investors out of gold and into U.S. Treasuries amid a weakening economic situation that eventually mutated into a recession.

Most of Howie's clients were bullish on gold, a stance that was in conflict with the actual price action. This is where a blend of fundamental and technical analysis was critical because the lack of technical confirmation kept fundamentally bullish traders out of harm's way.

Something else happened at Lehman that had a big impact on me, and particularly on the future direction of my career although I never could have guessed it at the time. One of Howie's gigs was his appearances on the old Financial News Network (FNN) with Jennifer Bauman. One day during the December holiday season of 1989/1990, Jennifer called the desk asking for Howie, who was on vacation in Hawaii.

Jennifer asked me about my opinion on the stock market, and after my reply, she asked if I would appear on her show the next day to repeat my view. I willingly accepted, and the next day, I went up to their remote midtown studio (the station was based in Los Angeles) to do the show. Jennifer asked me about the stock market, and I provided my bearishly skewed reply based on the signs of weakness in the global economy and on the technical erosion evident in the stock index futures.

Feeling good about myself and my performance, I returned to the World Financial Center following my gig, only to be met at my desk by the Futures Division manager who ordered me upstairs to see the head of the entire derivatives and trading department. As I walked into the upstairs office, I knew I was in trouble. Yelling as if he were addressing a wayward child, the head of the division admonished me for going on television with the Lehman name, and talking bearishly about the U.S. stock market.

At first, I was taken aback.

What I had not realized was that over the weekend just past, the firm had launched a massive, multimillion-dollar advertising campaign featuring a bullish market call and their top stock market analyst. Apparently, the analyst, known in the industry for her volatility, blew her top as she watched my spot and had called for my head on a platter. After being told how close I had come to being fired right there, on the spot, I was commanded to abandon my budding television career.

It did not matter that, in the end, the stock market went straight south meeting all the downside technical targets I had highlighted on the air. What mattered was that I was speaking for a vested interest and not as an independent purveyor of the market. It was obvious to me that I had to shed the burden of conflicting interests to gain credibility. I approached Lehman's management and asked if they would have a problem if I appeared again (Jennifer had loved the spot, especially since I turned out to be right, and had invited me to return) without the Lehman moniker. They agreed, and my public persona was born and provided a prelude to what has become a regular spot on CNBC.

But, by far, the most important thing that happened to me at Lehman Brothers was my introduction to the gang who eventually formed Moore Capital Management.

The Show

In baseball, players toiling in the minor leagues strive to reach "The Show"—the major leagues. Six years into my career, I reached the trading industry's equivalent.

I had just turned 30 years old, and I finally felt like I knew what was going on in the world. I finally had a clue, no, more than a clue, I knew what was happening, and why.

I was about to discover how wrong I was.

Sure, I had a clue as to what and why the markets did what they did, but I had *no* clue about how to manage money, and more specifically, how to manage risk.

At Moore Capital Management, risk aversion was the rallying cry, coming first, long before more mundane things such as macrofundamental analysis and technical considerations. Of course, those mundane things also were critical and we expended a tremendous amount of energy tracking down specific information points when constructing bigger-picture secular macrothemes.

A primary talent within Moore Capital was our ability to envision what-if scenarios. We spent endless hours discussing potential nuances and applying them specifically to the dissection of economic data.

What if the payroll number comes out 100,000 jobs stronger than expected ?

What if the payroll number comes weaker than expected?

We were constantly playing what-if scenarios for every imaginable future event, from as many angles as possible. We contemplated all the possible outcomes, created a few nearly impossible outcomes, and then discussed at length how to react given an overall top-down bullish or bearish predisposition. It was not akin to trying to predict what would happen.

Instead, it was mental practice so that we would recognize when a certain scenario began to play out and could effectively execute a game plan during times of extreme stress, without the requisite thought process. We had already been through that process as one of a hundred possibilities.

Fundamental factors evolve and mutate. Successful traders must believe in themselves and have unquestioned confidence in their particular methodology, but they must also be pliable, flexible, and ready to react to any curve balls that the markets might hurl.

Knowing what is going on is not nearly enough.

Having a solid technical understanding, if not some kind of systematic approach to entry and exit points, is a must, but alone is not nearly enough.

Being flexible and prepared for any unexpected twists provides immeasurable value-added, particularly in the heat of battle, but without the rest of the game plan, even this is not enough to ensure success.

At the end of the trading day, it all comes back around to risk management.

By far, this was the most significant lesson I learned at Moore Capital. In addition to expanding my ability to back-test technical trading systems and deepen my fundamental understanding of the global capital markets as one entity, Moore Capital introduced me to the study of risk management.

While I was on the floor, single-trade risk was not even a consideration since things happened so fast and being on the floor offered extreme nimbleness in exiting a losing trade. At Lehman, as I began developing my first raw technical trading models, single-trade risk of 5 percent of total equity seemed reasonable.

Naturally, 5 percent single-trade risk is anything but reasonable. It is suicidal, and through a reluctant (at first) rewind into the world of probabilities and game theory, I came to realize that fact.

Terms like *value at risk* (VAR), *dollars at risk* (DAR), *standard deviation,* and *risk of ruin,* quickly became part of my vocabulary. Other popular risk-management elements were added to the mix such as the *Sharpe ratio* and an understanding of the importance of keeping maximum drawdowns to a minimum, preferably to less than 10 percent.

Soon, within my models, the single-trade risk limit of 5 percent was replaced with a maximum single-trade risk of 40 basis points, which the firm still considered high.

Correlated position risk was a major calculation and consideration, and I began working on a way to gauge the risk to an overall portfolio from both an intersector and an intrasector perspective.

Diversification was another concept that had been evolving in my mind-set since I first left the trading floor (and in fact was a big part of the reason I left the trading floor). Whereas the exchange floor is pure contained chaos and provides the raw energy on which the markets feed, and whereas the upstairs brokerage offices provide the blood vessels that keep everything moving, the trading firms represent the heart of the industry.

The floor was chaotic, Lehman was intense, but the environment at Moore Capital was electric and eclectic at the same time, producing a well-oiled trading machine that missed nary a single beat. There was all-encompassing coverage; we could trade any instrument in the world that might provide a fundamental or technical speculative opportunity.

I came to realize that I must capitalize on every possible opportunity. Not a single opportunity could be squandered, because each and every position became an integral part of the overall trading performance, both positively and negatively.

And capitalize, Moore Capital did. The firm grew from less than $100 million under management when I joined, to more than $1 billion, making it at the time, one of the biggest hedge funds in the world, and putting it on the top shelf along with Soros, Steinhardt, Tudor, and Tiger.

I had started to put my trading ideas on paper, preparing one- and two-page reports for one of the proprietary traders who expressed an interest in my thought process. In December 1991, with global economies reeling from recession, crude oil had begun to exhibit signs of technical weakness, thus providing both a fundamental basis and technical validation for a potentially bearish trading theme. I wrote up a two-page report on the crude oil market that suggested adopting a bearish stance.

Just as my first copy of the report came off the printer, "The Man" (Louis Moore Bacon) came walking by. Louis Bacon is a brilliant thinker, and the most intensely focused individual I have ever worked with. He could be aloof and cold, to the point of being nearly unapproachable, but on this day, he was walking right past me, and I thrust a freshly printed copy of my report at him as he passed. Without saying a word, he took it, and for all I knew at the time, it ended up in the garbage the instant he walked into his private office.

Crude oil cracked wide open later that afternoon, dumping 80 cents in what was one of the biggest one-day moves in many months, accelerating a developing bear move that quickly thereafter took crude oil from $23 to its January 1992 low at $17.75.

Later that day I looked up to see that Louis was standing in front of my desk, holding my report in his hand. "Nice job" he said, a big deal coming from a man who offered little recognition and even less praise.

He told me that he had sold two thousand crude oil contracts that morning on the basis of my report, and had thus cleared over $1.5 million in profit. He then told me that he had put a million bucks of that profit into an account for me to trade on my own, for him personally.

My first at bat in The Show, and I had hit a grand slam.

Six months later, the British pound was making news, reaching the 2.00 level against the U.S. dollar, but declining against the euro as talk focused on the United Kingdom and entry into the European Exchange Rate Mechanism (ERM). The Bank of England was busy hiking rates as part of the program to keep the GBP (Great Britain pound) in line with other European ERM-linked currencies, and the economy was suffering mightily.

A fundamental basis for a trading theme was born, as was the trade of the decade: being short the GBP in September 1992. I was, and returned an astronomical +12 percent that month.

Swing, and it's a long drive, deep to center; it's going, going, it is gone—another home run.

Soros got the credit for breaking the Bank of England, but I participated, too. The breakdown in the GBP, and my ability to foresee it, fundamentally and technically, gave me the final dose of self-confidence that I needed to devoutly believe in my methodology.

The lessons I learned at Moore provided the final stepping-stone to all my future success. I arrived at Moore as a rookie, raw and green, but full of passion and potential. I left Moore as a market veteran. I had developed a solid, top-down methodology much like the one that I still use, drawing from fundamental and technical analysis with a robust risk management overlay.

I learned more about trading, the markets, and the global macroeconomy during my tenure at Moore Capital, than I had in all my previous experience combined.

The Firm

I saw her from across the room, which—given my physical stature—is not so unusual.

She never knew this (until now), but I stalked her that day.

I had never seen her before, but I had noticed her name tag, and I had identified my target. As I watched her move around the convention center floor, I waited to pounce, positioning myself on the other side of a large pillar. When she turned the corner, I stepped out and thrust my 235 pounds of towering height right in front of her.

Sandra D'Italia was a diminutive woman, but much like Craig Bell, she possessed a presence that belied her petite size. Indeed, my plan succeeded. She walked right into me, slammed her face into my chest, went flying backward, and hit the floor.

I had just intentionally blocked the poor woman's path and unintentionally knocked her on her derriere. Thankful that I had not injured her, I extended my hand, and while helping her get off the floor and back on her feet, I exclaimed with feigned surprise, "Hey, you're Sandra D'Italia aren't you?" "Yes," she reluctantly replied, not sure who I was and still stunned from her encounter with my chest. I introduced myself, explaining that I was the guy who had called her office once a week for the past nine months, with nary a single returned phone call. I was the guy who had sent one letter each month, pleading my case to become an Associate Trader at the firm where Sandra worked, the venerable Commodities Corporation (CC) in Princeton, New Jersey.

Sandra D'Italia was the person responsible for choosing the traders accepted into CC's unique seed program, where unproven trading talent was given a stake and allowed to trade the firm's proprietary capital under strict monitoring and oversight.

After reintroducing myself to Sandra and acting as if it was pure coincidence that we had collided, I asked her why I had never heard back from her despite all my attempts to connect. She looked up at me and genuinely answered that she had never heard of me, had not received a single phone message, and had not seen the track record I had produced at Moore Capital.

In fact, Moore Capital had a close relationship with CC, and I had been told by their previous Head of Trading in Princeton that I could get into CC's Associates Trader Program on the basis of my successful trading at Moore.

Sandra knew nothing about this and promised to check into it when she returned to Princeton. The very next day I received a call, and an interview was scheduled with CC's talent-selecting team for the following day. Within the week, I had accepted a position as CC's newest Associate Trader. Moreover—and something I will never forget—Sandra told me that she admired my "tenacity" and "persistence" in pursuit of my passion.

It was fortuitous that while working with Howie Levine at Lehman Brothers, I had already handled several of CC's largest traders and had begun to cultivate relationships several years earlier, with the hope of someday joining the firm.

Commodities Corporation was more of a think tank, one that was started in the 1970s by some of the most brilliant macrothinkers in the world, and it has since produced some of the greatest traders of the modern market era. Louis Bacon, Grenville Craig, Paul Tudor Jones, Michael Marcus, and Bruce Kovner all had received original seed money from CC.

I could finally use my 12 years of studying and experience to manage a portfolio of a significant size. I had arrived in a place where the sole focus was honing a trader's skill; making money was a secondary benefit, but not the ultimate goal. The ultimate goal was to become the best trader you possibly could be. This offered a cerebral pursuit that excited me to no end. I spent the next two years at Commodities Corporation, trading markets and trading stories with some of the greatest fund managers in the world.

Under the associates' program, we were required to submit monthly reports on all our trading, detailing every trade, why we did it, what was the fundamental idea behind it, what were the technical considerations, and what was the ultimate outcome, profit or loss. We were required to keep full statistics on all our trades, our won-loss percentages, average losses, average wins, largest losses, drawdowns, and gains. Everything was monitored statistically and analyzed. The experience and insights were invaluable.

Commodity Corporation encouraged dialogue between traders, and I seized that opportunity to produce reports on market topics throughout my tenure there. These reports, which piggybacked the ones I had prepared at Moore Capital, provided a more comprehensive presentation and served as the feeding ground for the well-known daily macro-market research reports that are now produced by Weldon Financial and are the cornerstone of my publishing business.

By blending all my experience and knowledge, I had great success at Commodity Corporation, returning over 60 percent in 23 months with a maximum drawdown of 11 percent.

I realized a sizable contribution to that return in the middle of 1997, and like the opportunity presented by the British pound's ERM implosion, this opportunity appeared in the currency arena. In fact, I recall the exact moment and the precise catalyst that gave me the idea of selling the Thai baht short: in August 1997, I saw a chart that plotted the year-to-year pace of cumulative export growth in (what was then known as) Asian Tiger nations.

Export growth had been the sole driving force in the sudden emergence of Asian Tiger nations as trading powers to be reckoned with. Suddenly, currencies such as the Thai baht, Malaysian ringgit, Singapore dollar, and Korean won needed to be closely monitored for clues to the dominant macroinfluences. Less than two weeks after I saw the chart of Asian export growth revealing a near collapse in what had been persistently rising, double-digit rates of expansion, I had taken a sizable short stance in the Thai baht forwards. With competition heating up and export growth eroding, the fundamental fodder for a trading theme incorporating a strategy designed to profit if the Asian Tiger currencies began to depreciate. I felt that currency depreciation would be specifically utilized by the local monetary authorities as a means to support the maintenance of export market share, amid a slowdown in final demand.

So the next step was a technical examination that revealed a long-term bullish trend in momentum and an upside pivot point above which the USD would likely accelerate, defined by the July 1997 high in dollar-baht, at the 33.0 baht per dollar level. In late August, the July trade data for Thailand was released and revealed yet another month of severe erosion in export growth, a fundamental revelation that drove the USD-THB through the July high, thus taking the Thai baht to a new all-time low against the greenback. The baht was ripe to be sold short, and that is exactly what I did.

By January 1998, the Thai baht had collapsed, with the USD soaring all the way to 56.0 baht. Subsequent to this move, my rolling 12-month rate of return at CC exceeded +50 percent.

I had identified and harnessed the power of momentum, using a blend of fundamental and technical analysis, covered by a complete risk management overlay.

I had become a successful trader.

Character

This is the time when a man's character shows.

Those were the words the head of Commodity Corporation (CC) uttered when Goldman Sachs announced that it had bought out the partnership and would be adjusting salaries and compensation packages, implementing significant cuts in the process. Moreover, the entire Associates Program would be changed, and Goldman would replace seed traders with their own inbred talent to be displaced from Manhattan.

I was shocked and felt as if the rug had been pulled out from under me. With an intense desire to ensure that this would never happen to me again, I chose to leave CC and start my own firm.

In founding Weldon Financial and *Weldon's Money Monitor,* I had just undertaken my most challenging task yet—starting my own business. I needed a support net, so I called an old client of Howie Levine's, a guy I had talked to every day while I was at Lehman Brothers. I called Bill Darby of Darby Trading, former head of commodity trading for 'Ace' Israel at ACLI Commodities, one of the most powerful commodity firms in the world during the 1970s and 1980s. From the offices of Darby Trading and AC Israel, in Westchester New York, Weldon Financial began operations in late 1998.

As I laid out my game plan, I decided to work my entire secular macrothematic thought process into the mix to get my business off the ground. It was (and still is) my belief that since the delinking of the U.S. dollar (USD) from gold in 1971, all paper currencies are in a trend of monetary debasement. Further, as a result of that long-term persistent debasement, gold will again shine as the only purely safe store of wealth. I was fundamentally bullish on gold, from a secular standpoint.

The problem was that gold was in a bear market, perhaps its worst ever, as the Fed kept pumping money into the financial system ahead of the year 2000, money that was not flowing into gold but into the U.S. dollar, the U.S. Treasury market, and mostly, the highly reflated tech stocks. At the time, my technical trading models were bearish on gold, and for my own account, I was short. Nonetheless, I had received word that Prudential Securities was moving to cut costs (part and parcel of the early days of the deflation wave that is now dominating the global labor market), and was laying off overpaid, underworked research staff. Pru was shaving staff that had been with the firm for years during the era of fat commissions and scant competition.

Now, however, competition was fierce and intensifying with the onslaught of online brokers, discount brokers, and a cheaper rate for floor brokerage. Suddenly, a new wave was on the rise, and I sensed it, I saw it, and I climbed on my surfboard to catch it.

That wave is now known as *outsourcing*.

Prudential Securities (Pru) was among the first of the major Wall Street houses to move in that direction, and luckily, I was already riding my surfboard. I had heard through inside channels that the metals analyst would be laid off, and that Pru would seek to direct that responsibility to someone outside the firm, for a cheaper price than the inflated salary being paid to the in-house research writer.

To prepare for this event, I created a daily research letter focusing on the gold and silver markets, calling it the *Metal Monitor*. I believed that gold would bottom in the following year or two and would reverse into an uptrend that would define a new secular bull market. Gold would then rally against all paper currencies, including the USD.

I also recognized that research in the metals arena had diminished into near nothingness as gold fell to new bear market lows amid new highs in bank stocks and the high-flying, capital-sucking technology sector. In 1998, there was not a solid daily research piece on metals being produced by anyone in the mainstream Wall Street business. There was a dearth of solid macroresearch in the metals sector, and given my background on the COMEX, I felt that I was the perfect person to fill that void. I circulated the *Metal Monitor* among the guys at the Prudential bullion desk in New York, headed by my good buddy and fellow Colgate alumnus John Fallon, the best gold broker in the world bar none. The gang on the desk loved the work and sent it along to a few of their clients, who also liked it and thought it provided value-added à la my all-encompassing top-down way of looking at things.

With John Fallon in my corner, I easily captured the Prudential business and solidified my own business. I was now an authority on the gold market, a scary thought; but it was a level of expertise that I knew I could live up to, thanks to my unique writing style and a robust trading methodology.

Whereas most research writers come from an academic or supply-and-demand background, my research was driven by a trading mentality that was rare among researchers, most of whom rarely want to go out on a limb to make a specific recommendation.

Instead, I had no problem making strategy calls, since all my research is merely a function of my own daily regimen as it relates to my own trading. The beauty of it all for me, was that I would be doing the research anyway, even if I were not publishing a daily newsletter.

Fortune smiled on me again in September 1999, when the Group of Seven nations got together and decided to limit the amount of gold that central banks would be allowed to sell into the open market, thus restricting a practice that had flooded the market with official gold supply. Here again, an official event, presaged by a change in the market's momentum, gave ample read to anyone paying close enough attention that a major change was taking place.

On Tuesday September 21, 1999, the gold market rallied sharply, rising $7, and ending a long period of dormant volatility. Indeed, the 100-day volatility measure applied to the cash gold price had been trapped in a very tight range for months and months, vacillating between 9 percent and 10 percent, but not having moved above or below those levels throughout the entire year to date.

On September 21, the volatility rose above 10 percent, and two days later, before the official announcement came, the "Vol" had exploded to more than 12 percent. Further, the Commodity Exchange (COMEX) calendar spreads and the cash forward swap rates moved sharply in a way as to indicate a dramatic tightening in supply, with calendar spreads narrowing, and swaps flirting with negative territory.

Something was going on, and the market was telegraphing it.

Loading up on the long side, and putting out a research piece indicating such, proved to be prescient, and helped solidify my stature in the metals community, as a top-shelf research writer. By the time the smoke had cleared, gold had rallied from below $250 per ounce to hit a near-term high of $342, in just 10 short days.

More importantly, from a secular perspective, the move by global central banks to systematically liquidate their gold reserves solidified my macrobeliefs about the persistent (and now accelerating) debasement of paper money. As a result, a major low had finally been established in the gold market, defined by the August 25 trade at $251.70 (basis spot market), and the market has not looked back since.

From the personal-business side of the ledger, the buzz generated by my bullish gold call earned me my first spot on CNBC-TV (cable financial news channel). I appeared shortly thereafter with Ron Insana on his *Street Signs* show. I have continued to make regular appearances on CNBC ever since, with Ron, then with the always affable Ted David on *The Edge,* and later on his version of *Street Signs.*

I recall an appearance with my buddy Ted, in which I was pounding the table bearishly (again, yes) on the U.S. stock market, with a particularly bearish opinion provided for the NASDAQ, which was already into its decline by that time.

The NASDAQ was trading around 3,400, having peaked just above 5,000 a couple of months prior to my appearance. When Ted David asked me how far down I thought the NASDAQ might go, he surprised me with that question, since usually I prefer not to make price predictions. I was caught off guard, but I was also prepared since I had worked out the technical numbers for the NASDAQ earlier that week. I had come up with a very low target for my short position, and I blurted it out without really thinking about what I was in fact saying—"1,300, Ted" . . . I exclaimed.

In other words, I was on global cable television forecasting a 60 percent decline in the NASDAQ from its level above 3,000. Ted nearly fell off his chair, literally. Although I was ultimately right on, it was such a negative comment that it marked my final appearance with Ted.

One show to which I have never received an invitation is CNBC's most popular morning show, *Squawk Box.* There is a reason for this, and it makes for a good story. It was Halloween and the associate producer for the *Morning Call* show telephoned me to see if I could appear as a last-minute replacement for a guest who had canceled (at the time, I lived close to their studio in Fort Lee, New Jersey).

I told her that I was on my way to my daughter's school dressed as I am on every Halloween, as Frankenstein (come on, what else am I supposed to be for Halloween, since my boots make me nearly seven feet tall?). My costume consists of a very authentic rubber mask, green paint, a way-too-small-old-worn suit jacket, hockey shoulder pads, and my boots. I can honestly say that this is a very good costume, and has won me numerous competitions over the years.

Well, the associate producer thought it would be fun to have me come to the studio dressed as Frankenstein, to participate in the *Squawk Box* Halloween-theme show. Little did I know that her boss had told her it was not a good idea, since he was not sure how the people on the set might react. Nonetheless, the associate producer told me to come anyway, and I did. I walked the Frankenstein walk right out onto the set in the middle of the news, roaring, grunting, and moaning; my arms were straight out in front of me (like Frankenstein) and I was moving in a herky-jerky fashion (like Frankenstein). Immediately, I went after Joe Kiernan, CNBC's resident stock-guru, as if to attack him. Suffice it to say that the stunt did not go over well at all with Mark Haines, the fatherly host of the show, nor did it go over well with the producer who had passed on the idea originally. Subsequently, I was blackballed from appearing on *Squawk Box.* Luckily, Ted was kind enough to refer me to the always gracious and vivacious Conseulo Mack, who "adopted" me and allowed me to appear regularly in her Strategy Sessions segment of the *Morning Call* show.

The *Metal Monitor,* and its sister publication born not long after, *Weldon's Money Monitor,* are now circulated around the globe, with clients in Asia, Europe, the Middle East, Canada, and South America as well as the United States. Our focus is top-down macroanalysis, intertwined with intense technical analysis, volatility, and momentum based, with significant doses of intermarket analysis, Elliott Wave theory, candlestick charting, Fibonacci analysis, and more.

This book is not about me, nor is it my story. It is merely a means to relate how I formed, cultivated, and evolved my methodology, and where it is today. Mine is a somewhat simple methodology. It only gets complicated in that there are many layers to it, each of which is equally important to the bottom-line conclusion.

Peeling back the layers, one by one, to see how many line up in this direction and how many line up in that direction is the process that I describe in this book. It is a method that anyone can undertake.

Ironically, when I first walked out onto the trading floor of the COMEX, more than 20 years ago, I had absolutely no clue about what made the markets tick. But over the years, I have learned enough to write about how anyone can trade the bullion market.

The United States is a great country. It is the land of opportunity where anyone who wants to work hard enough can accomplish just about anything imaginable. I should know: I am living proof.

The following chapters peel back the layers of my methodology.

PART TWO

Evolution of a Macromonetary Era

"Top-Down"—
It Starts at the Top

Gold is the child of Zeus
Neither moth nor rust devoureth it.

Pindar, c. 522–442 B.C.

This statement does not apply for any paper currency or debt obligation issued in the history of mankind. In fact, virtually every type of paper currency or debt obligation ever "created" or "printed" has eventually succumbed to moth or rust, in one sense or another.

A chart I saw in *Grant's Interest Rate Observer* (I think) sometime in the late 1980s or early 1990s had a profound impact on me. As anyone who has followed the markets during the past 20 years already knows, whether they agree with him or not at any given time, James Grant is the authority in the history of interest rates and is one of the top purveyors of the global fixed-income markets in the world.

The chart was in the form of a pyramid, with the riskiest investments (e.g., penny stocks) lined up along the bottom row of the pyramid. Each successively higher row of blocks, with every block representing a single category within a broader spectrum of asset classes, contained fewer blocks and comprised less risky investments.

Toward the top of the pyramid for example, would be U.S. Treasury bonds, above agency debt, which would be above emerging market debt, and so on, just for the fixed-income class. For sure, U.S. Treasury bills were near the top of the pyramid, as one of the safer investment categories that would go bust long after penny stocks, real estate, and just about anything, except for, the U.S. dollar and gold.

The U.S. dollar gets the second spot, thanks to its still undisputed reign as King-Dollar, the last resort safe-haven paper currency that serves as the reserve currency to the world. It may be obvious, but the fact is impressive nonetheless. The U.S. dollar is the means for facilitating transactions for all kinds of goods and services, globally, nearly anywhere on the face of the planet.

But, gold holds the top spot, at the pinnacle of the pyramid.

Throughout the ages, in every corner of the world, gold has represented the ultimate store of wealth, the safest of all assets, including real estate. This is increasingly true in the present era, which has come to be defined by the greatest monetarily facilitated paper wealth reflation ever witnessed. It is only on the short-term historical time horizon that the USD (U.S. Treasury debt, to be specific) has reached the second tier on the pyramid.

In Part Two, I explain the reasons for these trends.

The Golden Bull

While gold is the safest store of wealth, even more so than real estate, you may be skeptical.

Recall the plight of Moses and the slaves he led out of Egypt. As told in the Book of Exodus 32:4, Moses' brother Aaron fashioned a "golden calf" as an object of sacrifice while Moses scaled Mount Sinai. Struggling against Mother Nature, without claim to any land, short on water and food, the Israelites maintained their wealth in gold, mostly in the form of jewelry and trinkets. According to the story, Aaron took up a collection, mostly of gold earrings, melted the gold down, and created a near-life-size calf (cow, or bull).

To say the least, the moral of the story is skewed away from the mind-set of a present day, capital markets speculator. On his return from the mountain, Moses was enraged at the sight of the golden calf, slammed the commandment tablets to the ground, and ordered the golden calf burned.

My point is simple. Gold as a store of wealth outdates the U.S. dollar, and all paper currencies, by many centuries. From the Roman Empire, through the Mongolian Empire, to the English colonization, right down to the printing of the Ecuadorian sucre, paper currency regimes have come and gone, but gold has remained constant.

Of course, the price of gold is anything but constant. This is what makes the current environment so exciting and, at the same time, so ominous. Beginning in 2001, the price of gold began to rise relative to nearly every paper currency on the planet. The Russian ruble, the

Chinese yuan, the Brazilian real, the Eurocurrency, and the U.S. dollar have depreciated versus the value of gold, with most of these currencies reaching new all-time lows.

I don't pretend to be a historian, but today, more currencies than ever are making all-time lows versus gold. The historical focus here, from the perspective of a market participant, is the evolution of gold to the point where it is again claiming its spot at the pinnacle of the wealth storage pyramid.

It seems that the tablets have been broken as monetary officialdom has slammed the most sacred credit commandments amid a mad dash to out-reflate "thy export-competitor neighbor." The golden bull (calf) is being melted again, this time by global central banks through the debasement of the buying power of all paper currencies at a historic rate.

Bretton Woods and the "System"

I t is important to distinguish between European and North American philosophies surrounding inflation and monetary policy during the post-World War II period. Europe's philosophy was driven by Germany's experience with hyperinflation in the 1920s and the collapse of the domestic currency. The North American experience was defined by the Great Depression of the 1930s and the boom-bust phenomenon that led to it, with the appropriately named *Roaring Twenties* culminating in the crash of the U.S. stock market in 1929.

These spectrum-defining philosophies set the stage for the postwar era and the monetary system as we know it. During July 1944 in a somnambulant setting known as Bretton Woods, not far from Mount Washington in New Hampshire, the soon-to-be post-World War II Allied nations met to discuss and define a new global monetary system, to be put in place once victory over the Axis powers had been secured.

In Bretton Woods, the foundation was laid for the construction of the International Monetary Fund (IMF), the World Bank, and the International World Organization, which later morphed into the World Trade Organization (WTO).

In all, 730 delegates from the 44 Allied nations gathered at the Mount Washington Hotel, and following three weeks of intense negotiations, the Bretton Woods System was born. Achieving agreement on the structure of the postwar monetary system was far from easy. Essentially, at issue, was the balance of monetary power and global monetary domination.

And to the victor goes the spoils: the United States won, and thus a tectonic monetary transition moved into its final stage. Prior to World War II, the British pound had been the primary global *reserve currency* for hundreds of years. But when the Allied nations met in the United States during 1944, Great Britain was far from being in a position of strength, let alone dominance—monetarily, economically, or militarily.

Moreover, by the time nearly one thousand monetary and political officials descended on a sleepy New Hampshire town in the peak of the summer season, the U.S. Treasury had accumulated two-thirds of the world's monetary gold reserves. This simple fact made the U.S. dollar an obvious candidate to serve as the next international reserve currency.

Since the British are defenders of the Crown and Queen, the contingent from the United Kingdom refused to let the British pound slip away quietly into the summer night. A battle developed between the U.S. and British. The U.S. team was headed by international economist Harry Dexter White, and backed up by U.S. Secretary of State Cordell Hull. Britain's team was led by famed economist John Maynard Keynes.

Keynes proposed creating a new international currency that would serve as the reserve unit for the global economy. At the closing Plenary Session of the conference, Keynes opened his speech with the following words:

> Mister President, we the delegates of this conference have been trying to accomplish something very difficult to accomplish. We have not been trying each one, to please himself and to find the solution most acceptable in our own particular situation.
>
> That would have been easy.
>
> It has been our task to find a common measure, a common standard, a common rule applicable to each, and not irksome to any.

Keynes called for the establishment of a single global essential bank, to be called the International Clearing Union, which would print a new currency to be called the *Bancor Unitas*. It would have been a broader, global version of the euro, and indeed, Keynes's proposal at the Bretton Woods Conference became the blueprint for the creation of the euro decades later. Alas, Keynes did not even have the backing of the

U.K. government that, along with France, was heavily indebted to the U.S. Treasury. Consecutive world wars had destroyed the principal manufacturing capacity and industries in both the United Kingdom and across the European Continent.

Subsequently, amid rising demand for funding to rebuild, the United States lent the United Kingdom $3.8 billion and France $1.0 billion. In return for the loans ($4.8 billion was a sizable amount of money in 1945), Europe and the United Kingdom acquiesced to the U.S. monetary plan, which featured the U.S. dollar as the new reserve currency to the world.

It seems almost too ironic, in hindsight, to suggest that the evolution into the current macrosituation was specifically accelerated by what amounted to the export of U.S. dollar hegemony. Just 60 years later, those exports have reached epic proportions.

Rewinding to the mid-1940s and Bretton Woods, Harry Dexter White had drafted his own monetary blueprint, which would provide the global economy with access to liquidity in the form of the U.S. dollar.

With the U.S. Treasury in possession of two-thirds of the world's monetary gold at the end of World War II, every dollar was redeemable at $35 per ounce. (That rate represented a previous devaluation of the U.S. dollar from $20 per ounce, enacted by Franklin Roosevelt, to help pay for the New Deal. The common link . . . accelerated debt creation and fiscal deficits.)

In his best-selling book, *Economics in One Lesson* (New York: Pocket Books, 1946), esteemed *New York Times* economic editor Henry Hazlitt wrote:

> The most important contribution that this country could make to world currency stability would be to declare unequivocally its determination to stabilize its own currency. It could do this by announcing its determination to balance its own budget at the earliest practical moment after the war and by announcing that the U.S. dollar would no longer be on a 24-hour basis, but firmly anchored to a fixed quantity of gold.

More than 60 years later, these words ring out with as much pertinence as ever, amid the intensification of every single imbalance that was ultimately generated by the agreements reached at the Bretton Woods conference.

Seniorage

Within the context of the power struggle and the competition to dominate global trade, a major issue is that of *seniorage,* or the privilege bestowed, by default, on the country producing the world's reserve currency. Seniorage refers to the difference between the value of the bullion in a coin, the value of the bullion needed to produce a coin, and the value of the coin itself, within whatever monetary system is dominant. The difference in the value of bullion in a coin and the purchasing value that the coin carries becomes the layer of liquidity coursing through the global capital markets at any given time. In other words, seniorage is the means to monetary debasement of a currency.

Under the Bretton Woods system, the value of the U.S. dollar (USD) was fixed to gold, which was convertible for dollars only for international center banks and governments, with all other currencies aligned to the dollar-gold anchor. Thus, the United States gained unprecedented advantage through seniorage, and it provided the liquidity necessary to fund war reparations in Europe.

Key to my own monetary mantra is that seniorage, over time, has increased on a theoretical basis, as a percentage of the real value of any currency, including the world's reserve currency. In fact, ever since the U.S. dollar gold standard was abandoned in 1971, seniorage really has been 100 percent, given that every dollar now created is nothing more than a paper credit, backed by faith, rather than gold.

Perhaps, instead of "In God We Trust" being printed on the U.S. dollar, it should read "In Perpetual Monetary Reflation We Trust," as the greenback is merely an IOU—a pledge by the U.S. Treasury to make good.

This thought embodies the evolution that has led us from the time when the Bretton Woods system was implemented, right down to today's macromonetary environment. Of all the market moves experienced in human history, the most ferocious and longest running has to be the current bull market in seniorage. This bull market is the bloodline for the global economy, more so than ever before, amid intensified codependency among global trade partners.

Any retracement (reduction) in global seniorage from its current level near 100 percent would be devastating for the global economy, given the magnitude of debt that has been created using seniorage liquidity as collateral. From this perspective, the current bull market in gold, a price appreciation that incorporates nearly every paper currency on the planet, is a sign of contracting seniorage and intensifying risk of a debt-asset implosion.

As of the end of World War II, of an estimated $40 billion in global gold reserves, the United States held $26 billion. Thus, as stated earlier, the United States held 60 percent of the world's monetary gold. As the United States used the power of seniorage to rebuild U.S.-friendly regimes in war-torn Europe and to promote capitalism in Eastern Europe, world trade accelerated rapidly throughout the 1950s.

Moreover, it became easier for the United States to maintain a military presence overseas, which completed the transition to the era of *Pax Americana* from the era of Pax Britannica dominance that had lasted several centuries following the era of Pax Romana, as defined by the Roman Empire of the first century. As a result of its victory in World War II, the United States claimed seniorage, and the current era of monetary debasement, credit creation, and paper wealth reflation was born.

By the later part of the 1950s, the size of the gold base held by the United States had barely changed, while the seniorage linked to the value of the U.S. dollar had already intensified somewhat dramatically. This imbalance, the first of many that would occur, was reflected by the fact that in 1958 the U.S. trade balance swung into deficit.

Following the Bretton Woods conference, the U.S. reserve holdings of gold covered 100 percent of the U.S. dollar money supply. By 1956, that ratio had practically collapsed, plunging to 16 percent, and in the four years after the U.S. trade balance first posted a deficit in 1958, the ratio declined further, reaching a lowly 11 percent in 1962. In other words, in 1962, the United States had only enough gold to convert 11 percent of the U.S. dollars in circulation. It took less than 20 years for the U.S. dollar to be devalued by 89 percent, relative to the holdings of gold reserves.

Exacerbating the situation was the cost of the Korean War, and when the U.S. trade balance posted a deficit in 1958, it prompted a response from the Eisenhower administration, which imposed import quotas on oil and placed restrictions on exports. Arguably these actions intensified the recession that began in 1959 and likely contributed to the U.S. election of Democrat John F. Kennedy to the presidency in 1960.

As the U.S. deficits expanded, the price of gold began to creep higher and monetary authorities became concerned that there was not enough gold in the world to meet the theoretical, potential demand for a full-scale U.S. dollar conversion/redemption. As a result, in 1961, European nations, the United Kingdom, and the United States agreed to contribute gold to a fund to maintain the price of gold at $35 per ounce. More accurately, a pool of gold was created to support the value of the dollar. Essentially, it was an attempt to squelch the raging bull market in seniorage and force the value of the dollar higher, thus causing a reversal in the trend toward ever-larger U.S. trade deficits.

It seems all the more ironic today, as these same imbalances are far more intense than ever before, yet there is far less anxiety about convertibility issues. In line with the permabear market in the USD, and the permabull market in seniorage and debt creation, complacency has experienced yet another stunning bull market of its own.

The fund created in 1961 to hold the USD at $35 per ounce of gold, became known as the *Gold Pool*. This scheme kept the price of gold at $35 per ounce for five years, until 1966, when a trend toward increased speculative purchases of gold began to emerge. This forced Gold Pool member nations to provide their own tightly held gold reserves to meet the expansion in demand and keep the price pegged.

On several occasions, such as in response to the Cuban missile crisis, the price of gold spiked as high as $40 per ounce. In 1967, there was a speculative attack on the British pound, and a subsequent run on the Gold Pool. On November 17, 1967, the British government was forced to devalue the pound.

U.S. President Johnson was thus faced with a critical decision stemming from the resultant change in the value of the USD relative to the British pound. He could move to institute protectionist trade measures; he could move to dramatically reduce the burgeoning U.S. fiscal deficit (expanding as a result of skyrocketing costs linked to the Vietnam War—sound familiar?); or he could accept the risk of a full-blown run on gold, and thus the U.S. dollar.

Walt Rostow stated to LBJ on March 19, 1968:

> The world supply of gold is insufficient to make the present system workable, particularly as use of the dollar as a reserve currency is essentially to create the required international liquidity needed to sustain world trade and world growth.

Without the ability to perpetually devalue all paper currencies, global trade would stagnate, and the global economy would pay the price.

From (Walt Rostow) Lyndon Johnson to Ben Bernanke, the song remains the same.

As the pressure intensified in line with the escalation of the war in Vietnam, the United States strong-armed (West) Germany to hold the USD in reserve, rather than gold, amid a push by the German government to contemplate some degree of redemption of their expanding export receipts, for gold.

France, another reconstruction-facilitated holder of USD-based export receipts, was not so easily strong-armed. France was far more reluctant to hold USD in reserve than was Germany because classic gold-standard-economist Jaques Reuff had ascended to the position of primary monetary policy advisor to French President Charles De Gaulle. Reuff advised De Gaulle to pursue an exchange with the United States, demanding gold for their USD reserves.

Meanwhile, in 1968 President Johnson imposed a series of measures to stimulate American exports and crimp the outflow of gold to Europe. This outflow came against a backdrop highlighted by growth in Soviet U.S. dollar reserves derived from Russian petroleum export receipts known as *petro-dollars*. From its inception in 1957, to the end of the 1960s, the Soviets funneled nearly one billion dollars worth of petro-dollars into European banks, thus creating the eurodollar market.

By 1968, the European black-market price for gold in U.S. dollars had risen to five times the official price at which redemption was, theoretically, possible; and the outflow of gold from the United States had reached a crisis level. Before the end of the year, the Gold Pool had been disbanded, and a new series of meetings among global monetary officialdom had commenced, seeking a solution to the USD problem.

The International Monetary Fund met in Rio de Janeiro, leading to the birth of "Special Drawing Rights" (SDR), which was essentially a new "paper-gold" that prevented nations from purchasing dollars at a pegged price and then selling them at a higher open-market price. Moreover, the SDR program gave nations a reason to hold dollars, by generating a return of 1.5 percent.

Still, the return paid on SDR holdings failed to adequately bridge the widening gap in what was rapidly becoming a two-tiered monetary system.

Hence, when the energy crisis greeted new U.S. President Richard Nixon in 1970, he responded by lifting oil import quotas, which led to a flood of dollars flowing out of the United States and into the hands of petro-producing nations. By 1971, the United States had a reserves-deficit of $56 billion and had depleted most of its nongold reserves. In the first six months of 1971, another $22 billion worth of U.S. dollars flowed out of the country, and the demand by foreign countries to redeem dollars for gold had become so great that it drove President Nixon to take a dramatic step.

This step would come to define an era and would lead to the birth of a new monetary mantra, defined by the *goldbug* mentality.

The Goldbug Is Born

On August 15, 1971, without consulting the U.S. Federal Reserve or the State Department, President Nixon closed the "gold window" by suspending the convertibility of dollars for gold thus abolishing the gold standard (peg). Nixon also imposed a 90-day wage and price freeze, and imposed a 10 percent import surcharge on all good and services shipped into the country.

The resultant political crisis caused monetary officials to meet in Washington in late 1971, a pow-wow that resulted in the forging of the Smithsonian Agreement. Under the terms of the agreement, the United States raised the official price of gold from $35 per ounce to $38 per ounce. Also, the United States revalued the dollar versus the yen by 17 percent (dollar devaluated), versus the German mark by 17 percent, versus the British pound by 9 percent, and versus the French franc by 9 percent. In all, the dollar devaluation of 1971 was equivalent to (–) 8.57 percent.

More importantly, the price of gold was allowed to float, and by early 1972, it had soared to $50, as noted in Figure 10.1.

Early in 1973 the price of gold broke out above the then high at $70 per ounce, and in February the United States moved again to devalue the dollar, amid a deepening economic recession and virulent asset-disinflation risk.

Along with another increase in the official price of gold, to a well-below-market price of $44.22 per ounce, the United States allowed the value of the U.S. dollar (USD) versus other foreign currencies to float freely.

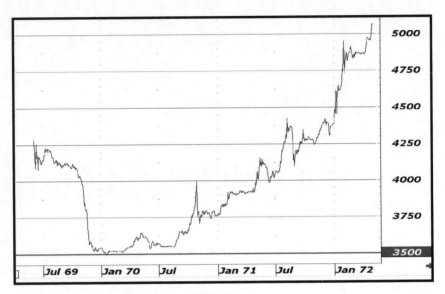

FIGURE 10.1   Spot gold: daily close 1969 to 1972
Source: Weldononline.com.

Subsequently, the foreign exchange (forex) market, as we know it today, was born; and not long after that, currency futures were introduced, allowing transparent open market flotation of the dollar on a second-to-second basis.

Initially, foreign central banks purchased dollars, with the Bank of Japan (BOJ) alone buying over $1 billion in the first week following the float. And, while this would prove to be a small sum, relative to the since-accumulated $900 billion in U.S. reserves held by the BOJ, offshore demand for dollars was short-lived and the greenback collapsed anew in March 1973. This in turn intensified the demand for gold from foreigners, and came in line with the previously mentioned vicious economic recession, and the first real oil shock.

As a result, gold soared. Evidence is in the daily chart shown in Figure 10.2, reflecting the movement in the price of USD-based gold during this period. From $50 in 1972 to nearly $200 by the end of 1974, the price of gold quadrupled in less than three years.

Conversely the international value of a dollar collapsed to 25 cents. Certainly some responsibility for the deep depreciation in the dollar needs to be ascribed to the Watergate scandal that led to Richard Nixon's memorable path toward resignation.

FIGURE 10.2   Spot gold: daily close 1972 to mid-1975
Source: Weldononline.com.

As things stabilized, so, too, did the dollar stabilize on interna-tional markets amid a less intense risk assessment associated with the United States. Gold went through a deep correction that took the price all the way back down to $100 per ounce in 1976.

In dissecting the current environment amid a deepening downside correction in gold's present price, it is important to spotlight that the downside correction, from a peak near $200 to a low just above $100, plots a textbook Fibonacci retracement pattern (see Chapter 20).

In hindsight, the correction offered one of the greatest buying op-portunities of all time, as the march higher resumed in the face of growing tension in the Middle East and President Carter's problems in Iran. (This again sounds eerily familiar to events in 2006.)

Throughout 1977, and right on into the fourth quarter of 1978, gold reclimbed the mountain, eventually reaching a newer, higher, peak, as $200 was violated in the second half of the year (see Figure 10.3).

Another U.S. political mess, combined with another petroleum crisis and volatility in the Middle East conspired to drive the U.S. Dollar Index from 107.60 as of June 1976, to a secular low below 82.00, and to a second low of 84.00 in July 1980. The end result is visible in Figure 10.4,

FIGURE 10.3   Spot gold: daily close mid-1976 to mid-1979
Source: Weldononline.com.

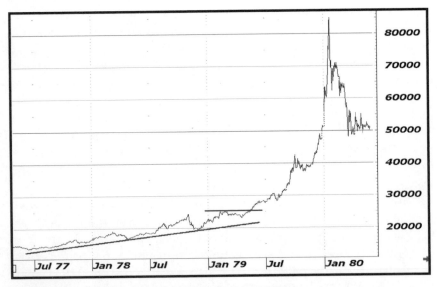

FIGURE 10.4   Spot gold: daily close mid-1977 to mid-1980
Source: Weldononline.com.

which reveals the historic spike in gold prices to a secular high that stands today at $875 (basis spot price), set in January 1980.

It was not long after that I first walked onto the trading floor of the Commodities Exchange.

To many, the abolishment of the gold standard remains the key monetary event in sowing the seeds for the current environment of perpetually intensifying imbalances.

The Emperor with No Clothes

L et me repeat: To many, the abolishment of the gold standard remains the key monetary event in sowing the seeds for the current environment of perpetually intensifying imbalances.

I find it difficult, philosophically, to disagree.

- The reality—the global economy is more dependent than ever, on credit.

- The reality—the global economy is more dependent than ever on the U.S. dollar (USD).

- The reality—the global economy has been built to produce the cheapest goods possible, for consumption in the United States, and the competition to do so intensifies every day.

- The reality—the U.S. consumer has no savings.

- The reality—the real wage-derived income is deflating.

- The reality—the U.S. consumer is more dependent than ever on housing for paper wealth.

- The reality—China, Japan, Korea, Singapore, Malaysia, India, Taiwan, and the Philippines are simply unable at this point in time (nor any time in the foreseeable future) to consume anywhere near the volume of goods they produce.

■ The reality—China, Japan, Korea, Singapore, Malaysia, India, Taiwan, and the Philippines have been willing to perpetually accumulate U.S. dollars in return for competing to sell their goods to the U.S. consumer.

In short, reality can be defined with four sentences:

1. Every single day for more than 30 years, since the abolishment of the gold standard (and before), global imbalances that are linked to trade, savings, reserves, exports, output, consumption, and debt have intensified and have reached a new peak intensity level of imbalance.
2. The global economy is incestuously codependent in its reliance on the U.S. consumer, and thus the health of the global economy is now dependent on the health of the U.S. housing market.
3. The global economy is dependent on a perpetual debasement of the USD to lead all paper currencies to devaluation relative to gold, as the only means to avoid a catastrophic debt deflation and global depression.
4. Someday, things will change.

When that day comes, the Emperor will be revealed as having no clothes, the U.S. Treasury will face the "exercise" of a mountainous USD put (in option terminology, a put gives the owner the right to sell at a given price) and some most difficult choices will be made.

I have no answers, no solutions.

The time for an academic approach is long gone. Reality now prevents the application of weed killer, for fear of killing the entire lawn.

My only goal is to monitor that reality and uncover opportunities for wealth appreciation within the market through risk-adverse speculation.

Someday, when things change, goldbugs will be proven right. The problem is that the macroscenario will be so hyperinflationary or debt deflationary that likely no one will feel like celebrating.

There will be a choice between two options:

1. Facilitate a recession and hope that debt can be paid down without an economic implosion, led by a cocooning of the U.S. consumer.

2. Facilitate a reflation, press the "Monetary Armageddon" button, and pay down all the U.S. debt with freshly printed U.S. dollars, acquiescing to the steepest devaluation of the U.S. currency ever witnessed, in an attempt to reflate domestic U.S. consumption and bail out the U.S. housing market with even cheaper liquidity.

Again, how familiar are these options? It is no surprise that gold is back above $600, and the U.S. Dollar Index is pushing 85.00 again.

The simple truth is that humans want to avoid pain; so as global central banks look at the economic abyss represented by the risk of a U.S. debt deflation, the solution will always "appear" to be monetary reflation through currency debasement.

The Emperor is wearing no clothes. Someday, everyone will notice. I want to be an owner of gold on that day.

PART THREE

Capital Markets: Looking Inside the Market

Welcome to My Boot Camp

I can't give you everything you need to know about precious metals, and I don't presume to say that I'm the most knowledgeable about this subject, especially about mining. But, you do not need to be an expert in the mining arena to successfully navigate the precious metals markets.

There is still, however, much that you *do* need to know before you can start trading. You must have a basic understanding of the mining industry's supply-and-demand (S/D) fundamentals, along with deeper insights into the dominant top-down macrodynamic. You also need to have a complete overview of the technical structure of the market including a comprehensive integration of intramarket (within) and intermarket (among other markets) analysis.

From that point, it is up to you—as an individual investor, trader, and speculator—to make your own decisions. You have to determine your risk profile (see Chapter 41 for information about assessing your risk) and how you can combine these factors into the investment decisions that make the most sense for your circumstances.

To help you learn the process for making an investment decision, I describe all the relevant information, how to dissect it, and how to devise a useful trading strategy. Because you have your own risk-reward situation, I can't offer a universal trading strategy. Instead, I describe my own routine including all the data that I want to know every day when speculating in the precious metals markets.

I catalog my own daily routine in my capacity as the sole researcher, writer, technical analyst, and editor of the *Metal Monitor.*

Welcome to my office.

Welcome to Weldon's Capital Market Boot Camp.

Intermarket Analysis— The Tape Tells a Story

First thing, every morning (which normally begins for me before 4 A.M. EST), I want to know how much the prices of gold and silver have changed since I last looked. Then, I want to know the price changes in everything else. And I mean everything—every market sector around the world, all macromonetary and mining fundamental input, and everything in the metals markets.

On my desk is the quote board—three computer screens that give me the information for many market sectors. I'm not always looking for the same thing. Sometimes, I'm looking for the market sector that has had the largest change while I was sleeping. I may be anticipating that a certain market sector will soon begin moving, reversing, or accelerating, and I will look at that sector first. Or, I might first examine whichever market sector has been making the biggest headline news lately, or the market that has been dominant in leading other markets directionally.

It all depends. But, over the course of the day, I will examine every sector. Usually, I start off by peeking at gold and silver, followed by fixed-income and then foreign exchange, key market indicators. Finally, I'll review all the global stock indexes, and sectors within each country. Then, I'll turn my attention to the entire commodities markets, from grains to petroleum, from base metals to tropical commodities and the meats.

Having a complete, top-to-bottom image of the most recent price changes in every global market proves handy when I examine the fundamental, macroeconomic data input, and the geopolitical dynamic. An in-depth knowledge of the intricacies of the most important price changes allows you to hone your focus, seeking the most pertinent happenings, on both a macrobasis and a microbasis.

Starting from the back end (from a book-writing perspective) so I can conclude with the metals sector, I first peer to the far right of my multi-screen display to find the commodities sector (sans metals).

For potential clues about the dominant trend in global food prices, I examine the soybean complex (beans, meal, and oil, and all the resultant calendar spreads and ratio relationships), along with wheat and corn, not to mention rice (a commodity that is underrated by most all traders when it comes to providing potential clues to the dominant trend in global food prices).

 It is time to enter the market laboratory and look at some examples, starting with rice, as seen in Figure 13.1. Rice prices can be very volatile.

More interestingly, looking at Figure 13.1, you can see how the 12-month rate-of-change in rice prices might be used as a proxy for the year-over-year statistically based pressure on

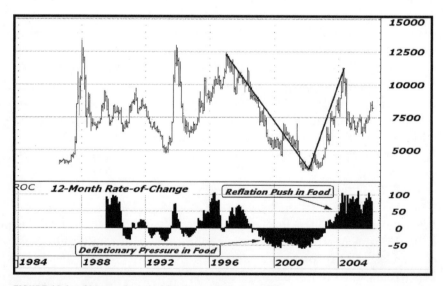

FIGURE 13.1   Chicago Board of Trade rough rice monthly
Source: Weldononline.com.

consumer price food components. During the period preceding the recession and near-tilt into deflation experienced in the United States in 2000, rice prices had been signaling the deflationary influences still emanating from the Asian foreign exchange (FX)-debt crisis of the late 1990s. Conversely, the 12-month rate of change in the monthly closing price of rice bottomed in line with the secular low in the Commodity Research Bureau (CRB) Index (an index of commodity prices that is actually agriculturally weighted), and within months of a significant bottom in other commodity markets, including several base metals.

Another reason I like to monitor the rice market is its heavy Asian trade, which offers a unique insight into the near-term pressure in food during the dark of morning, hours before wheat and corn begin trading in Chicago.

I'm not suggesting that rice or grain should be the dominant factor in weighing inflation or deflationary pressure trend dominance. But it can prove to be a small but valuable piece of a bigger-picture puzzle.

You can do the same thing just by being more observant on a daily basis. Information is available all around you, everywhere. My dad still calls me to report on the latest changes in the supermarket prices for orange juice, butter, milk, eggs, and particularly coffee. A change in the price of orange juice alone might not mean anything. However, a change in the prices of a majority of these items would say something about the dominant pressure in the prevailing reflation or deflation trend.

Usually, the first changes are miniscule. My dad pointed out a change in the old consumer food staple, the can of coffee. The can remains the one-pound size, yet it usually contains only 13 ounces. The "Giant" Hershey's Milk Chocolate bar was originally a seven-ounce bar that was sold at retail outlets for 99 cents and frequently contained a bonus ounce, making it eight ounces of chocolate. Now, the so-called Giant bar weighs six ounces, but it still costs 99 cents. My dad and I know this only because we both love Hershey's chocolate.

Indeed, for example, during 2006 there is a heightened awareness of gasoline prices. More people than I could have imagined now know the price changes in the natural gas market—a market that did not even exist when I first started in the business.

 The price of orange juice is an example of something that the average consumer can note, and I follow it daily on my quote board.

My dad often reminds me that not long ago, two half-gallons of premium OJ could be purchased for $4. Now, that same deal costs $5 (see Figure 13.2). That is a *huge* +25 percent rate

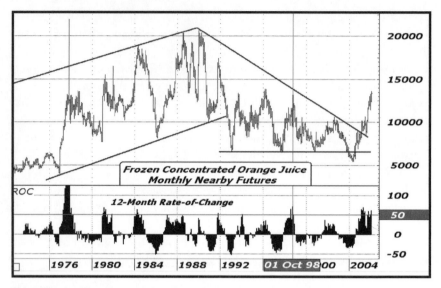

FIGURE 13.2   Frozen concentrated orange juice monthly nearby futures
Source: Weldononline.com.

of inflation and is worthy of note in examining the global markets for clues to determine the best strategy in the precious metals arena.

Right now, as is evident in Figure 13.2 of the frozen concentrated orange juice (FCOJ) market, orange juice is reflating. For those of you in boot camp, the lesson is that the OJ market represents a supportive intermarket influence on the precious metals sector.

If I am following data such as the price of rice, I must also keep abreast of the macrosituation in major producing and export nations. In the case of rice, that means monitoring the economic scene in Vietnam. I must also watch the action in the Vietnamese currency, the *dong*. In fact, Vietnam has become a semisignificant player in the commodities markets as a major exporter of coffee and rice.

Similarly, I watch rubber. Thus, I keep an eye on Thailand and on the Thai baht as well as on the intermarket relationships among all the Asian currencies. My reasons for doing so include the export competitive dynamic as it applies across a broad range of commodities.

By now, you should start to see how all this information is so intricately intertwined that everything matters. You haven't even looked at currency, but you are already seeing the Thai baht and Vietnamese dong as factors that might impact precious metals.

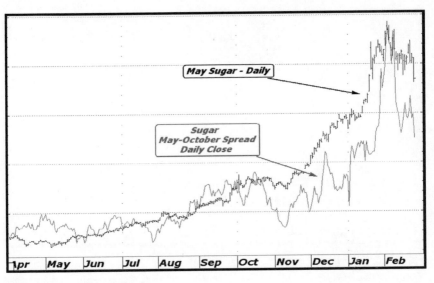

FIGURE 13.3   Sugar: daily close
Source: Weldononline.com.

Observe the current situation in the sugar market, which has rallied to near 20 cents per pound, leading to the highest prices since 1981. When I look at a market and dissect it by means of the spreads, this is the perspective I seek, since it reveals clues to the dominant pressure within the market.

In the case of sugar in late February 2006, you can review Figure 13.3 and determine that the spread did not lead prices higher. Subsequently, the probabilities suggest a hard-core shortage in the near term is not the most likely outcome. When the spread then breaks to the downside, as a precursor to a similar technical breakdown in the price of sugar, as occurred days later, you know it means something.

It definitely means something to active traders in the precious metals arena. Sugar, like oil or rice, is a key global commodity that is exported and imported in size and one that matters in the economies of the major producers. Even more relevant is that sugar and silver prices seem to have been highly correlated in the past, at least directionally speaking, if not in terms of the relative magnitude of price change.

So, you should plot the sugar market versus the silver market in the near-term overlay (Figure 13.4), a chart that I might pull up on any given (still-dark) morning while surveying the price changes flashing on my quote board.

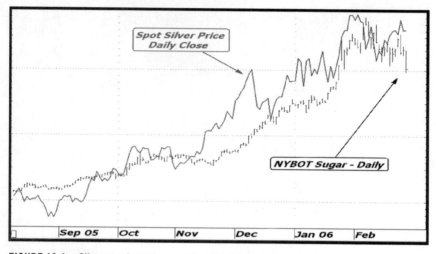

FIGURE 13.4   Silver market versus sugar market
Source: Weldononline.com.

Subsequently a breakdown in sugar spreads might be of significance to holders of long exposure in silver. I am not saying I would dump a silver position, or even less so, a core silver equity holding solely because sugar spreads are weak. But, I might tighten my protective sell stop-loss order based on this information, in conjunction with other information I might come across later in my quote board examination.

As I progress through the market sectors flashing on my board, I begin to single out specific noteworthy data. When I reach the end of the board, all this information is in the forefront of my thoughts as I approach the macrodata and news.

I look at each commodity, first by change in price and then via a daily chart overview, a perspective that incorporates my proprietary momentum indicators (see Chapter 34).

I move through the soft-tropicals, including sugar, cocoa, coffee, milk, butter, and orange juice, along with cotton. Again, I break down each market on an outright basis, per the calendar spreads in each, and each relative to various currencies, relative to the Commodity Research Bureau (CRB), and relative to gold. I look at each market individually using a chart view and my momentum indicators, along with multiple canned technical overlays.

I want to know whether these markets are moving together, up or down. If so, is this a signal in terms of the inflation-deflation impact on the CRB, the U.S. dollar (USD), and thus precious metals?

Moreover, if these commodities markets are moving in tandem, one way or the other, I want to know whether the majority are experiencing a tightening in the physical market that might be reflected in changes in the calendar spreads. For example, I want to know whether the sugar spreads and the silver spreads are moving in the same direction. Or, have they both reversed, suggesting a trend reversal in the flat price of both commodities, or even in all commodities? A widening *contango* (front month price discount to the back month deferred contracts, symbolic of ample supply for near-term delivery) and a decline in all grains might indicate a less intense inflationary push from the food sector. Or, it might even mean a deflationary push is developing.

Either circumstance might mean something for precious metals. Because every little thing matters, I want to know everything that is going on.

Food prices matter, and even more so, oil prices matter. The petroleum markets are critical to the direction of the CRB Index and the Goldman Sachs Commodity Index (GSCI, energy weighted), and thus energy is critical to the precious metals sector. Therefore, I monitor the energy markets on a constant basis, noting the changes in West Texas Intermediate Crude Oil (WTI, traded on the New York Mercantile Exchange), on a nominal basis, and relative to the rest of the global crude oil prices. Other important crude oil prices include North Sea Brent, Dubai Sweet, Mexico's Mayan grade, or the African Sour grades.

It is within this context that the Chinese factor has become increasingly important. The Chinese are directly competing for longer-term contracts for the sweeter grades of crude oil, now that their refinery infrastructure has been modernized. The shift away from using African sour grades toward the lighter, sweeter grades means that when China signs a deal with the Saudis or Venezuela for the delivery of crude oil, it is essentially absorbing supply that would normally be consumed in the United States.

With this in mind, I keep a close eye on the Chinese dynamic as it applies to crude oil, petroleum products, aluminum, alumina, steel, and all the base metals, looking for clues to help define a bigger-picture environment that may influence gold and silver in a similar way.

I focus on the WTI strip, too, seeking clues to changes in sentiment as it applies to expectations for future energy price (see Figure 13.5). I want to know if the market is paying for supply, or enticing product holders to put supply into storage. Or, is this the case of a forward spread that collapsed, counter to an outright flat-price appreciation, as

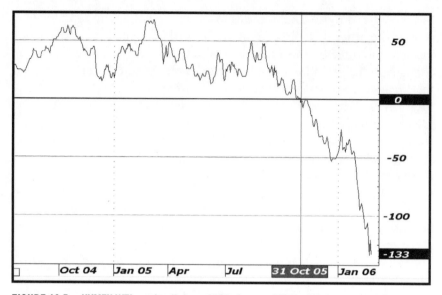

FIGURE 13.5   NYMEX WTI crude oil, June 2006–August 2006 calendar spread: daily close
Source: Weldononline.com.

seen in the petroleum markets in the second half of 2005 amid the Katrina-disaster price rally?

Even this catastrophe, which drove flat prices toward new all-time highs, failed to generate enough bullishness to erase the contango structure that dominated the crude oil spreads. On the contrary, that the spreads failed to move into a state of backwardation (nearby price premium, a market-derived mechanism for drawing supply out of storage and into the market) was a sign that there was no real shortage of supply resulting from the storm. Observe the action in the spread, which plunged from October 2005 into the end of the second quarter of 2006 (Figure 13.5) while the flat price of crude oil has remained above $60 (as seen in Figure 13.6).

I also monitor the relationship between U.K.-traded North Sea Brent Crude, and WTI. I want to know if there is an "open-arb-window." In other words, is it financially feasible (and profitable) to ship crude oil, or energy products across the Atlantic or Pacific, from the United States? If so, an examination of the forward strip becomes more relevant as I try to determine if supply is being moved.

Drilling deeper into the petro-patch, I observe the changes in product prices: nominally, relative to one another, relative to crude oil, and

FIGURE 13.6   NYMEX WTI crude oil, spot contract: monthly close
Source: Weldononline.com.

most importantly, on a seasonal basis, relative to forward prices, and of course, relative to the implications found within the fundamental supply-and-demand energy market data.

The relative movements in the summer-season calendar spread for gasoline often confirms or refutes significant changes in the near-term supply dynamic. Certainly a decline in U.S. gasoline production and a drawdown in supply in storage during April that causes the May-to-August spread to shift from contango to backwardation, is far more significant than a decline in supply during November that has no impact on a forward contango price structure.

The spreads in gasoline, heating oil, and natural gas can provide revealing information about the market's dominant psychology. You need to review Figures 13.7 and 13.8, which reveal a key summer seasonal gasoline spread (defined as May–July 2006), and one of the key winter seasonal spreads in natural gas (January–February 2007).

A spike in storage additions to U.S. gasoline inventories during the first quarter of 2006 led to expectations of ample summer supplies in gasoline, which caused the summer spread to move to a deep discount situation (Figure 13.7). This coincided with a decline in pump prices back below two dollars. More recently, thanks to intensified geopolitical

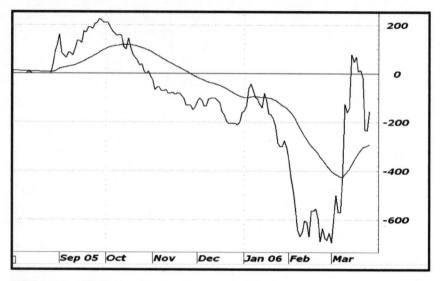

FIGURE 13.7 NYMEX May–July gasoline spread: daily close
Source: Weldononline.com.

risk that applies to any number of petromacro hot spots such as Venezuela, Nigeria, Iran, the United Arab Emirates (UAE), Saudi Arabia, and Indonesia, the spread spiked back to a slight (nearby price) premium structure, which helped support a push in pump prices back above two dollars. The slight contango structure evident at the end of the first quarter 2006 implies that supply-and-demand risk is evenly bal-

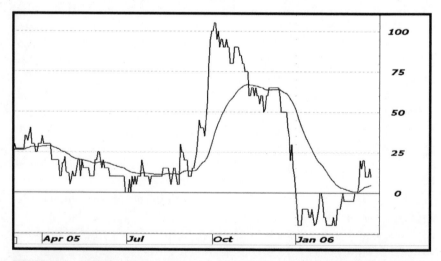

FIGURE 13.8 NYMEX natural gas spread, January 2007 versus February 2007: daily close
Source: Weldononline.com.

anced at the approach of the peak 2006 summer driving season. I would look for a change in this dynamic, in either direction, as part of my daily routine for intermarket oversight and analysis.

Similarly, in natural gas, I am looking for changes in the spreads to indicate potential shifts in the dominant underlying supply-demand balance, as it applies to the market's changing perception of supply-demand risk.

In the case of the example using the winter spread in natural gas (Figure 13.8), you can clearly identify the time period in which anxiety affected supplies during the period surrounding Hurricane Katrina. Then, the decline into a state of contango as 2006 began was indicative of a historic supply build. Enough natural gas was injected into storage during the fourth quarter, in line with the warmest January ever in the northeast United States to create a historic supply surplus.

As with gasoline, supply and demand were fairly evenly balanced in underlying risk when the second quarter began. That is why it is critical to monitor these relationships in the near future.

Why, as a precious metals follower, do I focus so much on the petropatch? The answer is simple. Price action in petroleum product markets often leads the entire commodity sector, including the precious metals.

I want to know whether gasoline is the upside leader, more so than crude oil, more so than gold. Is it rallying as denominated in all global currencies? I want to know whether a rally in gasoline relative to crude is the reason the WTI-Dubai spread might be widening, or vice versa.

To me, all these things matter, at all times.

A major influence in the gold market is the rampant reflation in paper wealth seen in energy-producing nations, much of which has been parked in gold. As this dynamic intensifies, so does the influence of the energy markets on the precious metals markets. Consequently, I go even further, by taking the relationships and comparing them back to the market that I am monitoring.

An example of how this works, using crude oil and gold, can be seen in Figure 13.9, in which I compare the price path of the crude-gold ratio spread (simply, crude's price divided by gold's price) with that of gold alone. I am particularly interested in the interplay between the two from the perspective of crude oil's leadership, most clearly exhibited during the 1999/2002 period.

From this perspective, the divergence seen in the first quarter of 2005 might be troubling in the context of the petroleum sector's continued ability to provide upside reflation leadership for the precious metals.

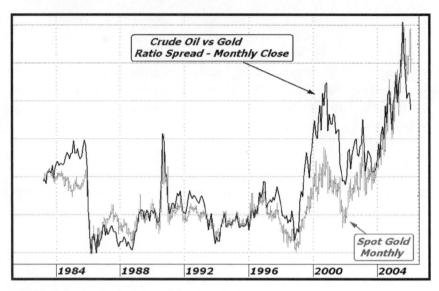

FIGURE 13.9   Crude oil versus gold ratio spread

Source: Weldononline.com.

Subsequently, a breakdown in crude oil might sway my expectations for gold and cause me to tighten protection on any risk exposure I might be carrying. Still, the primary reason to monitor the petroleum markets so intently, from the perspective of trading gold and silver is the reflation-disinflation angle, within the macro top-down methodology.

I am constantly seeking new angles from which to observe the macromessage offered by market action. As I monitor the moves in crude oil, I want to know what impact this activity is having on the bigger picture, as it relates to the energy-heavy Goldman Sachs Commodity Index, or GSCI.

When I seek to uncover the macro trend, I take a long-term perspective, using relative rates of change as a guide. In the case of the crude oil market, for its potential impact on the precious metals, I would look at Figure 13.10 plotting the 36-month rate of change in the GSCI.

From the inflation angle, there is justification for the multiyear high prices in gold and silver, since the three-year rate of commodity inflation as gauged by the GSCI reached its second highest rate ever in the 2004/2005 commodities bull market.

More recently, the correction in crude, the decline in gasoline, and the plunge in natural gas, all of which took place in the first quarter of

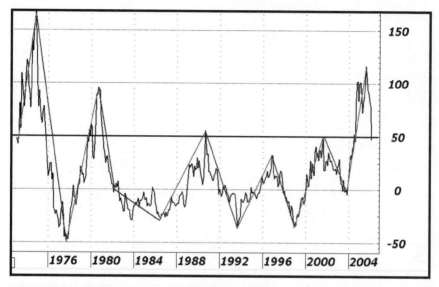

FIGURE 13.10   Thirty-six-month rate of change in GSCI
Source: Weldononline.com.

2006, have conspired to alleviate some of the reflationary pressure, as determined by this rate-of-change (ROC) indicator. Hence, the first-quarter stall in gold's bull market seems more reasonable, given the sharp deceleration in the ROC.

On the other hand, as of the end of the first quarter 2006, gold remained well bid above $550. Despite the deceleration in the ROC, it stayed historically high, hovering around the rampant-reflation-defining +50 percent level (Figure 13.10).

In fact, just weeks later, gold was at new highs, gasoline was back to $2, and crude was approaching $70 again, all while Figure 13.10 had mutated into Figure 13.11. Monitoring these relationships on a constant basis provides invaluable input when determining the validity and credibility of other forms of input.

Most of all, when multiple inputs are in sync and sending the same bullish or bearish message, I know that it is almost time to take action.

As I move through the energy sector, I also survey all the major global energy equities, and then examine all the global stock markets, including each country's main index, the internal sector indexes, and the external regional indexes and exchange traded funds (ETFs).

Immediately, I can determine how the metals and energy stocks "fit" within the near-term trend in the broader market averages, particularly

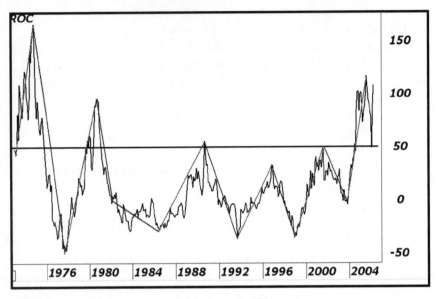

FIGURE 13.11 Thirty-six-month rate of change in GSCI
Source: Weldononline.com.

in countries that are producers, drillers, miners, or refiners of metal and energy commodities.

I begin by looking at the overnight performance in Asian indexes, focusing on China, Taiwan, Korea, and Australia, the last because of its direct link to base and precious metals.

Japan is a major focal point in Asia, and I check out each sector's performance. I am always particularly interested to see what is leading the Nikkei. I want to know whether the Japanese banks are leading the overall stock market. And, I want to know whether it is the regional, or the city banks, that are the driving force in that leadership. The answer just might matter.

In the second half of 2005, the banking sector was among the hottest performers in a rising Japanese equity market. The regional banks led the way within the sector, in conjunction with an upside leading expansion in lending by regional banks versus continued, albeit less violent, contraction in lending by the major city banks.

As a result of my constant monitoring and open-minded assessment and re-assessment, I was fully aware of this factor as a major, supportive background feature, in line with bullish technical readings emanating from gold priced in Japanese yen. This is a prime example of macrofundamental input falling into sync with technical indicators to increase the comfort level when initiating a position.

A reflation in regional bank lending in Japan, a feature that had been glaringly absent for years, provided a solid fundamental reason to believe that the bullish readings offered by my preferred technical indicators were valid. Once this thought process has been established, I am getting near the point where I am willing to assume risk in the market, through ownership of gold, against a short position in the Japanese yen.

Not all ideas work out as succinctly and successfully as did this one, but a look at Figure 13.12 reveals just how successful this methodology can be in pinpointing acceleration pivots and catalysts.

In mid-2005, gold priced in Japanese yen broke out technically to reach new bull move highs at the same time that the data revealed the first year-on-year increases in regional bank lending in Japan.

I was ready and recommended this position to my clients.

It does not take a degree in rocket science to make these observations, but it does take hard work and thorough research. It takes a boot camp mentality, every day.

FIGURE 13.12   Gold priced in Japanese yen: monthly close since 1989
Source: Weldononline.com.

Continuing the boot camp morning regimen, I compare the action in the Japanese equity market with the action in other Asian markets such as Singapore, China, and Taiwan. I want to know whether Japan is leading the rest of Asia or is just following. If Japan is following, who is leading? If I observe that Japan is leading the rest of Asia and that in Japan, the banks are outperforming, this potential macro-message could be a red flag to bullion traders and investors.

One way I monitor these relationships can be gleaned in Figure 13.13, where I have plotted the long-term 52-week moving average of two different stock indexes, the Japanese Nikkei, and the Morgan Stanley Capital International (MSCI) Taiwan Index.

In Figure 13.13, you can see that Japanese equity market outstanding performance and upside leadership, relative to Taiwan, became significantly more pronounced in mid-2005, at the same time that our Japanese bank-relationship perspective was coming into focus.

Again, it is worth stressing that everything matters in the macrosense, no matter whether it matters on any specific day. Naturally, gold priced in Taiwan dollars reacted as well, at the same time, a reaction that was intensified by expanding domestic Taiwanese money supply, credit, and trade.

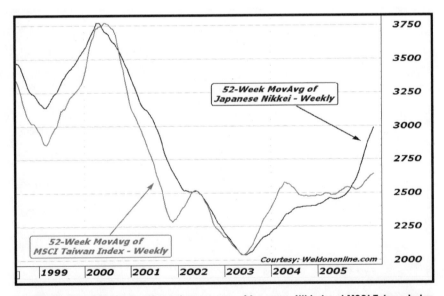

FIGURE 13.13 Fifty-two week moving average of Japanese Nikkei and MSCI Taiwan Index

Source: Weldononline.com.

In fact, as you can observe from Figure 13.14, you can consider linking the growth in Asian foreign exchange reserves, to the beginning of the secular uptrend in gold priced in Asian currencies, with a look at gold in Taiwan dollars in the 2000/2001 period.

I want to point out how you can make a single micro-observation within a bigger-picture observation. An important part of my approach is to store away mental observation notes, or micro-observations, for future macroexamination. The clues are everywhere, but you have to search for them, and usually, they are first evident in the microspecifics of the macroeconomic data. When I note several similar microimpulses, I begin to hunt for more, trying to link them with some potential change, interruption, or acceleration in the predominant macrotheme influencing the markets at the time.

Continuing with boot camp, I want a morning breakdown of the global equity markets. I want to know if the metals-heavy equity indexes are rallying, outperforming, breaking down, or what. The Australian equity market was among the best-performing markets during the 2004/2005 reflation period, with metal mining shares turning in the best relative performance, all of which occurred against a backdrop defined by a rallying commodity currency, the Australian dollar (AUD). I established that upside leadership was being exhibited by

FIGURE 13.14   Gold priced in Taiwan dollars: monthly close since 1984
Source: Weldononline.com.

specific mining names (e.g., *Rio Tinto,* a large industrial metals mining company) linked to Australia via their mining properties.

Upside global equity market leadership by an index represented by an appreciating commodity currency—within which the metals mining sector is leading the charge—is a bullishly supportive dynamic for the underlying metals markets from an intermarket analysis perspective and from a macrodefining thematic perspective.

Observe the weekly chart of Rio Tinto (Figure 13.15) and focus on the fact that the bulk of the price appreciation since 2001 occurred in the second half of 2005, in line with all the other intermarket-focused charts. Pay attention to the resumed rally to a new high in early April 2006, in line with a spike in industrial and precious metals prices, to its own new multidecade highs. The push to new highs in the Aussie stock market, as led by mining shares such as Rio Tinto, is a confirming and supportive feature of those rallies to new price highs in the metals markets.

To monitor risk, I am always looking for hints that run against the predominant theme. At the same time that Aussie stocks, as led by the mining shares, were pushing to newer new highs, mining shares in another gold-producing country were not confirming this move.

FIGURE 13.15   Rio Tinto PLC RPT: weekly close
Source: Weldononline.com.

Observe the failure of major-producing AngloGold, to reach its own newer new high in 2006, while gold was spiking toward $600 per ounce. This might mean one of several things (Figure 13.16). Note that Anglo-Gold led the way in the bullion bull phase discernible on the chart from 2001 to 2004. With that in mind, and Anglo failing to conform to that same pattern in 2006, you might think the issue was specific to Anglo, except that other major gold mining shares were not confirming the move in bullion either. Thus, it might mean that monetary influences have become more dominant and that paper gold might be inherently subjected to the same risk factors as the broader equity markets. This is particularly true when I incorporate my fixed-income overview to reveal that an upside breakout in global bond yields was taking place at the same time.

I want to know whether the emerging equity markets are generally underperforming. I want to know if there is something unique to the South African rand. I also want to know the stance of the Reserve Bank of South Africa, the core Consumer Price Index (CPI) rate, and so on as the macrofundamental analysis begins to kick in.

Simultaneously, I'm dissecting all the pertinent mining data provided by each country, and each company. This routine lets me monitor

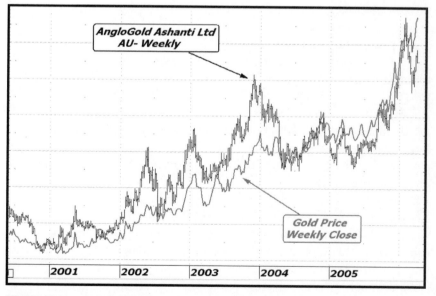

FIGURE 13.16   AngloGold bullion bull phase 2001 to 2004
Source: Weldononline.com.

the specific supply-and-demand fundamentals that apply at any given time to any given country or company.

The next relevant segment is "knowing the players."

If South African gold mining data reveals a decline in output, and I hear that South African producers are buying metal in the deferred forward market it likely means something. Does it mean they have overhedged their output and are buying back coverage for metal that will never be produced?

Knowing as many facts as possible may or may not explain the action. When the data does matter, it creates an edge for those who are aware of it.

I want to know whether emerging Asian markets are leading, or whether Eastern European markets are the market's focal point. If the Eastern European stock markets are exhibiting upside leadership, and I hear from one of my contacts that the buying of industrial metals in Hamburg is originating in the Eastern bloc; and then someone else says that gold purchases made in Zurich this morning were done on behalf of German banks, well just maybe I have identified a microcosm of a macroclue.

I look at everything I can, for clues. It really is that simple.

Getting back to my morning regimen, I shift gears and focus on the upper left portion of my massive price screen display, which flashes the prices for U.S. fixed-income markets. My display is cluttered with Treasury issues, covering all maturities, with information such as yield, price, and curve spreads shown.

I then observe the pricing structure revealed by the forward Eurodollar Deposit Rate strip. The strip provides an excellent proxy for the anticipated changes in official U.S. short-term interest rates.

I also monitor the credit spreads, including the Emerging Market Bond Index (EMBI+), which represents the yield (risk) premiums offered by emerging market bonds as a whole. Going deeper, I keep a close eye on the changes in each country in the EMBI+ and their individual spreads over U.S. Treasuries.

Credit spreads, in the form of U.S. corporate bond spreads and agency spreads, are also monitored on a daily basis.

From there, I scroll to the downside to observe the symbols representing non-U.S. fixed-income markets. These symbols include all the major industrialized bond markets in Europe, Asia, and North America, along with quotes for yield curves in each country. I also look at a full boat of quotes detailing prices, yields, spreads, and strips in the short-ends of the yield curves in all major economic countries and a number of emerging markets as well.

But, I am not yet finished with fixed income. I also compare countries, at the long-end, the short-end, as per the yield curve differentials, the differences in the forward deposit-rate strip, and the foreign exchange (FX) rate swaps. Monitoring all the major FX rate swaps, which become tradable proxies for changes in relative short-term interest rate differentials over various time frames, provides a nice segue into the next area of coverage—foreign exchange (FX).

While anticipated changes in relative interest rates, and thus potential rates of return, might be second only to capital-trade flow (and just ahead of relative money supply and credit growth) in influencing foreign exchange, the resultant changes in foreign exchange quotes likely provide the predominant intermarket influence on precious metals pricing. Therefore, a large percentage of my price display is dominated by foreign exchange quotes. The list is long and includes every major currency versus the U.S. dollar, every major currency against the yen, every major currency against the euro, most major currencies against one another, almost every emerging market currency relative to the USD, and a host of interregional, and intercommodity cross-rates.

Foreign exchange and fixed income are inexorably linked, and yet at times, they can offer completely different macro-opinions from an intermarket perspective.

Here is where things get even more complex. At the bottom line, we come to the USD, the U.S. consumer, the intensified trend toward global reliance on exports for income growth, and the willingness of global monetary authorities to perpetually allocate the overwhelming majority of trade income into U.S. dollar denominated assets.

When I look at currencies and interest rates, I cannot help but immediately think of the global imbalances in capital, wealth, savings, and trade that can be traced to the delinking of the USD from gold.

I am talking about 36 years of persistently intensifying imbalances—rips in the macro-fundamental-fiber that are worsening daily. They are breaks that were supposed to have been repaired in the 1980s with the Plaza Accord, and then the 1990s by the Louvre Accord as well as by the Washington Accord of 1999.

The imbalances are worse today than ever before—except of course, for tomorrow.

Nowhere are these imbalances more influential than in the forex and fixed-income arena. Trillions of dollars in debt, and trillions of yen and euro of paper wealth, are moving, changing hands, inflating, and deflating, all at the same time. Of all the markets, gold, as the global monetary currency, is at the center of this universe. What makes the current time unique (and thus so glaringly evident in terms of its macromessage) is that nearly every currency on the face of the planet is now depreciating relative to gold.

Simply, we have not encountered these circumstances since the last great bullion bull market, from 1978 to 1981. I cannot overstate the importance of looking at the relationship between every currency, and the U.S. dollar and gold.

Just as I have examined pertinent country-specific stock and mining share price action, in line with our macroeconomic data overview, I now begin to observe the price of gold in those same currencies.

Note the explosive rally in the price of gold denominated in South African rand. Except for the post-U.S.-bubble period of 2000 through 2003, the trend in rand-denominated gold has been reflationary, case closed.

From a low of 98 African rand per ounce in the mid-1970s, rand gold has trended higher for decades, to reach the recent 2006 high above 3,600 rand per ounce (see Figure 13.17).

Similarly, observe the appreciation in rupee gold, as bullion denominated in the currency (Indian rupee) of the world's largest gold-consuming nation, has reached 25,000 rupee per ounce.

FIGURE 13.17   Gold priced in South African rand: monthly close
Source: Weldononline.com.

There is another message within the long-term chart of gold in Indian rupee, as defined by the accelerated bull moves that have occurred sequentially. In other words, each successive bull market has been more intense than the previous one. The most recent bull phase has been nothing less than explosive, with the price of gold denominated in Indian rupee soaring from an already high 20,000 rupee per ounce, to an even higher 25,000 rupee per ounce, for an additional appreciation of +25 percent, in just six months' time (see Figure 13.18).

But, there is more to this picture than meets the eye. There are two sides to the forex-gold coin, the gold price side and the currency side. Hence when you observe the explosive rally in rupee gold, you must also observe the cause and effect unleashed when the Indian rupee stopped depreciating against the U.S. dollar, as noted in Figure 13.19.

From an intermarket perspective, you should focus on the mega-macro-monthly moving average (5-year moving average, calculated with a 60-month plot) that had been rising steadily, in line with rupee depreciation, since the early 1980s.

Then, in January 2004, the moving average turned to the downside directionally, signaling an end to the macrotrend in the rupee. In other

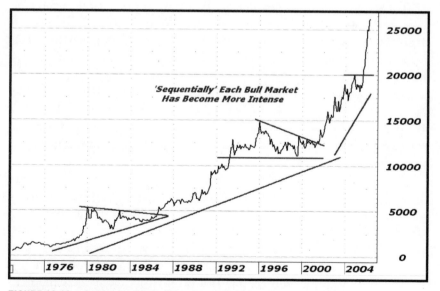

FIGURE 13.18   Gold priced in Indian rupee: monthly close since 1972
Source: Weldononline.com.

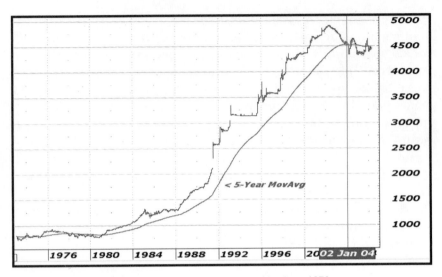

FIGURE 13.19   U.S. dollar versus Indian rupee: monthly since 1973
Source: Weldononline.com.

words, a depreciating rupee that had offered intermarket support for the rally in rupee gold for more than 20 years had vanished as a supportive feature, just as rupee gold exploded to the upside.

Gold's appreciation is now being driven by depreciation in the U.S. dollar, rather than being centered on rupee depreciation. From the intermarket perspective, note the overlay (Figure 13.20) in which the price of rupee gold is plotted against the value of the U.S. dollar versus the rupee.

You can also glean a macromessage from Figure 13.20 in defining the period of divergence from 1995 to 2001 as a time of price deflation and paper wealth reflation. As such, the current period of divergent price action can be identified as a time of price inflation, and paper wealth deflation.

It is no surprise that the global central banks are so reluctant to actually tighten credit conditions as opposed to their current campaign to raise the cost of funding, which has not yet inhibited the supply of, or demand for, credit.

So far, monetary officialdom has done a good job of offsetting the paper wealth deflation that might have otherwise accompanied the current trend in input and commodity price inflation. This is my personal reason for being so bullish on the price of gold from a secular perspective. Credit continues to expand, prices rise, and paper wealth

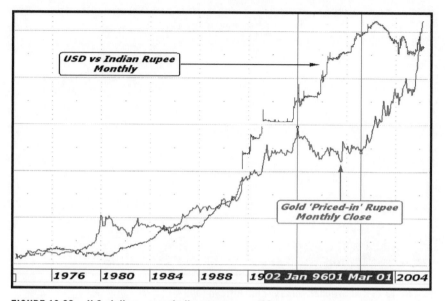

FIGURE 13.20   U.S. dollar versus Indian rupee: monthly
Source: Weldononline.com.

does not disinflate. Essentially, this is intensified paper currency debasement, reflected by a global rise in the value of gold relative to every paper currency, and in fact, relative to almost all paper assets.

Similarly, the overlay (Figure 13.21) reflects the divergence between the South African rand relative to the U.S. dollar, and the value of the rand relative to the price of gold.

Figure 13.21 leaves no doubt that imbalances have intensified dramatically, likely beyond the point of no-return, a point discussed in more detail in Chapter 14.

And, Figure 13.21 leaves no doubt that the price of gold is appreciating in all three currencies, the rand, the rupee, and the U.S. dollar.

Moving forward, in the current environment, any discussion about currency markets must include the Chinese yuan angle.

Not only does this apply from the commodity-demand juggernaut perspective, but more so, because China has surpassed Japan as the nation with the largest official holdings of U.S. dollar reserves.

In fact, in a recent edition of *Weldon's Money Monitor* (July 2006) I spotlighted the following updated data on the offer from Asian central banks, detailing their USD reserve holdings:

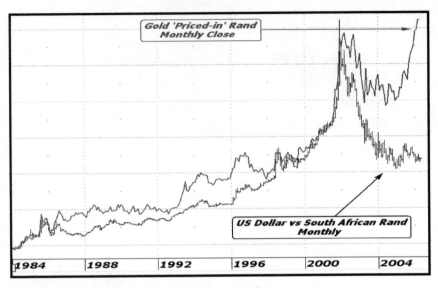

FIGURE 13.21 U.S. dollar versus South African rand

Source: Weldononline.com.

- India . . . Official Foreign Exchange Reserves . . . reached a RECORD HIGH of $151.62 billion, up nearly $3 billion in just the LAST WEEK ALONE.

- Singapore . . . Official Foreign Exchange Reserves . . . reached a NEW HIGH of $122.24 billion as of the end-March, rising almost $2 billion from the end-February total.

- Japan . . . Official Foreign Exchange Reserves . . . hit a NEW RECORD HIGH as of the end-March, reported at $852.03 billion, up nearly $2 billion from February.

- Thailand . . . Official Foreign Exchange Reserves . . . $55.3 billion . . . up by $1.5 billion over the last four weeks, and up by +16 percent since July 2005.

But most importantly, the release of these central bank (CB) reserves holding figures came within one week of the revelation by the People's Bank of China that China's official reserve holdings now exceed that of Japan's.

Compare that with the entire float of credit offered by the Fed, defined within the weekly money supply data as "Fed Bank Credit," which now amounts to $820 billion, on an average daily basis.

Never before, has one (let alone two) other central banks held more U.S. dollars in reserves than does the U.S. Federal Reserve itself.

Consider the tilt that could result from a potential shift in asset allocation by Asian central banks. Consider the corrosive impact on the ability of the Fed to most efficiently administer domestically focused monetary policy, particularly in the event of a global "event crisis." Essentially, Fed policy is being counterfeited. This is most bullish for bullion markets. Moreover, this is becoming increasingly evident in the markets.

Naturally, that the U.S. dollar is currently making new lows against the Chinese yuan (Figure 13.22) might be considered a sign, particularly given the subtle yet discernible acceleration lower in the USD since the beginning of 2006. The decline in the U.S. dollar versus the Chinese yuan could be a significant reason the price of industrial metals and energy products suddenly spike, on any given day. This has been true on many occasions, in the recent weeks and months. That is why I need to understand what the Chinese currency is doing, and why.

Within that context, and in keeping with our secular theme as it relates to counterfeited Fed policy mechanisms, I constantly monitor the price of gold, adjusted by a variety of yields. Figure 13.23 plots the

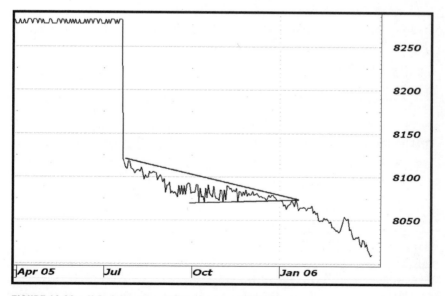

FIGURE 13.22   U.S. dollar versus Chinese yuan: daily close
Source: Weldononline.com.

price of gold divided by the yield on the 30-year U.S. Treasury bond. I call this my "Yield Adjusted Price of Gold," and it speaks volumes to the inherent reflation-deflation pressure in asset markets, as defined by the long-term yield and gold.

There is little doubt that the explosion to the upside in the post-2000 tech-bubble-collapse can be directly linked to the unprecedented degree of monetary stimulus provided by Alan Greenspan's Fed, when the Federal Open Market Committee (FOMC) took the Funds rate to a record low of just 1 percent.

At the end of the day, the relative value of all assets was reflated, a dynamic clearly visible in Figure 13.23, as the yield-adjusted price of gold has soared to a $1,200 per ounce equivalent.

(In fact, in my December 2005 interview with Ron Insana on CNBC Financial News Television, I highlighted this perspective when I was asked if I thought gold could rally to $1,000 per ounce. I simply stated that on a yield-adjusted basis, gold was already trading above $1,000.)

Of particular interest from this perspective is that the current 2005/2006 level of the bond yield-adjusted price of gold is nearly double the level seen at the inflation-gold peak in the 1977/1981 bull market. For the most part, this is a function of the difference in bond

FIGURE 13.23 Bond yield adjusted gold price versus 30-year bond yield: monthly close

Source: Weldononline.com.

yields, which were in double-digit territory during the inflation-plagued early 1980s.

Less discussed, however, is that the U.S. wage inflation environment was completely different in 1980, before the era of cheap global labor competition, which is the primary cause of the last wave of imbalance intensification.

Now, without any support from wage-driven reflation in the United States, European Union, and Japan, the natural level of yields is lower, by definition, even if that means the acceptance of a reflated gold price. This is true, at least as far as central banks are concerned, so long as the U.S. consumer-household does not suffer a bout of debt-disinflation.

Voilà—it comes time to monitor the U.S. yield curve and its recent trend toward what I term "pancake flattening," meaning that all maturities are flattening, in line with a move toward a zero interest rate differential in the deferred Depo strip (Eurodollar futures contracts, calendar spreads). The flattening in the U.S. yield curve has been caused by the same macrodynamic noted earlier, with lower long-term yields reflecting an intensified two-way, reflation-deflation risk.

 Another way to look at this comes in our boot camp regimen as we examine the U.S. fixed-income markets further, applying the same yield-adjusted method using the shorter-end yields. Observe the price of gold adjusted by (divided by) the yield on the U.S. two-year Treasury note (see Figure 13.24).

The Fed's tightening becomes evident with the steep price decline in the two-year note yield-adjusted price of gold. The focus here is on the period following the spike-high set when the two-year yield nearly fell below the record low Fed Funds rate of 1 percent, while hitting a low of 1.045 in June 2003.

With all this in mind, I proceed with my daily regimen, hoping to determine what the market expects from the U.S. Federal Reserve (and all central banks, as discussed in Chapter 14). Toward this end, I examine the short end of all global fixed-income markets, with a particular focus on the Fed, via the Eurodollar Deposit rate futures market. (The Fed Funds futures market does not extend out into the future as far as the more liquid Eurodollar market.)

First I determine what interest rate is implied by the front month (the month following the next FOMC meeting) by taking the price and

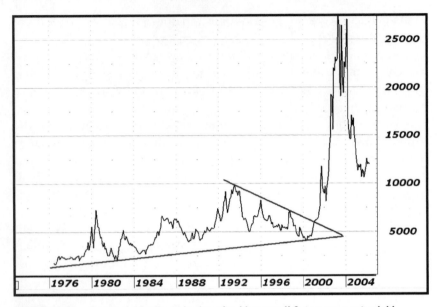

FIGURE 13.24 T-note yield adjusted price of gold versus U.S. two-year note yield: monthly close

Source: Weldononline.com.

subtracting from zero. For example, if the June 2006 contract traded at 94.75, the implied yield was 100 minus 94.75, which equals 5.25 percent.

Since a Eurodollar deposit must pay more than the Fed Funds rate, there is a spread over Funds that is neither set nor static. The spread moves and, in so doing, reflects the market's opinion about the risk profile of the entire global banking system. This spread is usually somewhere between 10 basis points and 25 basis points. So, to be consistent, I always use a spread of 25 basis points.

Subsequently, the 5.25 percent, June 2006, Eurodollar Deposit rate really implies the market's expectation for a Fed Funds rate of 5 percent, as of the end of June.

When you compare that with the current (July 2006) Fed Funds rate of 4.75 percent, just raised from 4.5 percent, you can see the market's near-term expectation forecasting another 25 basis point hike in the Fed Funds rate by the summer 2006. But that is not enough information. I need to know precisely what the market anticipates, over time, down the road, in the second half of the year, next year, and beyond. Thus, I also survey all the forward Eurodollar Deposit rate contracts, and, more importantly, the spreads between the forward months.

By slicing and dicing the contract months, and comparing the results of the individual spreads to the FOMC meeting calendar, you can accurately gauge the market's Fed outlook.

Look at Figure 13.25, showing the spread between the December 2007 and the December 2008 contracts. The spread had been trading at (–) 60 basis points (bp) in early 2004, meaning the nearby end-2007 yield was 60 bp less than the deferred end-2008 yield, indicating the market belief that the Fed will raise rates by as much as 50 bp during the year 2008.

During 2005, as the Fed raised interest rates in a measured way to remove policy stimulus, the expectations that the Fed would need to do more, down the road, lessened. This is reflected in the *rally*, or *narrowing*, or *steepening* in the spread (the spreads, sequentially noted, are known as the "Deposit Rate strip"), toward zero.

At zero, the market is indicating its belief that the Fed will not have cause to change the Fed Funds rate in 2008. Since the beginning of the second half of 2005, this specific 12-month forward spread gravitated within a few basis points on either side of minus (–) 10 bp, indicating the expectation that the Fed's measured pace of rate hikes would be completed before 2008.

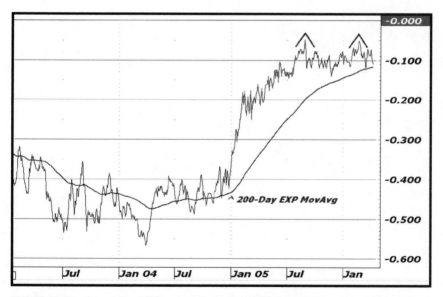

FIGURE 13.25   December 2007 versus December 2008 deposit rate spread 12-month swap: daily close

Source: Weldononline.com.

Thus, any significant deviation from this pattern would be noteworthy. A breakdown in this spread would be meaningful, particularly if the longer-term 200-day moving average were to turn back to the downside on the back of such a price move. Such a move would indicate a shift in the market's opinion as relates directly to the Fed and would reveal an intensifying belief that the Fed would be raising rates longer than is currently considered most probable.

I want to be constantly aware of these changes, not just in the United States, but everywhere. Having insight into the macro market opinion on global monetary policy provides key intermarket input, for bullion traders and investors. Considering the importance of intermarket input derived from foreign exchange and fixed-income markets, I dig deeper, for every nugget I can unearth.

One such nugget can often be found within overlay comparisons of different calendar spreads in the same market instrument. This is particularly effective in helping to gauge the expectations centering on a central bank through the comparison of deposit rate spreads.

In Figure 13.26, I compare the nearby 12-month (defined by the end-2006 versus end-2007 contracts) Eurodollar Deposit rate calendar

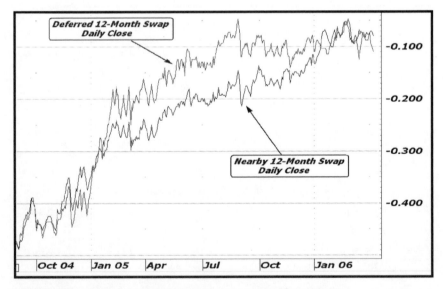

FIGURE 13.26 Deferred 12-month swap versus nearby 12-month swap

Source: Weldononline.com.

spread with the deferred 12-month spread (calculated using the end-2007 versus end-2008 differential).

The upside outperformance by the deferred spread (or swap) during the macrotrend toward narrowing is subtle yet meaningful. It might be considered normal to have the deferred spread move more violently than the nearby spread during times of opinion adjustment.

Subsequently, the recent role-reversal might be construed as a signal to suggest that the market's forward opinion is shifting, and the potential for a longer period of Fed hawkishness is being "priced" into the markets. Putting the pieces together, you might determine that a breakdown in the deferred spread on an outright basis leading to a downside outperformance by the deferred spread would be a clear-cut signal that the market's opinion is changing, as relates to expectations for future Fed policy. This is important input for bullion traders or investors.

As boot campers, you must dig even deeper, given the vast amount of market data to be mined on any given morning.

Combining the fixed-income and foreign exchange angles, as it relates to global central banks and their implementation of various monetary policies, I examine the quote screen segment dedicated to the forward FX swaps. These quotes are derived from the pricing of currency quotes for longer-term delivery and thus become a proxy for the expected changes in short-term interest rates, in both countries.

A six-month forward swap in the Eurocurrency versus the U.S. dollar will reflect the expected change in the interest rate spread between the six-month European interest rate, and the U.S. six-month interest rate, along with the expected change in the currency value. The majority of the pricing is determined by the expected interest rate differential in the future.

Figure 13.27 shows the six-month EUR-USD swap, which has soared to a steep U.S. interest rate premium over Europe from a USD interest rate discount when Fed Funds was 1 percent and the ECB repo (repurchase agreement) rate was 2 percent or higher.

But the crucial message to be gleaned from Figure 13.27 is that the expected forward interest rate differential is making a new high. This means that in six months, the rate premium in the United States is expected to be greater than it is now.

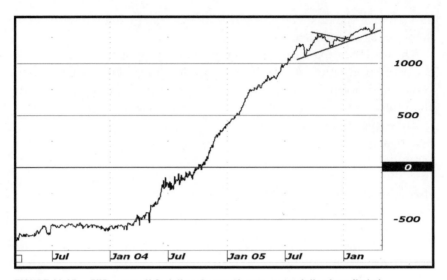

FIGURE 13.27   EUR versus U.S. dollar six-month rate swap: daily close (in bp)
Source: Weldononline.com.

A greater USD interest rate premium essentially would be accomplished in one of two ways. Either the U.S. interest rates rise more than European rates (or rise when Euro rates fall) or U.S. rates will fall less than European rates fall (if rates were to decline in the United States).

By now, you know from your earlier examination that the market expects rates to rise over the next six months in both the United States and Europe. Thus, you can conclude that new highs in the USD forward rate premium, as determined by the foreign exchange market, imply that the Fed will be unable to stop raising rates, particularly if the ECB begins to get more aggressive in its own pursuit of higher short-term interest rates.

More specifically, the market will not allow the Fed to stop raising rates. Even more specifically, if the Fed were to take the opposite view, the USD would be under big downside pressure, as implied by new highs in the swap.

Thus, you can continue to observe this dynamic as it plays out, and in return you receive "tells" to help determine where you might anticipate the next directional move in the USD, or what path the next move in interest rates will take. Again, this is invaluable input for bullion watchers.

The other side of this coin might be the capital flow angle, and while this dynamic is always reflected by the currency markets, often those reflections are created by changes in the fixed-income market relative to stocks, housing, gold, and other commodities.

For sure, the explosive growth in the amount of money under the influence of hedge fund managers is a key factor, as is the secular shift in pension fund managers' opinions, as it relates to the long-term investment potential offered by the commodities sector, specifically metals and energy.

Hence, as part of the daily routine, I am always looking at comparisons of asset classes to confirm or refute my broader macromarket thesis at any given time.

I will look at bullion, relative to fixed income, from an investment-capital flow angle, by examining the investment vehicles, rather than using the interest rate versus the price of gold. Figure 13.28 shows the ratio spread calculated by dividing the AMEX Gold Bug Index (HUI) by the Lehman Long-Bond Fund iShare (20-year plus maturity, TLT).

The picture speaks for itself, reflecting the bullishness of bullion assets, relative to the bearishness reflected by fixed-income linked assets. Indeed, the value of the HUI-TLT ratio spread has doubled since mid-2005.

FIGURE 13.28   AMEX Gold Bug Index versus Lehman Bond Index, HUI versus TLT ratio spread: daily close

Source: Weldononline.com.

Occasionally, something quirky happens. The rally in the AMEX Gold Bug Index relative to the Lehman Long-Bond Fund occurred at the same time as the action detailed earlier in this chapter concerning Japan, gold in yen terms, and the upside equity market leadership by Japanese regional banks amid an expansion in lending. Sometimes things really do fit, everything really does matter, and together, it all means something.

When I look at the fixed-income market, my centric focus is not necessarily on the U.S. markets, but rather, on the Japanese markets. My focus is on Japan for a simple reason—it is the world's largest creditor nation, whereas the United States is the world's largest debtor nation. This distinction is likely to become increasingly important for anyone making investment decisions. This distinction is why the USD has remained buoyant. It explains why Japanese interest rates have barely risen, despite all the peripheral commodity and asset market-based signs of reflation.

You must respect the influence of years of support from a central bank (the Bank of Japan) that has offered capital at a funding rate of virtually zero. The Fed has ended the open borrowing window "regime". The Bank of Japan has not. Thus, going forward, the BOJ will be critical to all reflated asset markets, particularly those built on credit, such as the U.S. housing market.

I could say similar things about the People's Bank of China.

Hence, my focus is sharp in my daily examination when it comes to the Japanese fixed-income markets. I offer what might be the single most important long-term chart, the Japanese government bond futures contract, now one of the most widely traded and tracked fixed-income instruments in the world, second only to the U.S. bond market.

As I write this in the summer of 2006, the Japanese government bond market is in the midst of a major technical breakdown, price wise, with a downward directional reversal completed by the long-term two-year moving average and violation of underlying support, and the multiyear uptrend line.

I monitor the chart shown in Figure 13.29 constantly and also keep a close eye on the Japanese deposit rate spreads, in the same way I do the Eurodollar Depo-Rate spreads, to gauge the (changing) expectations as they relate to the future direction of the Bank of Japan monetary policy.

 You need to monitor all the global bond markets for clues to assist you in trading (investing in) the precious metals markets. Observe the potential clues to be gleaned from Figure 13.30 in which you plot the yield on the 10-year Canadian government bond. Simply, the Canadian 10-year yield is breaking out to the upside at the same time that the

FIGURE 13.29   Japanese government bond price of 10-year JGB: weekly close
Source: Weldononline.com.

Japanese 10-year yield is breaking out to the upside. Moreover, both markets are violating the trend that began way back in the 1980s. You might even begin to think that the explosion in gold, as priced in nearly every currency in the world, including the Canadian dollar (see Figure 13.31), is part of the reason global bond yields are breaking out to the upside en masse. The explosive move in Canadian dollar based gold looks eerily similar to gold in USD, gold in yen, gold in Aussie dollar, or gold in Swiss francs. In fact, the yield on the U.S. 10-year note is doing the same thing, as is the yield on the Aussie bond, the European bond, the Swiss bond, and the Japanese government bond.

There is no doubt that a breakout to the upside in the yield on virtually every global long-bond, is a significant macroevent (should it continue) that will carry meaning for other markets, and for the global economy in general. At the end of the day, it is most important to be constantly aware of all the subtle shifts and swings, at least on a day-to-day basis. This is how every successful trader or researcher works.

This instinctive, constant, awareness extends to every market wherein we can detect subtle shifts in sentiment. Sometimes it means nothing. Other times, it means everything. It all depends on a top-down subjective read, and an understanding that there is no holy grail.

Maybe it is just 20 years of doing the same thing, but it comes naturally to me. I can't define exactly how I make these decisions, but you

FIGURE 13.30 Canadian government bond 10-year bond yield: weekly
Source: Weldononline.com.

FIGURE 13.31 Gold priced in Canadian dollars: weekly close
Source: Weldononline.com.

have to find the pieces of the huge macropuzzle, one piece at a time. You then begin to stack one clue on top of another clue, and another on top of those clues, and eventually, there will be enough pieces to allow you to solve the macropuzzle. You have accomplished that task when you feel comfortable enough—in identifying a market trend—to commit risk capital to that trend.

Trading and investing is much like poker in that you must make decisions based on incomplete and less than certain information. The more information you can gather, the bigger the edge you will have.

The sun is not yet visible on the horizon, and I've finished checking out the prices for just about every market around the world. Indeed, it is not even 7 A.M. EST, the U.S. markets have not opened, I have already been working for hours . . . and yet, my work has just begun.

Who's on First?
Know the Players

After I know what is happening, as defined by market prices, I set
out to learn why the changes are taking place. If there is going to be
movement, then I need to look for who is causing the movement.

I have cultivated many relationships over my long tenure in the industry and thus enjoy the privilege of speaking with contacts in all
areas of the business. I speak with bullion dealers around the globe,
mining company executives, foreign exchange players, hedge fund
managers, bank risk managers, reporters for news services, central
bank research employees, and on and on.

Even the most well-connected professionals can extend their contact base for exchanging information. Most of what we might hear is
noise. But often, just one offhand remark by a colleague—usually a
quip made without specific intent or meaning—can generate a spark
in your thinking that might tie up some loose ends or put a piece into
the bigger-picture puzzle. Individual investors can make an effort to
speak with a market professional, a broker, or family member, or ac-
quaintance, on a regular basis. I can derive insight into what other
market players are thinking, and more importantly, what action they
are taking. I want to know what the smart money is doing.

Indeed, sometimes knowing that the "smart money" is thinking
the same thing, all around, to the point of being fully invested, not

only financially but emotionally, suggests that a cautious approach is prudent.

A lopsided speculative dynamic can be meaningful and, at times, can be enough to overwhelm the more dominant fundamental influences, no matter how powerful those influences might be.

Conversely, a market that is devoid of investment, with an abundance of apathy, historically low and declining volatility readings, contracting volume, and uninterested open interest readings, can often be viewed as opportunistic.

If my top-down, macromonetary analysis suggests that the dormancy could be replaced with electricity, then I might start to look for an opportunity with the right timing, some kind of psychological mutation, and an adequately supportive technical setup.

Another source of valuable information is the Commitment of Traders Report, or COT, produced weekly by the Commodity Futures Trading Commission (CFTC). The COT Report details the prevailing "open" positions held in futures contracts, while providing details about the size and change in positions held by commercial accounts, and then positions held by large and small speculators.

The long-held belief within the industry professes that dead money is represented by the small speculator category, whereas smart money is defined by the commercial account activity. The belief extends from the thought that commercial accounts represent insiders and that most of their activity represents hedging of actual physical market supply (output) or demand (consumption), thus meaning it most accurately reflects the dominant support-demand trend.

Sometimes, this is true. Other times, this is totally not true. More to the point, it is the times when commercial accounts are caught on the wrong side of the market that market movements can become the most violent and one-sided, directionally speaking. The problem stems from a potential imbalance between the forward futures positions and the capacity of commercial accounts to deliver, or take delivery, of the metal. Movements in the calendar spreads often reflect the onset of such imbalances, as was the case in 1999, prior to the public announcement of the signing of the Washington Accord, in which the Group of 7 linked central banks agreed to limit the amount of official annual gold sales. In fact, the circumstance surrounding the signing of the Washington Accord and the subsequent upside explosion in the price of gold is a perfect example of finding clues and piecing together a bigger-picture puzzle.

First it must be noted that global central banks, led by the Swiss and British Central Banks, had disinvested out of gold, in the midst of a completely apathetic environment as pertained to bullion. The price of gold had been sliding to new bear market lows for months, amid declining open interest, with virtually no investment demand and historically low readings posted by all the mainstream volatility indicators.

Yet suddenly, seemingly out of nowhere, spreads began to tighten—a full week prior to "the announcement." Months of deepening contango were giving way to a state of tightening backwardation (where the nearby contract trades at a price premium, irrespective of carrying charges and interest rates, indicating a lack of supply available for immediate delivery). Phone calls to sources revealed that bullion banks had suddenly stopped lending metal and that borrowing rates were soaring as a result. Naturally, this left short positions within the market fully exposed to intensifying risk. A survey of the COT then revealed that commercial accounts had a high degree of short exposure. A few more phone calls indicated that some producers might not actually hold enough metal to meet all their delivery commitments and that a couple of specific producers might be experiencing margin-related difficulty in financing short-positions that were becoming increasingly unprofitable on paper.

The pieces fell into place, and when my momentum indicators confirmed that the market had evolved to the point of exhibiting trendlike momentum characteristics on a short- and midterm basis, I took the leap and called for bullish exposure. I didn't know the Washington Accord would be signed just days later. I didn't need to know. The pieces of the puzzle let me know everything I needed to know. Once in place within the puzzle, the pieces told a story in sync, strong enough—in conjunction with the technical overview—to allow me to be comfortable in assuming risk with my money. Needless to say, it was a profitable experience, but only because I was in sync with my routine.

Up next in boot camp is an exercise in how to conduct a technical overview of the precious metals markets.

PART FOUR

Looking Inside the Market Technically

Reading the Tea Leaves— Technical Analysis

Technical analysis and quantitative systems do not provide the holy grail to trading-investing success. They do, however, provide key input as part of an overall strategy and methodology.

I use technical analysis in the same way that I use intermarket analysis, fundamental analysis, and a psychological read of the market—as one part of the bigger-picture puzzle.

The beauty of technical analysis is similar to the beauty of macro-fundamental analysis. You can observe the market in multiple time frames, much as you can observe the trend of macrodata changes, at various rates, over various time frames, to get a more in-depth, micro-to-macro overview.

I apply the same thought process to technical analysis, observing a wide variety of indicators over various time frames, looking for certain setups that have proven time and again to indicate high-probability odds that a significant, sustainable price trend is developing.

Indicators can be used in different ways. The same indicator can be used to determine a price top or bottom and, under different conditions, to imply that a full-blown macrotrend is in place, or that a countertrend move is becoming more likely.

I try to keep all my technical indicators as robust as possible. I don't want to overoptimize by fitting each indicator to each market sector, attempting to find the most efficient indicators over whatever time frame might be back-tested or simulated. I much prefer to use the exact same statistical variables for every market.

While I have no doubt that different market sectors trade differently—each with its own unique characteristics, psychology, and nuances—it is critical to maintain a standard technical overlay, simply because the markets evolve. I have seen fund after fund come down the pike marketing the perfectly optimized program for a specific market sector, only to be brought down when that particular market's trading environment mutated.

One thing that does not change is the human condition. For that reason, I maintain continuity and a natural resilience in my indicators by using the same standard indicators across the entire spectrum of markets that I monitor.

Trends are created from within the same natural forces that drive the human condition. Trends provide the meat on which traders and investors feed. Trends, countertrend moves, and trend reversals can all provide profitable trading opportunities, but the long-term macrotrends offer the most fertile ground for investors to seed.

First and foremost, you need to identify the markets with the most robust trends. Then, you can use the intermarket skills you have just learned to determine the meaning for the metals markets. More specifically, you are trying to gauge, technically, exactly where each metal market is.

With respect to gold, I need to know: Is gold trending or not? If not, is it coiling, preparing for a springboard breakout, or breakdown? Is it just congesting, in a nontrending environment? Is it stuck in a range? If so, what has to happen for this to change? If it is in a trend, at what stage is that trend? Is it the beginning of a longer-term trend, in the middle, or toward a potential peak or trough? Is the trend overextended or exhausted?

Technical analysis provides insight into such issues and that is why you need to ask these questions on a continual basis. And while my quantitatively derived *Momentum Matrix* indicators, rank-

ings, and pivot points are produced by a complex sequence of calculations (I detail the Power Rankings in Chapter 34), my top-down
and bottom-up technical application follows one rule—KISS—keep it
simple, stupid.

Now it's time to look at the way you can dissect the precious metals markets, or any other market for that matter,
technically.

Charts

I still have the original point-and-figure charts that I kept when I started in the industry working for Stanley Bell on the floor of the Commodities Exchange. I used special engineering graph paper so that the boxes were very small, and thus I could jam weeks of price action onto a single page. When I ran out of room, I would tape another sheet of graph paper to the filled piece, cut the edges to maintain continuity, and wrap the old plot around the back, using a couple of pieces of cardboard as a clipboard of sorts.

Within a year or so, I had created a monstrously long string of chart pages that zigzagged in size as I cut the edges to keep a single continuous chart. My original point-and-figure chart of silver and gold stretches out over 10 feet in length, containing thousands of X's and O's, and years of price action.

Often, after my day on the trading floor, I went uptown to the New York Public Library, and researched past daily price changes by accessing microfilm of the *Wall Street Journal.* That seems archaic, but the experience was invaluable because I dissected thousands of days' worth of price series, covering dozens of markets.

From this handwritten data, I then created more point-and-figure charts, mostly for currencies, that I then began keeping in real time, while I was working in the gold and silver pits. It was this experience that inspired my interest in the foreign exchange and the (then new) overseas fixed-income markets.

There is nothing like trying to keep multiple point-and-figure charts in real time, while handling trades in the then frenzied gold and silver pits, particularly as word spread, and traders began to monitor the charts with me.

Little did I know then that it marked the beginning of many things—charting, studying, and mostly sharing. I have made the latter my primary business, which seems oddly fitting. Within that context, I still use point-and-figure charts today, though I no longer keep them by hand!

The premise behind point-and-figure (P&F) charts is simple. It is the identification of short-term resistance and support points that I now define as *pivot points* in my current work. Point-and-figure charts are created simply by tracking market movements on a continuous basis solely on price parameters, without regard to time.

Moreover, I use several price parameters to determine the trend over various time frames, without having to reference time at all. In gold, I use a $1 parameter, a $2 parameter, and a $5 parameter. This determines the size of each box on the chart. From there, we use a constant for the *reversal price parameter,* at three.

In other words, three boxes mark a reversal; thus in a $1 chart, $3 becomes the reversal parameter, whereas in the $5 chart, the reversal size is three boxes times $5, or $15.

An X marks a rise in the price, whereas an O in a box indicates a declining price, with X's, or O's strung in line until there is a reversal in the opposite direction. Thus, for a market that has made its last $3 move to the upside in the $1 chart, each $1 rise is marked with an X, until the market reverses (or, "swings," following a "pivot") a full $3 from its most recent high, rounded off to the dollar.

Confused yet? There is more, as these charts are kept on a continuous basis, meaning that every tick is calculated, so that there might be numerous swings from $3 upmoves to $3 (or more) downmoves in the same day. These gyrations are not captured by any other chart form, bar chart, candlestick chart, or line chart, unless it is the very shortest-term intraday chart, which even still, might miss a swing.

It sounds more difficult than it is, as exemplified by Figure 16.1, which reveals a simple, $5-by-$15 P&F chart of spot gold. In Figure 16.1, observing the most recent three columns of movement, you note the peak at $665, which could have meant a peak anywhere between $665.00, and $669.90, or the $670 box would contain an X. From there, the fact that the price three boxes below the most recent high box of $665, or $650, was touched before $670 was reached, means that we now draw three O's to the downside filling the $650 box.

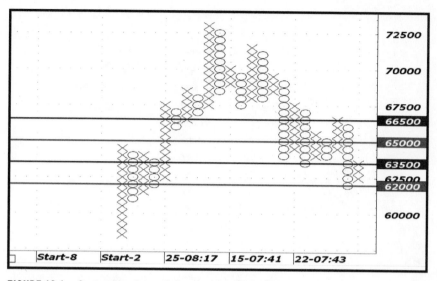

FIGURE 16.1   Spot gold point-and-figure chart: $5 by $15
Source: Weldononline.com.

On the one hand, at that point, it would take a $15 upside reversal to begin a row of X's. On the other hand, until there was an upside reversal, we would continue to put O's in the column with each new $5 level that was touched—$645, $640, $635, all the way down to $620. Finally, from the $620 level, there was a $15 upside reversal, to $635, and thus the new column of upside X's, ending the downside column of O's.

Since it can take days to trade within a $15 range (not that long ago, it used to be weeks within a $15 range, a side-effect of the secular bullish influence), it could take days before a new mark on the chart was required.

Hence, time is not a factor in the creation of these charts, except, in terms of sensitizing the chart by price-box parameter, which by nature shortens the time frame within which the chart generates movement. A smaller price parameter produces more swings, and the increased sensitivity causes the chart to move to the right more rapidly.

I use the $1 and $2 charts with greater regularity for discovery of near-term and midterm support and resistance pivots.

In Figure 16.2, observe the more sensitive $2 chart, defining $2 boxes with a $6 reversal parameter ($2 times the three-box reversal). Congestion and consolidation periods are clear, as are extensions and accelerations.

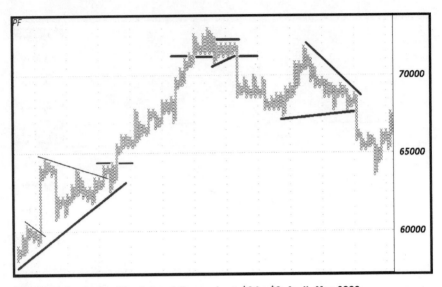

FIGURE 16.2   Spot gold point-and-figure chart: $2 by $6, April–May 2006
Source: Weldononline.com.

Within point-and-figure charts, geometric patterns become more defined and trendlines fit with uncanny accuracy, providing yet another way to use these charts, specifically to generate trading signals.

From your perspective, you want to use the P&F charts for timing the way to trade around a core-trend position. In other words, you want the macro-overlay and the trend-momentum overlay to be in alignment. Then you can use the P&F chart for timing. There are a couple of ways to do this.

Assuming a bullish trend has been identified with a supportive macro-backdrop, you would want to hold a core position that might be maintained over a longer time frame, but you might also seek to capitalize on the accelerated moves that come within the trend.

With a bullish bias established, you would use any spike to the downside that violates the most previous low (a column of O's that makes a lower low) as a buying opportunity.

Put an order in above the market basis the level that would define an upside reversal (as per a bullish bias), a stop-order that would initiate a long gold position, on a $6 upside reversal (in the case of a $2 chart).

Another technique is to simply buy an upside breakout, an X-high above a previously defined X-high, using the box that represents the breakdown pivot relative to the latest O-low as a protective sell-stop. Then, you move this stop order as the most recent box low "rises."

Charts 115

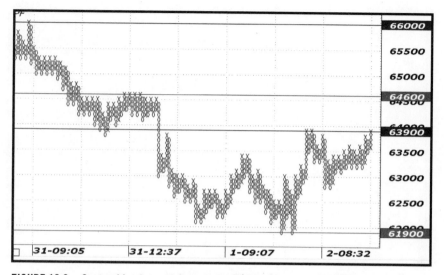

FIGURE 16.3 Spot gold point-and-figure chart: $1 by $3 as of June 2006
Source: Weldononline.com.

Observe the $1 (by $3) gold chart in Figure 16.3. The most recent lower O-low was seen below $630, with a more recent upside X-breakout above $635, meaning you might be getting long if a bullish trend-bias is established, using a breakdown below the most recent low as a stop-loss.

Or, you would have used that most recent spike low below $630 as a buying opportunity, purchasing the first $3 (three-box) upside reversal, which occurred at $631.

More importantly, since all these charts were created at the same time, I must spotlight the alignment, as all point-and-figure charts are skewed toward bullish breakouts, as the most recently dominant move.

As always, these instances of time (or, in this case, price parameter) alignment provide the highest probable circumstances, in terms of profit opportunities.

The P&F charting method also facilitates the use of technical analysis. Note the inclusion of a moving average (MA) overlaid on the point-and-figure chart shown in Figure 16.4.

You might decide to use short-term selling strategies when the action is below the MA, using downside reversals as position catalysts or, vice versa, using buy signals during times when the price is above the midterm MA.

Again, the sensitivity of the price parameters, as well as the moving average length, is largely dependent on bankroll and risk tolerance, at

FIGURE 16.4   Spot gold point-and-figure chart: $2 by $6
Source: Weldononline.com.

least from a trading perspective, as investors are likely to have less use
for shorter-term support and resistance identification.

Line charts provide a different perspective, most often a smoother
one with less noise than a bar chart, since a line chart plots only the
close, without the intraperiod gyrations.

When markets are trading in a frenzied, volatile, wide-ranging manner, line charts can be particularly useful for taking a step back to look
at the bigger picture net change.

This is especially true when using weekly and monthly charts. Observe the longer-term weekly close only chart of AngloGold Ashanti
Ltd., AU, as seen in Figure 16.5. From the close-only perspective, the
most recent close represents a breakdown in the price of this stock, on
a weekly basis.

If the most previous low (the one just violated), were set at the high
of the week, meaning that the low of that week, intraweek, was lower
than the current price level, then you know that a bar chart of the same
instrument would not reflect the breakdown visible in Figure 16.5.

Often when you get dragged into myopic oversight of the intraday
gyrations, particularly when market action is violent and volatile, you
can forget to note where the close is relative to the historical pattern.
Line charts provide this perspective.

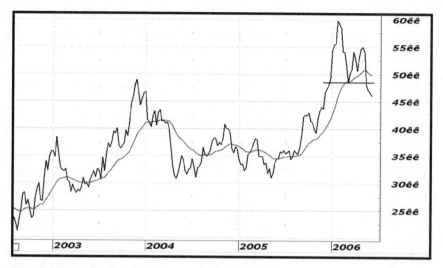

FIGURE 16.5   AngloGold Ashanti Ltd., AU: weekly close
Source: Weldononline.com.

More so, I use line charts for reading ratio relationships mostly because prices of two different instruments that trade separately cannot be charted on an intraday basis (most ratios really don't trade as such).

Rather, most ratio spreads (intermarket analysis) that I monitor are traded via transactions enacted in the individual components. Charting the path of these ratios is done by plugging a formula into whatever charting/quote software a trader might be using.

The end result is a line plot.

It's the same thing for calendar spreads and swaps. Line charts are used exclusively, since most of these instruments are not tracked or traded directly on an intraday basis.

You examine these dynamics (ratio spreads, calendar spreads, and swaps) from a "Looking Inside the Market" perspective, described later in Part 4.

And then there are candlestick charts, a method of charting that first appeared in Japan during the nineteenth century for tracking and trading rice.

The candlestick method of charting generates a multitude of specific chart patterns, and it is not the purpose of this book to provide a tutorial in their definition. Author, technician, and noted candlestick expert Steve Nison has written extensively on candlestick pattern recognition, as has Greg Morris. Candlestick charts offer the same thing that point-and-figure charts offer from a slightly different perspective, but derived from the same price input.

What makes candlestick charts unique is the appearance of a momentum-defining indicator visible within the plot of the price change. Candlestick charting accomplishes this by adding a body to the standard bar chart plot, covering the difference between the opening price and the closing price.

Then, the direction of the one-day momentum, from open to close, up or down, is marked by a different color. Light colors (or white, blank) are used to indicate a close that occurs above the open, while dark colors indicate a close that takes place at a price below the opening price. Thus, without concern for whether the market is higher, or lower relative to the previous close, the color of the body of the bar indicates the change from open to close, of whatever time period is being charted.

The daily candlestick chart of New York Mercantile Exchange (NYMEX) platinum is shown in Figure 16.6. Days with white bodied-bars indicate days in which the market closed higher than it opened, whereas dark-bodied candles indicate a close below the open.

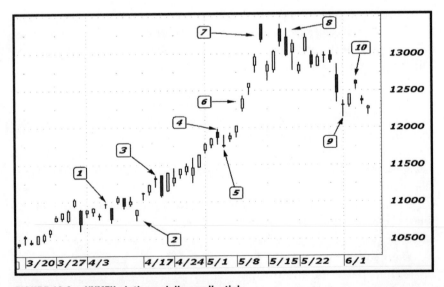

FIGURE 16.6   NYMEX platinum daily candlestick

Source: Weldononline.com.

Notice how the color of the bar is not related to the net daily change. This might be particularly evident at Point 7 in the chart, when the market gapped up to new highs, and closed significantly higher on the day, but is marked by a dark body candle because it closed below the level of the gap-up opening.

As it turns out, Point 7 reveals a potential reversal pattern, called a "Long Black Candle." Had this pattern been followed by a *Doji* day (a tight-range day with the close at the same level as the opening, creating a "plus-sign-looking" candle) it would have represented a very reliable topping pattern.

In Figure 16.6, a Doji candle is seen at Point 9, in fact with a longer downside leg (thus called a "Long-Legged Doji"). It represented a short-term bottom from which platinum rallied in the next two days.

Note Point 1, with a Doji where the open and the close came at the high of the day, known as a "Dragon Fly Doji," a short-term topping pattern. Observe that the following day brought a gap down and a steep (dark) downside slide.

Then note Point 5, a Doji where the open and the close come at the low of the day, known as a "Gravestone Doji," indicative of a short-term bottom. In the case of platinum's Gravestone Doji pattern, it appeared just two days prior to the big runaway bull move.

Within this bull move in platinum, observe Point 6, in which the market gapped higher on the open and kept trading higher throughout the day, to close above the open and near the high of the day.

Considering the gap, this is a very bullish continuation pattern, having implied steady demand from buyers, at (or despite) the new higher price.

On the flip side, observe the price action surrounding Point 10 in Figure 16.6, when a gap higher open was met with consistent selling throughout the day, causing the market to close below the open, while still leaving a gap. This pattern represents weak momentum, a dynamic subsequently unveiled the next day, with a gap down reversal.

Candlestick charts offer valuable insight and perspective and can be used smoothly in conjunction with point-and-figure charts, to gauge the short-term and midterm momentum that might dominate any given market, at any given time.

Moving Averages

I could probably write an entire book about the numerous applications of moving averages.

I'm not focusing on how these technical indicators are calculated. I am assuming that most readers already know what a moving average is, or how an oscillator is derived. I provide an overview into the basics in this chapter, but for an in-depth explanation into the math, I highly recommend two books that are classics in the field: *Technical Analysis of the Futures Market,* by John J. Murphy (Paramus, NJ: New York Institute of Finance, 1999) and *The New Commodity Trading Systems and Methods,* by Perry J. Kaufman (New York: John Wiley & Sons, 1987).

I employ a set of specific moving averages, and I prefer exponential moving averages, rather than simple moving averages. An exponential raises the quantity of factors used by weighting the input toward the most recent price data, thus diminishing the weighting of the input from the back end of the time frame being averaged. The exponential moving average still captures the entire range of price action during its assigned time frame; it simply gives more importance to the more recent action.

According to Kaufman's book, the technique of exponential smoothing was developed in World War II for tracking aircraft. By applying a geometric progression to a nearby weighted moving average, the U.S. military could project the future flight path of an airplane based on the *trend* of its movements and the short-term changes to such. Kaufman provides a thorough explanation of how an exponentially smoothed moving average is calculated (see *The New Commodity Trading Systems and Methods*, page 65). I sometimes use simple moving averages as well, but only to compare with the exponential moving average, to gain insight into the credibility of a given move.

In Figure 17.1, you see the most recent action in the spot gold market, with two moving averages overlaid (plotted over the price, as opposed to being displayed in a separate window, below the price plot). The solid line represents the 100-day exponential (EXP) moving average (MA), while the dashed line depicts the simple (SIM) 100-day moving average.

Clearly, the paths are not the same.

I want to know whether the exponential moving average, which gives more weight to the most recent price action, leads the simple moving average during an upmove or price decline. If it is leading the way higher, as it had been from August 2005 in our example, it provides a bullish trend confirming signal. For sure, the trend was to the

FIGURE 17.1   Spot gold: daily
Source: Weldononline.com.

upside in this period, and the price of gold never once declined below either moving average.

Now note the period between February and August 2004, when the EXP-MA fell below, and remained below, the SIM-MA throughout the first quarter 2004 rally that resulted in a double-top around $425.

The failure of the EXP-MA to lead the way higher, proved to be a prescient warning sign suggesting that the near-term momentum lacked the strength to drive prices to a new high.

This turned out to be the case.

Again, I am not trying to capture every short-term price swing, but rather to identify when the bulk of evidence robustly suggests that a trend is developing or reversing.

If you used only this moving average combination to make your decision, you would have missed the huge profit opportunity when gold spiked to the upside in the spring of 2003, leaving behind what ultimately became a major low. Still, you would have participated fully in the ensuing price rally seen throughout the second half of 2003.

That price move turned out to be a robust trend that lasted for months and witnessed a significant change in price, as gold rallied by more than $75 per ounce, or +20 percent, in that time frame.

Systems are created using these types of input, with the application of rules, whereby we might say that the EXP-MA must be above the SIM-MA, and the price must be above both before any signal can be issued.

Conversely, a liquidation, or even a reversal signal might be construed from a decline in price below one or both of the moving averages during an uptrend, or a rally above the moving averages to end a bear trend. You could take it even further by adding a rule that says we liquidate a position when the two moving averages narrow to a predetermined width, after having been expanding during a trend, as is the norm.

An application that I most prefer, is the three-average method, whereby I compare three different moving averages, differentiated by time, against one another, and against the price. This can be done in multiple ways.

Observe the same chart of spot gold used before, overlaid with three stock moving averages, the 50, 100, and 200-day EXP-MA.

First, I want to determine if a trend is in force. This is easily identi-fied when the shortest-term average is leading the intermediate term average, which in turn is leading the longest-term average, as is the most recent circumstance in the chart.

The moving averages must be sequentially aligned, either climbing up the time-ladder as in our example, or climbing down the ladder, if the 50-day was below the 100-day, which was below the 200-day (see Figure 17.2).

Indeed, if you were to eliminate the 50-day EXP-MA from the equation, and use just the 100-day and 200-day averages shown in Figure 17.2, there would not be a single downside crossover since before October 2004. This analysis would indicate that gold has been in a solid, well-defined uptrend for almost two years now, without interruption.

Or, suppose you removed the longest term MA from the equation and went with just the 50-day and 100-day. From that perspective, the most recent uptrend commenced in the third quarter of 2005, when the shorter-term MA moved above the middle-term MA, and began to lead higher.

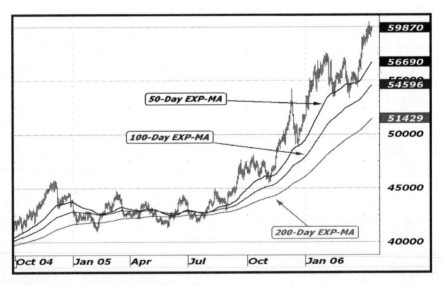

FIGURE 17.2   Spot gold: daily close
Source: Weldononline.com.

Since that time, the 50-day MA has not once crossed back below the 100-day MA. However, the price has declined below the shorter-term average on several occasions, twice with enough near-term momentum to change the directional trend in the MA.

These gyrations in the price, relative to the shorter-term moving average, the direction in the shorter-term average, and its relationship with the longer-term (in this case, the middle-term average) provide the basis for timing models.

The relative changes between two moving averages also provide the basis for the creation of oscillators, which measure the differential between the values of two different averages (see Chapter 18).

How each trader or investor uses these moving average techniques is largely dependent on an accurate and honest assessment of risk tolerance and bankroll considerations.

Traders with a deep tolerance for risk and with deep pockets (meaning excess capital to risk), who do not want to worry about the day-to-day intricacies of the market, might use the 100-day, or even the 200-day EXP-MA as their stop-loss level.

More nimble traders, who can monitor the market more closely, or traders with less risk tolerance or risk capital might employ the 50-day MA as their stop-loss level. However, one of the risks to being too short term and too risk adverse is the danger of missing a sizable price trend as a result of a failure to reenter a position, once the shorter-term moving average has stopped you out.

I find it far more frustrating to miss a move than to take a small loss, particularly when all the other factors continue to confirm the direction and validity of the dominant longer-term trend. This is why I insist on using a variety of time frames to view the price action.

Moving deeper, I go to an assessment of moving averages calculated on a weekly basis as a key determinant of that validity over the long-term trend. I watch the 26-week, 52-week, and the 104-week exponential EXP-MA, reflective of the six-month, one-year, and two-year trend, or lack thereof.

Here, too, I focus on the direction of the moving average's week-to-week change (on a day-to-day basis), the relationship to price (above or below), and the interplay with the other moving average.

Using gold's most recent history, which provides a fertile and robust uptrend, the chart shown in Figure 17.3 plots the weekly price action and the one-year and two-year (weekly) moving averages.

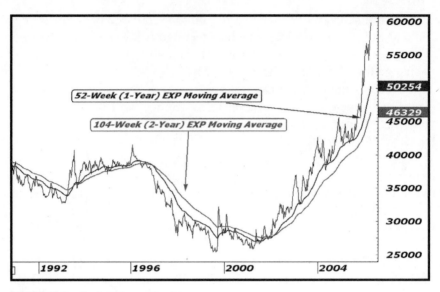

FIGURE 17.3   Spot gold: weekly close
Source: Weldononline.com.

Over the past 15-plus years, there have only been a few primary (crossover) signals issued on the basis of these two moving averages. The most recent signal was a bullish crossover executed in the week of February 11, 2002, with spot gold trading at $295 per ounce (see Figure 17.3).

Hence, within the context of being in sync over various time frames, there is no doubt that the trend in recent months and years has been for gold to appreciate on a secular basis, technically speaking.

Thus, you cycle back to the chart reflecting the daily moving averages, and with the knowledge that gold's weekly moving averages are aligned bullishly, an opportunity to make a trade, and in fact an investment in bullion, was offered toward the end of the third quarter of 2005. Again, you could identify this when the shorter-term averages accelerated and began to distance themselves from the longer-term averages, with price leading the way.

Even on the longest-term basis, the moving average dynamic has been aligned bullishly since 2003. This is defined in Figure 17.4, reflecting the monthly plot of gold with the 60-month exponential mov-

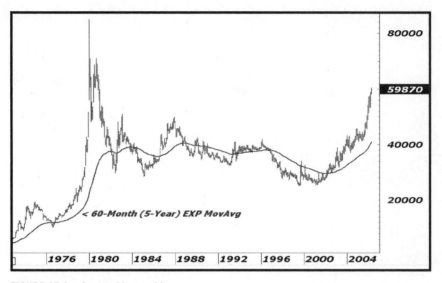

FIGURE 17.4   Spot gold: monthly
Source: Weldononline.com.

ing average overlaid on price, to provide a five-year trend indicator (see Figure 17.4).

As with everything else, moving averages don't offer a holy grail, since markets can trade sideways for months, chopping the moving average crowd to death.

Like all the other indicators, moving averages offer a small, but important technical piece of the puzzle.

Oscillators

Simply stated, oscillators represent the differential between two moving averages.

The idea here is to get a more sensitive reading on the market, using moving averages. By monitoring the differential between the 50-day exponential moving average (EXP-MA) and the 200-day EXP-MA, a trader can gauge the strength, or lack thereof, in the short-term move, on a relative basis.

An oscillator also provides a tangible signal that is visible for identifying when the shorter-term moving average crosses over the longer-term moving average. This is reflected by the change in the oscillator from a positive reading to a negative reading or vice versa.

You can define some examples within the precious metals arena noted in Figures 18.1 and 18.2. In Figure 18.1, from the end of 2003 through the first quarter of 2004, spot gold is in candlestick form, with my preferred oscillator. This midterm indicator simply measures the 50-day EXP-MA against the 100-day EXP-MA. The divergence is obvious, as the oscillator was into a well-defined downtrend following the first peak set in January 2004 and did not even come close to challenging the highs when gold rallied back above $425 in the spring of 2004.

On the contrary, the oscillator could barely generate a positive reading, with prices at a new high, a technically weak circumstance defined by a lack of near-term momentum. In this case, the oscillator's bearish divergence turned out to be a valuable sign of internal technical weakness, as the market failed to hold above $425 and promptly plunged $50, or more than (–) 10 percent.

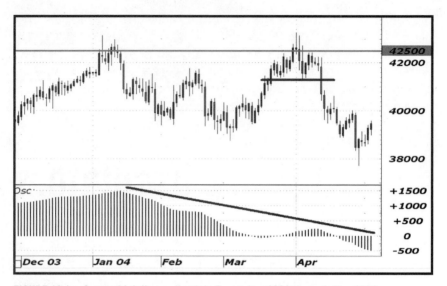

FIGURE 18.1   Spot gold daily candlestick, December 2003 through May 2004
Source: Weldononline.com.

Of interest is the supportive evidence provided by the candlestick perspective in this example, as the market spiked and probed above the $425 level on numerous occasions, but was rebuffed on every single foray, leading to a technical failure and breakdown in line with the bearish oscillator divergence.

Even more technical evidence provided adequate warning to would-be bulls, as defined by the head-and-shoulders topping pattern evident in the March-April period, with a downside violation of the neckline leading to a sharp price decline.

I look for this exact type of setup (Figure 18.1), with multiple signals.

In the context of what you have learned in boot camp, you would rewind to the day that the neckline was violated as defined in the candlestick chart of spot gold. The oscillator was signaling significant divergence, and the candlestick chart revealed a failure to hold above $425, in line with the head-and-shoulders topping pattern.

You would have been most interested that morning in observing any negative fundamental macrodata that might have been released within the preceding 24 hours.

When a confluence of circumstance presents itself, you should try to take advantage (from the perspective of the trader) by day-trading from the short side, looking for the type of breakdown that ultimately took place with a keen eye on that neckline going into the trade.

Another perspective on the value of monitoring the momentum of a market using an oscillator was provided recently in the copper market, as noted in the longer-term weekly chart of the London Metals Exchange (LME) three-month contract (Figure 18.2).

First you can observe the long-term (again, I use my stock 52-week EXP-MA versus the 104-week EXP-MA) oscillator's move from a negative reading to a positive reading in June 2003, with copper trading at less than $1,700 per metric ton. This became a primary buy signal on a stand-alone basis, but the real value of the oscillator is visible later in the upmove.

As the price of copper was attaining each successive new high during the late third quarter of 2003 and into the fourth quarter, the long-term oscillator was confirming by breaking out concurrently to its own new bull move highs. Even more importantly, you should focus on the action centered around Point 1, as labeled on Figure 18.2. Here, when copper's price went into a mini-downside correction, the oscillator kept moving higher and made newer new highs despite a multiday

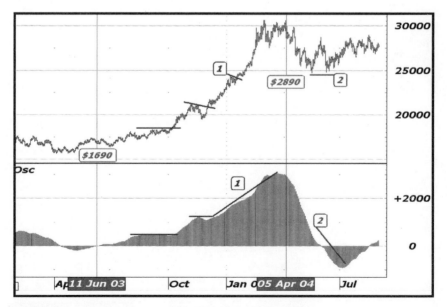

FIGURE 18.2   London copper: weekly LME three-month contract
Source: Weldononline.com.

price decline. This is a powerful signal, particularly when viewed within the context of the long-term weekly perspective.

Not long after that, copper went parabolic and exploded to new bull market highs above $3,000.

The other incident worthy of note is defined by the circumstance labeled Point 2, when after a sharp downside price correction that took copper back to $2,500, the price put in an apparent *double-bottom*, but the oscillator kept plummeting and turned negative (Figure 18.2).

At first, this would likely prevent you from being bullish again, as a potential sign of impending price weakness, but when prices failed to break, and the oscillator regained a positive position, the momentum created a powerful bullish circumstance. Copper continued its bull market thereafter and made new price highs, significantly above $3,000.

Again, as with moving averages, using oscillators becomes subjective, with much depending on the goal of the person who is tracking the market. Still, both traders and investors can benefit from doing so.

Rate-of-Change Indicators

Rate-of-change indicators are simple to calculate and can be exceptionally informative, particularly when applied to commodities, currencies, and fixed-income markets in conjunction with rate-of-change indicators applied to macroeconomic indicators, such as the Consumer Price Index (CPI) and exports.

I use rate-of-change (ROC) indicators to measure percentage changes in markets and economic statistics, as a nominal gauge, and more often, to compare with other ROC indicators.

One of the most effective ways to compare ROC indicators is over various time frames, which will allow you to assess whether momentum is accelerating, decelerating, or stagnating. If gold's 100-day ROC is trending higher, and the rate crosses above a rising 52-week ROC, this would mean that the market is appreciating more rapidly on a short-term basis, with both rates accelerating.

Naturally, I seek out this opportunistic situation to define a market that is exhibiting favorable momentum and trend characteristics. I look for this type of ROC setup in the context of an overlay from the macromonetary side, as might be presented by any number of ecoindicators, such as money supply or the CPI.

The example shown in Figure 19.1 was present in recent months.

In this case, rewind to the fall of 2005 and the situation surrounding the gold market, which had been probing a possible upside technical breakout above long-term over-head price resistance at $450.

From August 2005 through November 2005, the gold market built momentum while finally claiming and holding above the $450 level. Following a fall retracement (right back to the original breakout pivot at $450, a classic continuation-corrective action), the market broke out to the upside at Point 1, with the full support of a concurrent, confirming upside breakout in the 100-day rate-of-change indicator.

Following a spike high and consolidation, the market broke out again at Point 2, and again the ROC indicator followed suit, providing technical confirmation for would-be bulls.

Point 3 offers an example of bearish divergence, where the price of gold made a new high, but the ROC did not. This turned out to be a timely short-term warning sign to bullion bulls, as a sharp correction ensued thereafter.

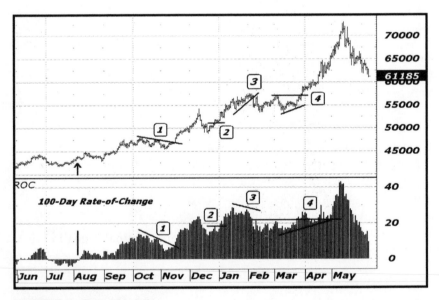

FIGURE 19.1   Spot gold: daily
Source: Weldononline.com.

It took a couple of months for this divergence to be reconciled, leading to a sideways congestion phase that culminated in the end-March resumption of the bull move, amid a breakout that was confirmed by a nearly identical pattern exhibited by the ROC, at Point 4 (see Figure 19.1).

What is not seen, is that you boot camp participants have been busy throughout the run in gold from August to the February 2006 interim high. More importantly, by following what you have learned in boot camp, you have focused on the rate-of-change indicators published by the U.S. Federal Reserve Bank during that same time. This macrodata revealed an eerily similar acceleration to the upside as seen in gold, in terms of the growth of U.S. monetary aggregates and commercial bank lending.

What made the macrodata so supportive was that the three-month ROC had accelerated to a more rapid growth rate than the six-month rate, which was more intense than the twelve-month rate in most of the data series. This represented one of the broadest based monetary reflations I have seen to date and came in contrast to the Federal Reserve's campaign to raise the cost of short-term funds.

Your boot camp's daily data dissection also revealed an acceleration in the ROC indicators applied to Fed data on custody holdings (holdings of U.S. debt by official overseas institutions) and overseas data on official foreign exchange reserve holdings. In fact, both of these monetary-based data series were (are) expanding at a record pace, to record levels, throughout the bull move in gold.

No wonder then, that the U.S. Dollar Index also provided confirmation, as its pace of depreciation accelerated rapidly from November 2005 (USDX at 92.00) to January 2006 (USDX at 87.8, down almost 5 percent), providing specific intermarket support for gold during its upside acceleration from Point 1.

This comprehensive perspective showed that the most pertinent influence was the monetary data, as the Fed failed to lift the cost of funds high enough or fast enough to squelch demand for credit.

The acceleration in growth and the record nominal highs in credit were the dominant market influence during the fourth quarter 2005 and the first quarter 2006. Within this specific context, rate-of-change indicators can be invaluable when applied over a multitude of time frames and a wide range of input, both market based and macroeconomic databased.

And finally, ROC indicators can be used as a precursor to a trend change, or breakout/breakdown.

 The most recent daily plot of LME Aluminum is shown in Figure 19.2. The completed head-and-shoulders topping pattern is obvious, as is the downside violation of and directional downturn by the midterm 100-day EXP-MA and the breakdown below the uptrend line in place since 2005.

Also obvious is the collapse in the midterm rate-of-change indicator, following sizable bearish divergence. In this case, the breakdown in the ROC came prior to the breakdown in the price of the metal, and offered a loud warning siren to bulls, as a precursor to a trendline violation.

As if that was not enough, as the ROC in aluminum began to soften, the rate-of-change indicators applied to the macrodata that China offered for their domestic output and export of aluminum products reveal a significant upside acceleration—in other words, more supply.

With that knowledge in tow, I am looking for this exact ROC setup, in concert with a concurrent macrodata-driven theme, with the hope of taking advantage from the speculative trading perspective.

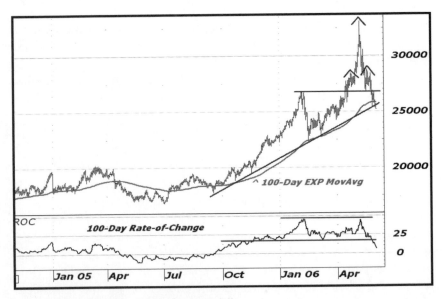

FIGURE 19.2   LME three-month aluminum daily

Source: Weldononline.com.

From the investment standpoint, such a convergence of technical and macrodata input might influence a longer-term holder of aluminum-based equities to consider a partial liquidation or a move to tighten protective sell stops.

In the case of aluminum, the sector's equities have failed to reach the same level of price reflation seen in the underlying metal, frustrating equity players involved in the metal stocks basis the bigger-picture macrotheme.

From the boot camp perspective, this fact is useful on its own merit and symptomatic of the general reflation outperformance by the actual commodities, rather than the commodity-linked equities.

Under these conditions, you want to be either long or short the underlying instrument, expecting more bang for the buck as long as the ratio spreads continue to imply that your thesis remains intact.

20

Fibonacci Retracements

Fibonacci Retracements

I monitor Fibonacci retracements, again, to gain as much information as possible, technically and fundamentally. Sometimes, the location of Fibonacci retracement levels can become a deciding factor in making decisions from both a trading and investing standpoint.

Retracement levels are derived through the work of Italian Leonardo Pisano and his *Liber Abaci,* penned in the thirteenth century and finally published in a mathematics text in 1857. Using observations linked to a study of the Great Pyramid of Gizeh, Pisano calculated the Fibonacci summation series, which measures relationships not only on the basis of space but also relative to the solar year, and thus time.

Hence, it might be correct to suggest Fibonacci retracements (many figures can be calculated using the Fibonacci summation series), but to keep things simple and robust across all markets, I use only three retracements—one-third (38 percent), half (50 percent), and two-thirds (61 percent).

As a result, Fibonacci analysis can be applied over any time frame and is equally effective in mapping short-term intraday swings and daily gyrations. However, the real value-added offered by Fibonacci retracements (Fibo) can be specifically gleaned from their application to long-term secular charts.

Traders often get caught up in the heat of battle, particularly when a trend is undergoing a correction, which can intensify anxiety and second-guessing. This is especially true among investors who fear that an alleged correction to an ongoing macrotrend might be a significant reversal instead. Luckily, Fibonacci retracements are very effective in capturing the bigger-picture perspective.

Figures 20.1 through 20.3 show multiple applications of the Fibo indicator. These charts plot the longer-term weekly path of spot gold during its spectacular bull move of the late 1970s and subsequent deflation in the early 1980s. During this volatile period fraught with macro-uncertainty, the high degree of correlation between major market pivot points and the respective Fibo targets seems almost surreal following the application of the Fibonacci retracements.

In Figure 20.1, the Fibonacci retracements are applied to the bull move from the 1970s into the 1980 secular peak, marked by a dashed line and stretching to the left edge of the chart. The overlaid Fibonacci retracements pertain to the deep downside move from that peak to the March 1980 spike low below $500.

Point 1 defines the postsecular peak's spike low at $480, which maps out a near perfect 50 percent correction of the entire bull market price appreciation to that peak, from the 1976 starting point.

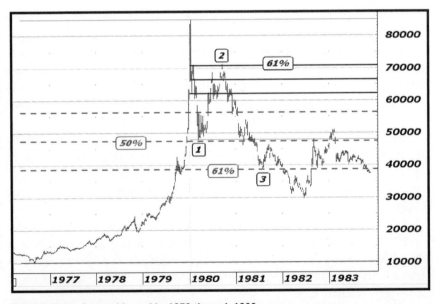

FIGURE 20.1   Spot gold: weekly, 1976 through 1983

Source: Weldononline.com.

Following that decline, the market rallied again, peaking at Point 2, which just so happened to represent a 61 percent correction relative to the decline from the January 1980 secular peak, to Point 1 (March 1980 low below $500).

The subsequent move back below Point 1 defined the rally to Point 2 as the corrective move within a corrective move and implied that the downside correction had not yet been completed. Of interest is that the ensuing breakdown took the market right to the last (61 percent) of the Fibonacci retracement targets relative to the original bull market (see Figure 20.1).

The downside penetration of Point 3 confirmed that the great bull market had ended, since it penetrated the final retracement level, thus implying that a new bear trend had begun.

Therefore, it should come as little surprise to discover that the next rally in gold, a move that was considered a minibull market at the time (1982 to 1983), failed on the 50 percent Fibo retracement level defined by the bear market from the second secular high set in 1980.

Not only did Point 1 in Figure 20.2 represent a 50 percent Fibo retracement from the second secular peak in 1980, but the same Point 1 in Figure 20.3 reveals that the 1983 peak was also a near-perfect 38

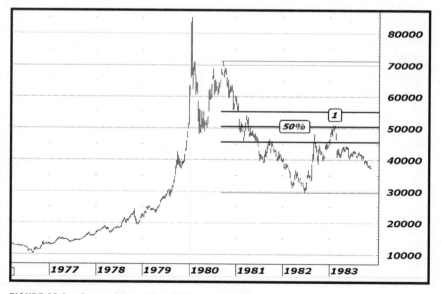

FIGURE 20.2   Spot gold: weekly, 1976 through 1983
Source: Weldononline.com.

FIGURE 20.3   Spot gold: weekly, 1976 through 1983
Source: Weldononline.com.

percent Fibo retracement relative to the decline from the original secular peak set in January 1980 at $850.00.

From the macrosecular perspective, the bull market of 1982/1983
represented a solid selling opportunity, as a corrective retracement in
an ongoing secular bear market. You cannot help but spotlight that gold
failed in 1983, at the 50 percent Fibo retracement, in conjunction with
the beginning of a spectacular bull market in the U.S. dollar. That rally
in the USD represented a massive appreciation in the greenback that
began in earnest during the second half of 1982 (USDX breaking out
above 110.00) and culminated with the March 1985 all-time USDX peak
at 164.72.

This near 50 percent appreciation in the U.S. Dollar Index coincided
(not coincidentally) with a plunge in the price of gold, to its (then secular) low of $284.25 in February 1985.

The announcement by the Group of Seven (G-7) of the Plaza Accord
in the spring of 1985 changed all that.

The point is, by applying Fibonacci analysis to long-term charts, we
can create a well-defined bigger-picture secular story, from which to
begin our top-down analysis. Again, the application and use of this indicator depends on the financial goals, risk profile, and temperament
of the individual trader or investor.

In the context of the current bull market and the more recent sharp corrective-looking decline, I am opening the boot camp door for a look at the present situation, as defined by the pertinent Fibo retracement levels.

In Figure 20.4, which shows an elongated daily chart covering the action in spot gold since mid-2003, the present decline does look corrective. In fact, despite its apparent violent nature, the current decline in gold (June 2006) has not even scratched the surface relative to the extent of the bull market, as defined by the distance remaining to the first Fibo retracement level.

Often the Fibo retracement levels will coincide with prices that previously defined congestion phases. You can see this when noting the current situation in gold, where the 38 percent Fibo retracement level lines up with the sideways congestion period in the first quarter of 2006.

The dynamic that has been detailed here solidifies the credibility of the support defined by the retracement level. In this case, the first Fibo level (38 percent) is pegged at $550, which is the center of trading range experienced during the first quarter's congestion period.

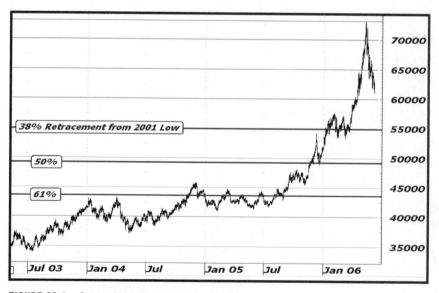

FIGURE 20.4   Spot gold: daily, 2003 through 2006
Source: Weldononline.com.

Additionally, the more robust 50 percent Fibo level in gold, relative to its 2001/2006 bull market is pegged right at the $490 level, which provided an upside pivot point during the steep and swift downside correction seen in mid-December 2005.

You may be wondering whether there is some other source of underlying technical support that converges with the Fibonacci levels. Of course there is, as you throw your robust long-term 104-week exponential moving average (2-year EXP-MA) over the weekly chart of gold. This chart also plots the same Fibonacci retracement levels seen in the earlier daily chart.

Bingo: The current position of the moving average is dead-on the 50 percent Fibonacci retracement level. In turn, it coincides with the December 2005 spike reversal low at $490 to provide solid underlying support for the gold market from the long-term technical, secular-trend perspective (see Figure 20.5).

Continuing in the boot camp mode, and given the steep correction currently underway in the precious metals sector, you decide to map the pertinent Fibo retracement levels in the silver market. The results are exhibited in Figures 20.6 and 20.7.

FIGURE 20.5   COMEX gold: weekly

Source: Weldononline.com.

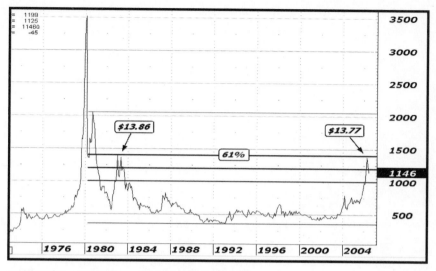

FIGURE 20.6   Spot silver: monthly close since 1973
Source: Weldononline.com.

First focus on the link between the 1982/1983 monthly closing high in silver at $13.86, and the most recent secular peak posted this year at $13.77. That the recent high came within a dime of the high from 23 years prior simply cannot be ignored (see Figure 20.6).

When you overlay the Fibo retracement grid defined by the decade-long move from the second 1980 secular peak, to the secular low below $5 in the early 1990s—surprise, surprise—the recent high is bang-on the 61 percent Fibo retracement level. The implication would be that the entire bull move from the 2001 low below $5, was merely corrective, relative to a multidecade bear market that remains intact.

Thanks to a plethora of other analyses, you do not think this is the case. Rather, based on the macromonetary backdrop, it seems far more likely that a deep downside correction is underway in an ongoing secular bull market that remains at an early stage.

Therefore, your boot camp exercise is to define the corrective downside targets in silver under the belief that a longer-term secular bull market is experiencing its first stiff test and downside retracement.

First apply the appropriate Fibonacci retracement levels, as seen in Figure 20.7. Then observe three specific points of interest.

First, the most shallow of our three Fibo retracement targets (38 percent) comes in dead-on the psychologically key $10 price level.

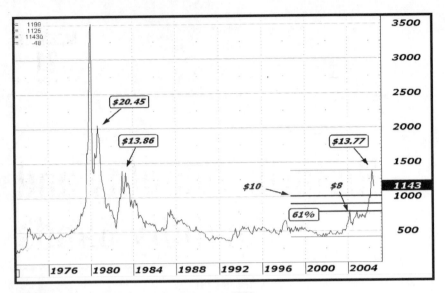

FIGURE 20.7   Spot gold: monthly close since 1973
Source: Weldononline.com.

Second, the deepest of the retracement targets (61 percent) matches the original upside breakout pivot that the silver market accelerated rapidly, pegged at $8.

And third, should the Fibonacci levels ultimately hold and should the silver market move toward mapping out another upside bull leg in a secular bull market, the next overhead resistance is defined at $20 per ounce.

Historic Volatility and Volatility Bands

Reading volatility is yet another subjective exercise. There are two primary ways I look at volatility:

1. I observe volatility from a historic perspective.
2. I look at volatility for the application of bands to intraday charts, for use as a timing mechanism, and for the definition of short-term pivot points.

Looking at historic volatility, the intent is to learn something about the trending characteristics, or lack thereof, exhibited by a market. I do this by comparing historic volatilities over multiple time frames.

A market where the 21-day volatility is rising and is higher than the 50-day volatility that is also rising, and has just moved above the 100-day measure would be signaling an acceleration in whatever direction it was moving.

The subjective nature extends from the fact that a volatility alignment such as the one just described could define either a significant trend reversal in the making, following a prolonged low-volatility trend or a fresh breakout and newborn trend in the making, extending from a sideways, nontrending market.

In the first case, I might look to employ some countertrend techniques on a low risk, shorter-term speculative basis. Or, as an investor, I might seek to tighten my stop-order protection. This would most likely occur where giveback is intensifying, in terms of holding what is still a longer-term profitable investment, but where the reversal is accelerating and causing pain.

In the second case, a volatility alignment taking place in a market that is breaking out of a sideways pattern confirms whatever other trend signals my indicators might be flashing. In other words, the pedal gets pressed to the metal. This becomes particularly true if there is a compelling macrothematic canvas on which our statistical and volatility alignments are being drawn.

Again, it is that lightbulb popping when the alignments become visible and the global-macro backdrop is painted with the same color scheme. It is then that the trade idea crystallizes, and conviction is born. A proper volatility alignment can be a simple, yet powerful, signal in spotlighting an opportunity-spiked acceleration in any given market.

Turning to volatility bands, you need to observe a couple of specifics.

First, observe the bands in Figure 21.1 that plot the hourly path of spot gold. Note how they expand and contract, whereby the differential between the upper band and the lower band is either widening, or narrowing.

A widening dynamic signals acceleration and range extension, whereas a narrowing band signals a tightening trading-range environment on a short-term basis.

The action in price relative to the bands is the next specific focal point. A market that has last touched the upper band is said to be in a bullish mode, whereas a market that last touched the lower band is considered to be in a short-term bear mode.

The overall picture suggests that a market where the latest touch is to the upper band, when the band is widening, would imply an upside price acceleration that should last for a short-term period. Likewise, a market that touches the lower band, amid band widening, would be accelerating lower accompanied by increasing volatility.

Conversely, a market that touches the upper band while it is narrowing is unlikely to become a sustainable move. In this case, if I were looking to sell strength, this would be a signal to do so. The same is

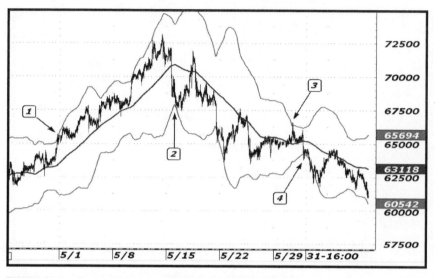

FIGURE 21.1   Spot gold: hourly, mid-April through June 2006
Source: Weldononline.com.

true for buying weakness when the lower band is touched in conjunction with a narrowing bandwidth dynamic (see Figure 21.1).

Within this framework comes my use of volatility bands as a timing mechanism, specifically in the placement of stop orders.

When holding a long position, I might use the lower volatility band as my initial stop-loss order placement point.

Likewise, I will use an upper band defined price as a buy-stop loss against a short position.

While I manipulate my stops dependent on the overall trade dynamic, risk profile, and macroenvironment, this methodology might be useful to a longer-term investor in the precious metals arena, or any other marketplace. A longer-term investor might use daily volatility bands to provide deeper stop-loss order placement than is offered by intraday charts.

The following example shows how I might use a band methodology to determine the placement of a trailing stop order.

Figure 21.2 plots the intraday path of gold. The buy signal is elicited at Point 1, when the upper band is touched and the band is clearly widening. Using the lower band as my initial stop-loss order placement point, I have a sell-stop at $544.95.

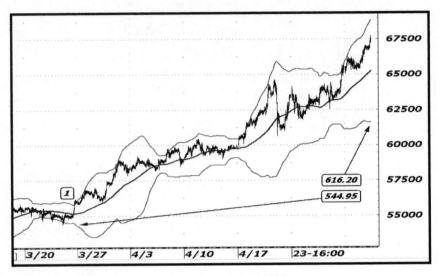

FIGURE 21.2   Spot gold: hourly, March through April 2006
Source: Weldononline.com.

As the market rallies, the bands widen, narrow, and then widen again, and yet, both have been rising throughout the process.

As gold trades higher, the untouched lower band moves higher, too. About a month later, my stop has risen substantially, in sync with the price rally, to stand at $616.20. In this way, my stop is said to have trailed the market (see Figure 21.2).

Volume, On-Balance Volume, and Money Flow

Volume, on-balance-volume (OBV), and money flow go hand-in-hand in providing valuable information to traders, speculators, and investors.

Money flow can be identified from data produced by Dow Jones & Company, as provided for individual stocks.

I watch the data to help determine the overall investment demand and sentiment within each market sector. This information is particularly valuable in the precious metals sector because the mining stocks are not widely traded issues and are mostly shares with a relatively miniscule float.

When the money flow figures for mining shares, petroleum shares, or banking shares rise rapidly and reach into the billions of dollars over time, I begin to take notice. When the money flow first starts to rise, this signals the early stages of investment demand for precious metals from equity market players and longer-term investors.

When headlines are blasting the win-win merits of some particular sector on a "can't-lose" basis and money is pouring into the individual shares, I begin to take notice from a contrarian standpoint. Often, I can

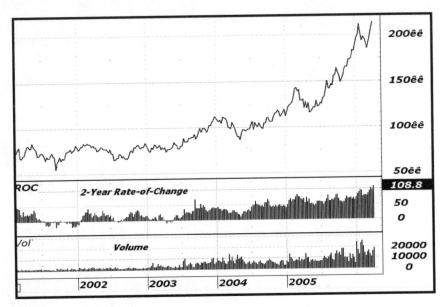

FIGURE 22.1 Rio Tinto PLC RPT: weekly close

Source: Weldononline.com.

combine a study of historic volatility and money flow to identify when the odds are intensifying for a trend reversal or a significant corrective move.

Rapid money flow that has reached high nominal levels, combined with a reversing price push defined by a realignment in the historic volatility readings, is often a signal of a saturated market that is ripe for a liquidative purge. In this case, depending on the macro-backdrop, I might look to deploy countertrend trading tactics.

A look at straight volume readings can also provide similar signals. Figure 22.1 shows a popular mining share, with a two-year rate-of-change (ROC) indicator and a plot of weekly volume. Note that as the stock price was hitting new bull market highs, and the ROC was confirming that move, the volume was lagging and failing to match its own previous bull market peak.

This divergence pattern would suggest caution from a bullish perspective, and is an example of how volume can be utilized.

The Commitments of Traders Report

The Commodity Futures Trading Commission (CFTC) produces the Commitments of Traders Report (COT). It can offer valuable tidbits of information, though its overall usefulness has diminished with the explosion in over-the-counter (OTC) derivative trading in commodities and currencies.

The report breaks down the open interest in each commodity, currency, and financial futures contract, detailing information relating to positions held, long and short, by commercial accounts, large speculator accounts, and small speculator accounts.

The general wisdom is that large money is smart money, representing the sharks; and small money represents the fish on which the sharks feed. Thus, when the large speculative accounts and the small speculators are on opposite sides of the market, the trend is often pushed in the direction that hurts the small traders.

By nature, the commercial accounts and the speculative accounts should combine to have offsetting exposure from the long, short, and spread position perspectives.

Again, in contrast, speculators are said to be the shallow-pocketed trade, whereas the commercial accounts have deep pockets because they are most often hedging price exposure in the physical market.

In the case of precious metals, the commercial accounts are represented by bullion banks, mining companies, and industrial consumers, to name a few of the primary players.

In general, commercial accounts are believed to be the most "in the know" about the specific supply-and-demand fundamentals that apply to their individual commodity or financial contract interest.

Thus, it is often worth noting when commercial accounts and speculators take extreme positions on opposite sides of the same market. Usually, something will give, and either the specs will get mauled or commercial accounts will get squeezed. These extremes, and the most sizable week-to-week changes in exposure can offer information that you can incorporate into a broader, overall strategy.

PART FIVE

Looking Inside the Market: Top-Down Macro

Again, Everything
Matters!

In the same vein that I monitor the markets, from a constant price change perspective within a universe of instruments, when I look at the market's fundamentals, I want to know everything. I want to dissect every detail in microcosm, so that I can fully assess the top-down environment.

In the same way that I approach each instrument, spread, or ratio from a technical perspective, when I look at the macroeconomic data, I want to slice and dice the data in every way possible, over as many time frames as possible, to get the full picture. Just as things evolve technically, the macroeconomic fundamental backdrop evolves from the bottom-up, with evidence of a potential shift in trend first exhibited in the microdata.

Herein lies the conundrum in approaching the markets with a top-down strategic methodology: analysis, as it applies to macroeconomic trend reversals, appears first at the bottom and evolves upward.

I am always seeking the time frame when the macro-overlay is in sync with the technical overlay and vice versa, particularly when countertrend nuances are synchronized. This occurs when the 3-month rate of change (ROC) of the U.S. monetary base is moving lower against the continued uptrend in the 12-month ROC, and I note that the 100-day exponential moving average (EXP-MA) in gold has turned lower in the face of a continued climb in the 52-week MA. Then I can say there is synchronicity between these technical and fundamental indicators, implying a countertrend decline in an ongoing macro-uptrend dominant environment.

In this way, everything matters—every data point from every location in the world. From industrial output in exporting nations to trade balances and export/import growth statistics, nearly all sectors are covered.

Moreover, with trade data, I dig deeper, looking into which products are more actively trading. Are they finished goods, raw materials, or intermediate materials? From whom are they being imported, or to whom are they being exported? Is export market share rising? Is volume the cause for statistical changes, or is price a larger influence over any particular time frame?

I dig deep, as the best nuggets of information can be mined from the microdust that many speculators consider insignificant. Such analysis is somewhat out of the reach of average investors. However, those same investors can change that to some extent.

A focused reading of specific types of research is key, whether newsletter based, or your own data mining. Decide which indicators matter most, in terms of your approach, methodology, risk tolerance, and goals.

Find the best sources of information and dig. For me, those sources are virtually endless. Anecdotal macroinput can be invaluable, but poor timing may make it useless. Moreover, macrofundamental analysis is tricky even at its point of origin because the most dominant influence will change, and then it will change again. Last year's all-important, do-or-die data release might be ignored next year, depending on the broader macrolandscape. From this perspective, you can use global capital flow and savings imbalances (current account and balance of payment deficits) as a prime example. There is no shortage of highly credible thinkers who understand that these imbalances are simply not sustainable.

Yet, this is no different from the way it was in 1990. It has not mattered, despite the focus on it. It has not mattered that this single macro-dynamic has intensified in a massive way, over just the past two years.

One day, it will matter.

Your goal, in using a micro-to-macro top-down approach is to understand the purest facts, such as the unsustainability of global capital and saving imbalances, while looking for a transition to a period where such data matters within the changes exhibited in the micro-data. Your goal is to recognize what things matter and when they matter most.

Often, the market will not realize which influence has become dominant until the data evidence has worked its way toward the midlevel surface and become more pronounced. It is within that gap that opportunity lies, particularly when there is synchronicity with a confirming technical setup.

I have always loved what legendary trader Bruce Kovner told research guru and *Market Wizards* (New York: HarperCollins, 1989) author Jack Schwager. Kovner likened trying to figure out the macroenvironment, to trying to play chess on a three-dimensional chessboard.

We must cover all the angles and dig as deep as possible. It would be impossible for me to include every global macroindicator that I might monitor at any given time. However, I can shave things down to the point where you can extract information to continue your own exploration.

When talking about the precious metals, and gold specifically, there are a host of macrofundamental data and intermarket analysis points that any active participant should monitor. Most of all, from the macroperspective, what matters for precious metals is the Fed. As much as I hate to admit it, it all starts and ultimately will end with the Fed. And, as much as the global macromarket scene is shifting to Asia, and as much as monetarily reflated paper wealth gravitates toward Asia and away from the United States, the U.S. Federal Reserve could change all that with the push of a single button.

I have termed this circumstance *Monetary Armageddon*. I have linked this to my entire secular thematic thought process. This refers to the choices that will ultimately be forced on the Fed as the "buyer of last resort," when global investors put their bonds and reserve dollar holdings to the U.S. Treasury.

A debt-deflation liquidation would be viewed as too painful, and given the human condition and the drive to avoid pain, central banks will choose to reflate, by printing more paper, even past the point where it no longer works, to create wealth. This is the primary bullish support for gold, in the secular sense. Furthermore, this is exactly the same support that has held gold high in the eyes of global investors, over and over, for centuries.

When faced with the prospect of a collapsed currency and sky-high interest rates, the Fed will choose to push the Monetary Armageddon button by creating as many paper dollars as the Treasury requires to repurchase every USD bond on the global offer.

The macrodynamic that will be experienced in the interim and the length of time it will take for such a worst-case scenario to play out are a complete mystery.

This is what I mean by the puzzle.

 Attention Readers!

Now it is time to dig in and do what you need to do every day.

U.S. Monetary Fundamentals and the Federal Reserve System

You start putting the macro-monetary puzzle pieces together with the Fed and the U.S. money, credit, debt, and banking statistics.

There are multiple overlays and interconnections between the monetary and credit statistics based on the components used to compile different money supply aggregates, or the breakdown in bank lending data, debtorwise. Some numbers might be important under one set of circumstances and not significant in another.

When I first started in the business on the floor of the Commodity Exchange (COMEX) in the silver pit, the single most important nugget of information that was released on a regular basis was the Thursday afternoon money supply data. To this day, I give great weight to these figures in defining the flow and change in the supply of money and credit.

This is first and foremost on my mind, as I try to discern the Fed's true policy intent. I have often used the terminology in discussing global central banks that "talk the monetary talk," but fail to "walk the monetary walk." In other words, there is often monetary misdirection.

My, experience at Lehman Brothers in the 1980s was invaluable, with guys like Stan Jonas, Howard Levine, Frank Maganella, and Martin Lysaght coming together every morning at Fed time. They tried to discern Fed policy by dissecting micronuances related to the daily add or drain of money market liquidity.

It used to be difficult to figure out what the Fed was really doing. It was an art, and institutions had entire teams dedicated to trying to read the Fed's "tea leaves." Transparency was a nonstarter, with a veil of mystery draped over central bank activity. Indeed, it is from this fact that the goldbug conspiracy theorists have built their case. They believe that the central bank (allegedly in conjunction with bullion bank co-conspirators) is responsible for gold market manipulation.

I refuse to join the debate except to say, of course there is manipulation. This is an epic battle, a monetary war, in an ever-escalating effort to sustain paper wealth reflation on a global scale. There is manipulation on many fronts, largely and undeniably in global currency markets.

A major monetary misdirection obviously is taking place, and as players, you must simply deal with it and perhaps find a way to turn these dynamics to your advantage. Dissecting the macromonetary data is one way to carve out a slight advantage.

Are global central banks, the Fed first and foremost, adjusting rates to the point where money supply and the supply demand for credit begins to contract? *Does what?*

If they are acting in a way that leads to expanding money supply and expanding credit, while talking "dovishly," then they are walking the walk.

Similarly, if the Fed is talking hawkishly and raising the cost of money, and the result is a contraction in, or disinflating growth rates of both money and credit, then they are also walking the walk.

But, if, as has been the case more recently, the Fed is talking hawkishly, while raising rates but not doing so with enough force to cause a contraction in growth of either money or credit, then they are merely talking the talk.

The difference is significant in the impact on the capital markets, particularly currencies and gold.

How can you figure out if the Fed is walking the walk or merely talking the talk?

Is it the fact that the Fed has announced it will no longer report the data compiled for the broad money supply aggregate (known as "M3")? Look at the breakdown of the most recent data available at the time of publication. Perhaps the reason the Fed is reluctant to keep tracking the path of M3 can be gleaned in Figure 25.1, as the aggregate had reached more than $10 trillion. In other words, M3 had expanded more than 10-fold since the USD was delinked from gold and had more than doubled since the mid-1990s.

Data is available in charting format at www.economagic.com as supplied by the U.S. Federal Reserve Bank in St. Louis. The data is also available on the St. Louis Fed's web site, at www.research.stlouisfed .org/fred2/categories.

Observe in Figure 25.2, the most recent long-term chart of total narrow money aggregate (known as "M1"), which is reaching for $1.5 trillion and accelerating to the upside in the year 2006 to date (YTD).

There is far more information to be gleaned than the simple reflection of a monstrous, massive, ongoing, paper monetary reflation that is being facilitated by the talk-the-talk monetary policies of the Fed.

I take the Thursday data (weekly money supply figures) and grind out the rate-of-change (ROC) analysis conducted in the report by the Fed. This provides weekly and monthly comparisons on 13-week, 26-week, and 52-week time frames, along with 3-month, 6-month, and 12-month calculations.

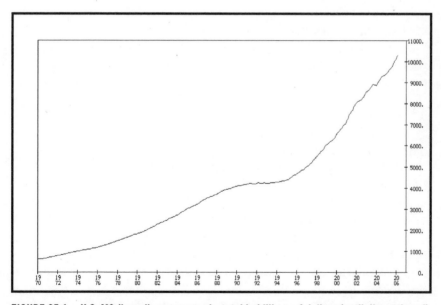

FIGURE 25.1   U.S. M3 (broad) money supply, total in billions of dollars (until discontinued)
Source: St. Louis Federal Reserve and Economagic.com. Data is available at www.federalreserve.gov /releases/H6. Chart courtesy of Economagic, LLC. All rights reserved.

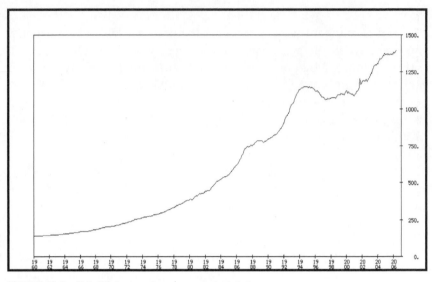

FIGURE 25.2   U.S. M1 (narrow) money supply, total
Source: Chart courtesy of Economagic, LLC. All rights reserved.

Note the year-on-year percentage change in M1 money supply dating back to 1960 as plotted in Figure 25.3.

A simple top-down examination of the gyrations unveils a connection between accelerating growth in money supply and the degree of paper asset reflation. Conversely, when money supply growth is disinflating, or worse, contracting, it usually coincides with periods defined by intensifying deflation risk.

There can be varied reasons for this, but usually the bottom-line dynamic can be traced to demand for credit that has been stimulated by a loose monetary policy and ample liquidity.

Since the stock market peaked in 2000 to 2001, the growth in narrow money supply has surged on two occasions to a +10 percent year-on-year rate, as the Fed drove rates to record low levels to stave off a debt deflation. The unprecedented period of year-to-year contraction in narrow M1 money supply was symptomatic of the intensified debt-deflation risk. More recently, you can identify a shift to the downside as the deluge of Fed rate hikes finally began to take effect by lifting the cost of money enough to at least slow the pace of credit growth.

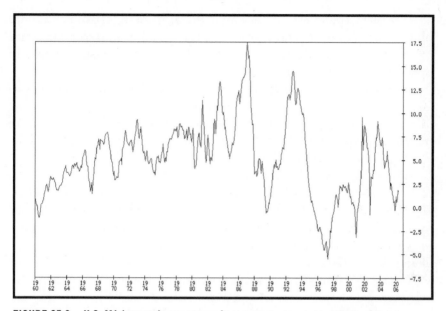

FIGURE 25.3   U.S. M1 (narrow) money supply, year-over-year percentage change
Source: Chart courtesy of Economagic, LLC. All rights reserved.

To provide a practical example from data on display within the Fed's web site, observe the following shift in growth rates of both M1 and M2 since the discontinuation of M3:

■ The 13-week rate of change posted for narrow M1 on April 3, 2006, was +3.9 percent, while the same ROC for headline M2 money supply was +6.5 percent.

■ By May 8, 2006, the 13-week ROC of narrow M1 had slowed to +2.4 percent, while that of headline M2 had slowed to +5.2 percent growth.

In the data, for the week ending July 10, 2006, the 13-week growth rate of narrow M1 was reported at a barely positive +0.1 percent, a virtual collapse from the near 4 percent rate in April.

In the meantime the growth in M2 has moderated to just +3.5 percent, barely more than half the growth rate seen in April 2006.

Is it mere coincidence that gold prices peaked for this cycle (to date) during the first week of May, just weeks after the short-term and long-term growth rates in most money supply measures peaked?

Is it mere coincidence that employment growth, consumer spending, housing, stocks, and gold have all entered a midterm corrective move to the downside at the same time that the money supply growth has slowed on a midterm basis?

While a multitude of factors are involved, the relationship can be skewed, and slowing money growth might simply reflect the slowdown in spending and housing. But, for the most part, the growth in money supply and credit are significant factors for gold, and all monetarily reflated paper wealth.

At the end of the day, the money supply and credit statistics reflect the attitude and stance according to the Fed's stated monetary policy. The sustained surge in the supply of paper currency and credit can be directly attributed to decades-long monetary stimulus and the continuous support for paper wealth reflation provided by global central banks, led by the Fed.

Taking this thought further, it is not a coincidence that as the nominal aggregate levels of credit and paper dollars climb to ever-newer all-time highs, gold and paper have become positively correlated from a wealth reflation perspective.

Even more impressive is that gold has broken out against and is appreciating against almost every paper currency printed on the planet. It all rewinds to gold, as the purest reserve currency.

A look at Figure 25.4 should dispel any doubt that gold might in fact be significantly undervalued at $600 per ounce. The parabolic multi-decade explosion in the monetary base is exhibited in the mega-macro long-term chart that tracks the U.S. monetary base dating back to 1918 (see Figure 25.4).

From 1918 through the late 1960s, the U.S. monetary base expanded gradually, perhaps even in line with economic growth and the expansion in gross domestic product. The adjustment to the price of gold in the 1940s can be discerned with a sudden bloat in the monetary base, and then the real action began in the early 1970s following Nixon's abolishment of the U.S. gold standard.

Since then the monetary base has exploded increasing from less than $100 billion to the current level in excess of $800 billion.

Is it any wonder that the USD price of gold has finally begun to play catch-up?

Another way to dissect U.S. monetary data is to use the Fed's "MZM," shown in Figure 25.5. The MZM represents the most liquid components of M2 money supply, including money market funds.

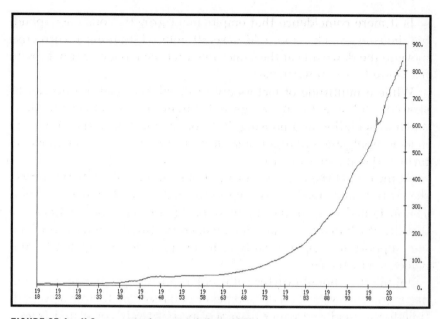

FIGURE 25.4   U.S. monetary base, total since 1918
Source: Chart courtesy of Economagic, LLC. All rights reserved.

First you must focus on the steep upslope and accelerated reflation in the most liquid money supply aggregate that supported the intensified paper asset reflation that took place in the mid-to-late 1990s. From 1996 through 2003, the MZM aggregate more than doubled as it rode the wave of paper wealth reflation defined within the technology-driven stock market boom.

Note that when MZM dips, so too does the pace of paper wealth reflation, as they essentially reflect one another. You need to dig deeper, to see what is really happening beneath the surface picture shown in the plot of total MZM (see Figure 25.5).

You can look at it in another way. The chart shown in Figure 25.6 on page 169 plots the actual dollar change on a rolling year-over-year basis; that is, the 12-month change in dollars, dating back to 1960. This is a totally different picture, with several obvious points of interest.

First and foremost, look at the peak 12-month increase, posted in mid-2003 when the previous 12 months had experienced a $100 billion increase in MZM.

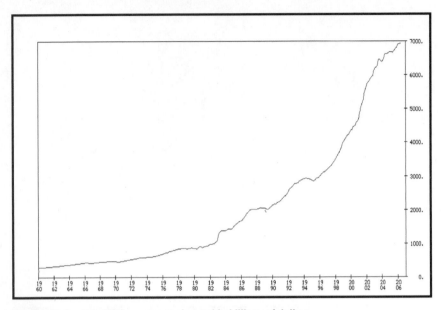

FIGURE 25.5   U.S. MZM money stock, total in billions of dollars
Source: Chart courtesy of Economagic, LLC. All rights reserved.

Is it a coincidence then that the Fed had taken rates to near zero during this period, essentially providing as much cheap liquidity as
debtors could possibly consume?

Of course not.

The perspective offered in Figure 25.6 is troubling because of the
parallels in the conditions witnessed when the 12-month change in
MZM reflects no growth, or a contraction in liquidity. Paper wealth
disinflation has accompanied those periods, usually in line with economic contraction and recession.

Depending on the Fed, this is important input for precious metals
traders and speculators and investors in all global capital markets. It
is particularly key for precious metals, known as history's "reserve
currency."

History is making note of the outrageous bloat in liquidity offered
not only by the Fed, but also by the Bank of Japan and the European
Central Bank, just to mention a couple.

As for the macrobullish secular impact on gold and silver, along
with other precious metals, you need to ask the following two simple
questions:

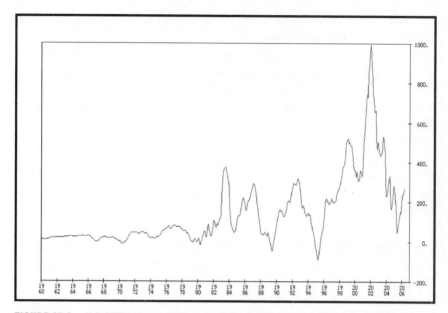

FIGURE 25.6   U.S. MZM money stock, actual change in dollars from one year ago
Source: Chart courtesy of Economagic, LLC. All rights reserved.

1. When the next contraction appears on the horizon (and it may already be visible), and the Fed must reflate the debt-ridden, savings-devoid U.S. consumer with even more excess liquidity, won't the 12-month pace of MZM growth need to exceed $100 billion?

2. If the answer to the first question is yes, then you can only ask, isn't gold cheap at $600?

The risk is a deep debt deflation in which the price of everything disinflates, including precious metals. When Fed stimulus and excess liquidity provisions no longer can reflate debt-saturated, savings-starved consumers, then gold is attractive only on a relative basis. If the Fed fails to respond, or alone, is not enough in the face of continued hawkishness by other global central banks, such a path would likely drive the USD price of precious metals lower at first, but it would also set the stage for a possible monetary Armageddon scenario.

There are numerous theoretical scenarios. The stakes are high, fortunes are on the line, and fortunes await those who are properly positioned. This is why it is so important to monitor these statistics and to keep your finger directly on the monetary pulse, which provides invaluable clues to reality versus the verbal monetary misdirection sometimes offered by the Fed.

Back to the present, Fed Chairman Ben Bernanke has written that he has his sights set on avoiding the asset-collateral paper wealth deflation experienced by Japan. In Japan, bank lending had contracted for years, literally years, until just recently. To read the Fed and monitor the support for and robustness of the reflation of paper wealth in the United States, you can closely observe the weekly commercial bank balance sheet data, reflecting lending activity.

Of all the bank lending statistics, by far the most impressive, if not ominous, is that the total outstanding lending by U.S. commercial banks to the real estate sector now exceeds $3 trillion.

Moreover, as noted in Figure 25.7, which shows the total outstanding real estate loans made by U.S. commercial banks, the amount has doubled in just the past six years and tripled since the 1997/1998 global currency crisis and debt-deflation episode.

Much of the paper wealth reflation, not just in the United States, but in the world, has been predicated on a massive housing-linked credit

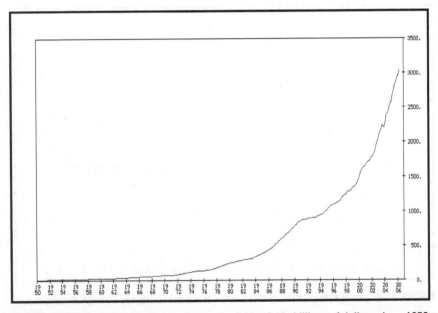

FIGURE 25.7   Real estate loans at all commercial banks in billions of dollars since 1950
Source: Chart courtesy of Economagic, LLC. All rights reserved.

expansion. As boot camp participants, you already know this because of the evidence that you have observed from the climb in this figure, on a week-in and week-out basis. Having watched this figure rise weekly for years, I am truly shocked that it has reached $3 trillion.

A different perspective offers invaluable insight as to how this has transpired. Figure 25.8 plots the week-to-week change in real estate lending by commercial banks on an annualized basis, charted weekly.

Simply stated, the chart of the weekly change in real estate lending, annualized, spotlights the increased codependent relationship between banks, mortgage debt, and the U.S. consumer-homeowner. The week-to-week swings have become wildly wide and are severely skewed to the upside, particularly since the mid-1990s. Obvious is the increased number of weekly expansions that exceed +500 percent annualized, all of which have taken place since the stock market peaked in 2000/2001.

By examining the data in several ways, you can more clearly see the unprecedented reflation in U.S. housing that has resulted from a loose monetary policy defined by cheap and limitless liquidity.

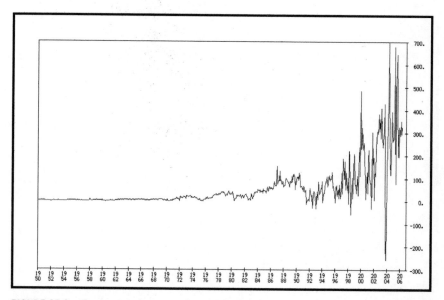

FIGURE 25.8   Real estate loans at all commercial banks: weekly change at annualized rate

Source: Chart courtesy of Economagic, LLC. All rights reserved.

This path of paper wealth reflation, as defined by the trillion plus extraction of that paper wealth through mortgage equity withdrawal (MEW) may have been paved by the Fed purposefully. The goal would have been to offset a massive wealth disinflation that might have otherwise accompanied the post-tech-bubble stock market environment.

Indeed, the Fed's plan worked.

It sparked a bull market in gold and silver, not to mention a host of other commodities, with a particularly acute reflation in the industrial/base metals sector.

The plot of the total outstanding commercial bank lending to consumers is seen in Figure 25.9. Since the year 2000, commercial bank lending to U.S. consumers has increased by +50 percent, rising to nearly $750 billion.

Focus again on the shorter-term change plotted on an annualized basis, as seen in Figure 25.10, using the monthly changes in total commercial bank loans made to U.S. consumers. The two huge upside spikes are eye-opening, amid

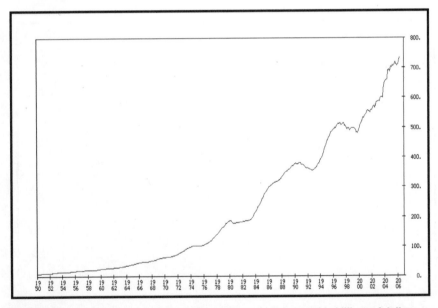

FIGURE 25.9   U.S. consumer loans at all commercial banks, total in billions of dollars since 1950

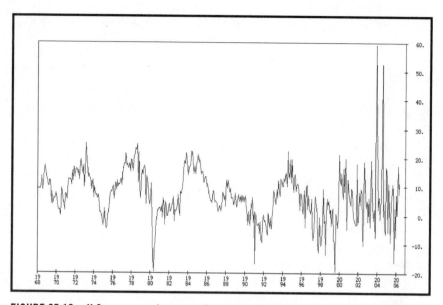

FIGURE 25.10   U.S. consumer loans at all commercial banks, month-to-month change at annualized rate

Source: Chart courtesy of Economagic, LLC. All rights reserved.

enormous short-term expansions in bank lending to consumers in 2003 and 2004.

More important though, in terms of the sustained rise in bank holdings of consumer debt, is the huge number of occasions since the year 2000 that the monthly expansion has spiked to a +20 percent annualized rate.

Does this mean that consumers, feeling flush with housing debt-linked paper wealth, were willing to borrow more? Of course it does, and this should lead you to an examination of inter-market analysis, as might be exemplified by the bull market in motor-cycle stocks (Harley-Davidson in particular) and boating stocks, as U.S. consumers have shown a seemingly insatiable appetite for adult toys.

But the MEW support has evaporated with the end of rabid home price reflation, as has the fiscal support offered by the U.S. government. Payroll growth has slowed leaving the consumer with big debt payments to banks, against less paper wealth reflation support.

You should begin to ask, when does increased consumer borrowing from banks reflect intensified financial stress?

Now it is time for you to twist the data and look at the actual dollar change in commercial bank lending to U.S. consumers plotted on a year-over-year basis, as exhibited in Figure 25.11. This is the actual amount of new debt over the most recent 12-month period.

Each time a negative 12-month period has occurred, it has been associated with macroeconomic contraction and paper wealth deflation. With that in mind, you can spotlight the multidecade trend toward higher highs in lending, which reached a mind-blowing $100 billion in the past two years.

Worse yet, the increased lending done since the last pay-down by consumers is numbing in aggregate, as even declines in the pace of bank lending to consumers take the growth rate down to a still-rapid 12-month pace of $20 to $30 billion. Incorporating some intermarket analysis might show that your macrofundamental read is accurate. Observe the long-term weekly chart of MarineMax in Figure 25.12,

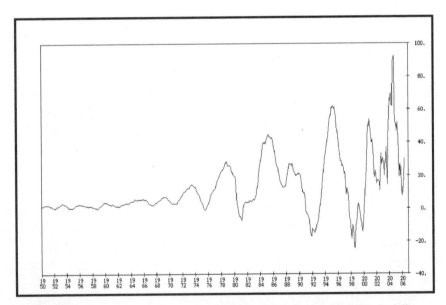

FIGURE 25.11 U.S. consumer loans at all commercial banks, actual change in dollars from one year ago

Source: Chart courtesy of Economagic, LLC. All rights reserved.

FIGURE 25.12   MarineMax Inc. HZO: weekly
Source: Weldononline.com.

which is breaking down amid liquidation as reflected by a negative on-balance volume (OBV).

In such a circumstance, you might be predisposed to be cautious in pushing a bullish bullion stance against this backdrop of paper wealth disinflation driven by a faltering macromonetary reflation evolution. It is no coincidence that during the same week that both Marinemax and Harley-Davidson stocks violated long-term uptrend lines, the price of gold flirted with its own midterm breakdown, while testing key support at $620.

Everything and anything can matter.

Back on point, the question quickly becomes would the Fed tighten monetary policy enough to cause liquidity to contract? This could put the consumer on tilt to the point of causing a debt liquidation or a pay-down driven contraction.

As boot campers, you have to dig deeper!

One of my major macrosecular themes has been, since the early 1990s, that technologically driven productivity gains and the globalization of the labor market produced a tectonic shift in wage-income dynamics. Simply, for a decade or more, technology has reduced the amount of human labor input required to produce an increasing level of output. Throw in that the globalization of labor markets caused a massive shift in output origins toward the lowest cost labor regions (China, India, and Eastern Europe), which has also exerted a disinflationary influence on global wage income. It has been a dual-edged sword, and the end result has been to severely restrain any push to the upside in wage-derived income reflation, particularly in Japan, the European Union, and the United States.

When you incorporate a rising level of the consumer price index (CPI), real U.S. wage-derived income has plummeted into overt deflation. This macrofactor is then respun back into your analysis on the credit situation as it impacts the debt-saddled, income-donked U.S. consumer. Debt growth is now far outperforming income growth. This might not have mattered when paper wealth in the stock market was reflating, or while paper wealth in housing was being channeled to the consumer through mortgage-equity withdrawal. But, without any reflation in paper collateral, there comes a breaking point. Income deflation has become a looming problem, as evidenced in Figure 25.13, which plots the 12-month

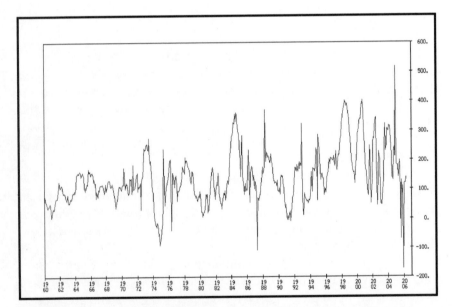

FIGURE 25.13   U.S. real disposable personal income, change from one year ago in billions of U.S. dollars: monthly since 1960

Source: Chart courtesy of Economagic, LLC. All rights reserved.

actual change in dollars of personal disposable income. Few players may realize the depth of income deflation over the past two years. The word *historic* comes to mind when you review Figure 25.13.

Subsequently, when you dig to the bottom of the pit to define one of the ultimate measures of consumer health that the Fed produces, you unearth the debt obligation and service ratio data.

Figure 25.14, the first of the two charts covering this all-telling statistical series, shows the surge to a new all-time high in the household debt service ratio (as a percentage of disposable personal income). Glaring is the steep slope seen in the past 18 months, as U.S. consumers feel the heat amid deflating income, rising interest rates, higher CPI, a complete lack of savings, and a monstrous debt load (see Figure 25.14).

And even worse than what is noted in Figure 25.14 (reflecting a near 14 percent financial obligations ratio) is the perspective noted within Figure 25.15. This chart reflects the Consumer Financial Obligations Ratio when the effect of mortgage refinance and Home Equity Loans are incorporated. Indeed, this ratio is breaking out toward 19 percent of income, thus reflecting an even greater degree of debt held by consumers, relative to income.

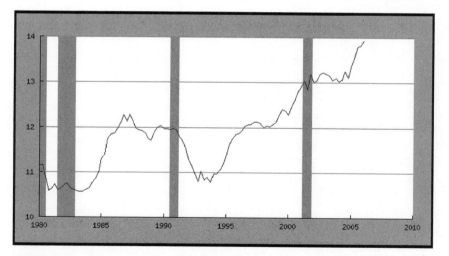

FIGURE 25.14   Household debt service payments as a percentage of disposable personal income

Source: Board of Governors of the Federal Reserve System, 2006 Federal Reserve Bank of St. Louis: research.stlouisfed.org. Shaded areas indicate recessions as determined by the National Bureau of Economic Research (NBER).

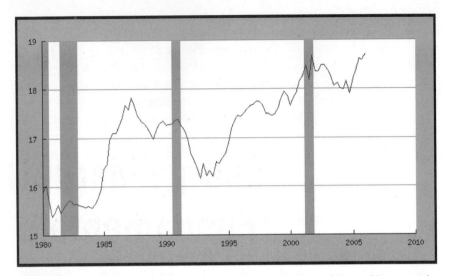

FIGURE 25.15 Household financial obligations as a percentage of disposable personal income

Source: Board of Governors of the Federal Reserve System, 2006 Federal Reserve Bank of St. Louis: research.stlouisfed.org. Shaded areas indicate recessions as determined by the National Bureau of Economic Research (NBER).

Mortgage refinancing and MEW had allowed consumers to restructure higher cost credit card debt, by incorporating that debt into their homes at (allegedly) cheaper rates. Rates were cheaper at the time, but most of the resultant credit is adjustable rate mortgage (ARM) home-equity debt. The more recent steep increase provides hard-core evidence that the loss of MEW and more recently the impact of ARM rate resetting are beginning to bite into the U.S. consumer's balance sheet.

This matters for all markets. It matters in the precious metals arena because of the current war taking place beneath the surface between the paper U.S. dollar and gold, as the world's safe haven store of wealth. The USD has begun to lose that war, for all the reasons highlighted over the past few pages.

Anyone can keep a finger on the pulse of the Fed, thanks to transparency. I hope that the road map I have offered so far provides something of a guide. The reaction of the Fed in the coming years will be key. Nonetheless, the Fed does not have control nor oversight when it comes to several other key pertinent factors affecting the health and well-being of the U.S. consumer.

Energy Market Fundamentals

Y ou must dig some more and focus on energy—one of the potentially most serious macrorisk land mines buried in the secular landscape of gold, precious metals, and all other investment asset classes. You must explore another whole world to understand the macromarket fundamentals that matter in the petro-patch. For your purposes, this chapter highlights a few key points.

First and foremost, the American Petroleum Institute (API) and U.S. Energy Information Administration (EIA) both publish a host of supply-and-demand statistics every week on Wednesday. I want to know everything about these two reports. Not only do I want to know the headline week-to-week change in overall supply of crude oil, heating oil, and gasoline, but I also want to know what is happening in distillates, reformulated gasoline, blending components, kerosene, propane, jet fuel (now ethanol, too), and refinery utilization rates.

Moreover, I want to know the breakdown in each product by "Pad," or delivery point. Pad 1 is the East Coast and Pad 5 is the West Coast; Pad 2 represents the Midwest, and the NYMEX delivery point at Cushing, Oklahoma; Pad 3 is the U.S. Gulf port; and Pad 4 is the Rocky Mountain region.

Heating oil data for Pad 1 is most important. For gasoline, Pad 5 is consistently short supplied, particularly when it comes to reformulated gasoline (RFG), which is also a major factor for Pad 1 and the Northeast, acutely so during the peak summer driving season.

It can be important to distinguish between the significance of the data, based on the specificity of the input regionwise and productwise. Refinery utilization rates are also informative because they reflect the amount of crude oil being consumed by refiners during the production of products. A build in product supply that came amid a decline in refinery runs and subsequent decline in the output of that particular product would speak volumes about diminished demand or consumption. The U.S. Energy Information Agency also provides detailed statistics related to demand.

Perhaps the most important data to be gleaned in these fundamental energy reports are the changes in the trend of the year-over-year supply deficit or surplus. In other words, is more or less supply available now than at this time last year?

Like a 52-week moving average, this macrofundamental statistical analysis is a means to determine whether a trend exists over time, and to monitor potential changes in that trend. Suppose a weekly API report reveals a rise in gasoline supply; let's say it's 2.0 mb (million barrels). Considering that U.S. motor gasoline (Mogas) supplies run just above 200 million barrels on average, a change of 2.0 mb is not insignificant, representing a one percent nominal change.

Markets might react bearishly, pricewise, to the increase in supply reported for the latest week. But, suppose this is a week where, normally every year, refineries come back online from regularly scheduled maintenance and produce more gasoline. Suppose the normal increase for this particular week, seasonally, is 3.5 mb. Hence, the one percent increase is *less* than the increase of 1.75 percent posted in the same week last year.

Now suppose that the year-over-year supply situation in gasoline had been flat, with no surplus and no deficit versus the same period one year ago. In this case, an increase of one percent in weekly supply would result in a supply *deficit* of 1.5 mb, which might actually be bullish for gasoline prices.

Another key report for the energy market is the natural gas injection data produced by the EIA, along with the U.S. Coal Production and Consumption report, also produced by the EIA. In natural gas, the analysis dynamics are similar to those used in crude oil and gasoline, à la comparisons of supply to historical and seasonal norms.

For natural gas, the key comparison is with the five-year average supply. At present, the U.S. supply of natural gas held in underground storage is more than 25 percent above the five-year average, and is more than 20 percent above the level a year ago.

The lack of weather severe enough to cause demand to spike, has left natural gas prices struggling, despite some seemingly positive secular fundamentals. The U.S. Fed is likely very happy that natural gas and electricity prices have remained in check and thus have not exacerbated the intensified pressure on the U.S. consumer as a result of high gasoline prices.

I also monitor the Baker Hughes rig count report, as a bigger-picture gauge of supply and demand. When prices reach a level conducive to profitable production and more important profitable (relative to risk) exploration dynamics, the number of rigs pumping oil in the Gulf, Mexico, or Canada will rise and vice versa. This in turn impacts the mentality of bullion traders. Thus, you need to monitor the energy macromarket fundamentals as well.

Figures 26.1 and 26.2 show the Texas and Louisiana rig counts, as reported by the Dallas Federal Reserve Bank.

It appears that the current supply situation was set up as a result of the collapse of the domestic oil industry in the early 1980s. Only within the past few years amid a return to high prices and expanding product margins (gasoline crack spread—the profit margin that oil refiners receive for "cracking" crude oil into gasoline) pushed to record highs during the first half of 2006 have the rig counts started to show signs of

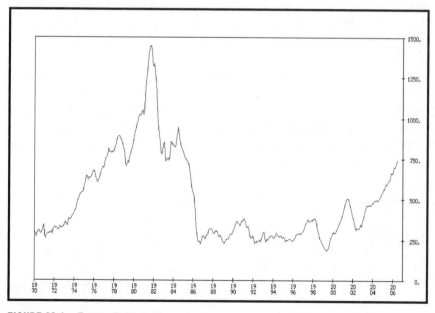

FIGURE 26.1   Texas oil rig count
Source: Chart courtesy of Economagic, LLC. All rights reserved.

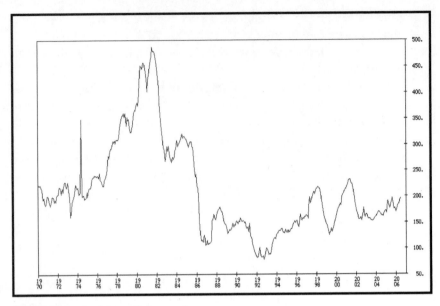

FIGURE 26.2   Louisiana oil rig count
Source: Chart courtesy of Economagic, LLC. All rights reserved.

life. This dynamic partially explains the divergence between rising crude oil supplies and stagnant gasoline supply, again spotlighting the primary problem in the United States, a complete lack of sufficient refinery capacity (see Figure 26.2).

This has become even more important with the spectacular inflation in gasoline as a macroeconomic factor, potentially an inhibitor to continued reflation in the U.S. consumer. Gasoline is important on many fronts for this reason, not least significant of which is the Fed front.

Thus, there is no debating the importance of bullion traders and investors knowing the energy fundamentals.

 Now you'll embark on a routine overview of the petropatch so you can make broader investment decisions, not only about precious metals, but about all assets.

First you can simply note the pure price explosion experienced in the crude oil market dating all the way back to 1946, the year after the end of World War II. A perusal of Figure 26.3 suggests that the current steeply sloped spike in oil prices appears to be more violent than that seen during the 1970s and 1980s, with prices having doubled in just the past three years.

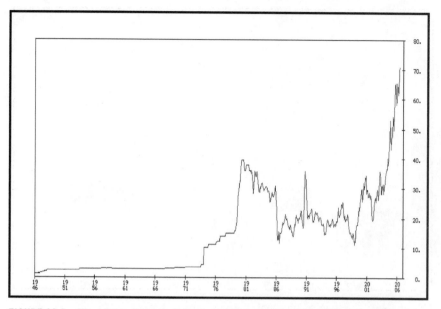

FIGURE 26.3   West Texas intermediate crude oil, spot price: monthly since 1946
Source: Chart courtesy of Economagic, LLC. All rights reserved.

Things begin to look even more ominous in Figure 26.4, which reveals that U.S. supplies of crude oil have risen significantly since the end of 2004.

In fact, as defined by the year-over-year rate of change (ROC), the 12-month supply situation has been in surplus since the end of 2004, but prices have skyrocketed nonetheless. This indicates that the driving force in energy prices has not been crude oil, but gasoline. More recently, you can note the breakdown in supply and the eroding year-over-year surplus.

The real problems are U.S. gasoline demand, the failure of the United States to expand refinery capacity, and heated competition with China for long-term supplies. The gasoline-specific side of the equation is evidenced in Figure 26.5, which plots the five-year ROC of crude oil supply (bars) against that for gasoline (line). The recent divergence is obvious, as ample supplies of crude oil are not bearish enough, given the inability to transform those supplies into adequate gasoline output (see Figure 26.5).

This situation can also be attributed to the high degree of intensified geopolitical risk currently evident in petroleum-producing regions from the Middle East, Nigeria, and Venezuela.

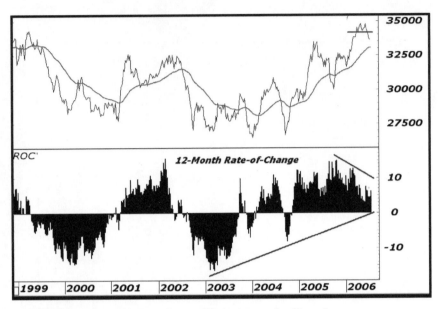

FIGURE 26.4 U.S. crude oil stocks: weekly in thousands of barrels

Source: Weldononline.com.

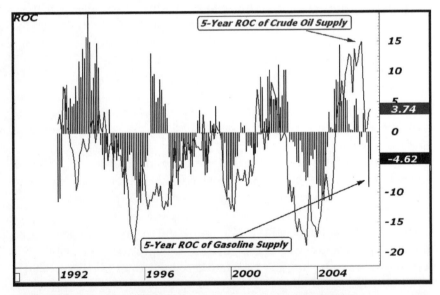

FIGURE 26.5 Five-year ROC of crude oil supply versus gasoline supply

Source: Weldononline.com.

What is problematic going forward, for U.S. consumers, and thus for the U.S. Federal Reserve, is the most recent downturn in U.S. supplies of gasoline, as measured on a long-term basis and plotted in the monthly chart shown in Figure 26.6. You may revel in the fact that the five-year rate of change in gasoline supply has fallen into a state of contraction, as has the 12-month MA of the ROC.

The bottom line for bullion traders, speculators, and investors is that the Fed is likely to be very sensitive to the intensifying pressure coming to bear on the U.S. consumer. It will be predisposed to tread lightly, monetarily, thus providing an underlying thread of support for precious metals, particularly in USD terms (see Figure 26.7).

In the United States, despite record high output of gasoline, the secular trend in supply is decidedly to the downside, as seen in Figure 26.7 reflecting the 24-month average of U.S. supply, plotted monthly since 1986.

As for that record high domestic U.S. output of gasoline, Figure 26.8 plots the daily average gasoline output recorded weekly and plotted monthly, dating back to the late 1980s. Not only has the trend been toward greater output over the past 15 years, but the daily average has just reached a new all-time record, exceeding 9.0 million barrels per day for the first time ever (see Figure 26.8).

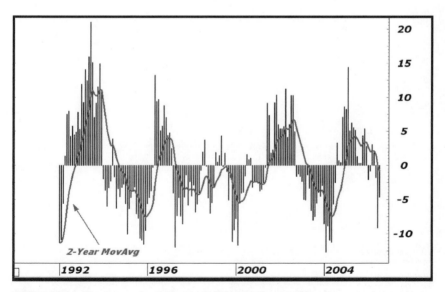

FIGURE 26.6   Five-year rate of change in U.S. gasoline supplies
Source: Weldononline.com.

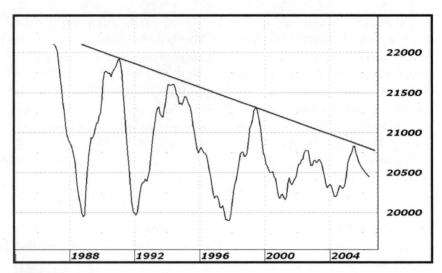

FIGURE 26.7 Twenty-four-month average of U.S. gasoline supply: millions of barrels plotted monthly

Source: Weldononline.com.

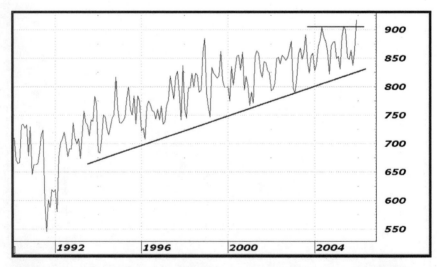

FIGURE 26.8 U.S. gasoline production: daily average in millions of barrels plotted monthly

Source: Weldononline.com.

Given record domestic output and record product imports, the fact that supplies maintain a long-term downtrend speaks volumes as to the enormous increase in demand that has taken place in the past 20 years. When contemplating the ferocity of the price changes in energy, look at Figure 26.9 reflecting the USD change from the year-ago period in NYMEX West Texas Intermediate (WTI) crude oil.

The global economy has never been forced to deal with the type of energy inflation experienced over the past three years, during which time the 12-month change has vacillated between $10 and $25 without a single decline, an unprecedented situation.

More to the macrometals point, you can safely say that record high gasoline prices have done absolutely nothing to squelch consumption demand. Until this demand dynamic changes, prices are most likely to continue trending higher, offering underlying support for a continued long-term appreciation in precious metals prices. In fact, one of the primary risk points, in terms of expecting a sustained intermediate-term bull market in the precious metals, would be a major breakdown (major meaning back below $45 to $50) in WTI crude oil.

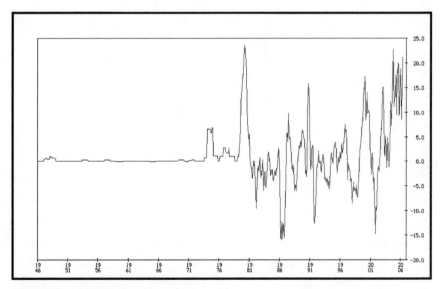

FIGURE 26.9   West Texas intermediate crude oil, spot price change in U.S. dollars from one year ago: monthly since 1946

Source: Chart courtesy of Economagic, LLC. All rights reserved.

Such an event would crush consumer inflation expectations. Further, such an occurrence might take place in line with significant softening in the global economy, perhaps as a direct result of a contraction in the U.S. consumer. Unless the Fed would respond aggressively with stimulative monetary policy, such a scenario would be unlikely to be bullion bullish. Or, perhaps a breakdown in energy prices would spark a consumer revival, offering the financial support that is now so lacking à la housing disinflation, wage income deflation, stock market stagnation, and fiscal paralysis.

It would be interesting to see how the Fed might respond to this scenario, open to easing by receding inflation expectations, but maybe restrained amid consumer enthusiasm.

Of course, you boot campers will be monitoring the data for clues every day and will fully expect to see exactly what is really happening. Again, the money and credit statistics will provide key clues.

The opposite scenario appears more probable. An upward spike in energy prices unleashes a wave of disinflationary influences, particularly in the area of U.S. consumer debt, creating a real conundrum for the U.S. Federal Reserve.

The writing is already on the wall, and the internal erosion may be too damaging for quick and easy monetary repair. This is one of the (many) reasons I have been a secular (non-goldbug) bull on bullion since 1999, as a replacement for the U.S. dollar and U.S. Treasury market, as the safest pure storage vehicle for wealth.

Figure 26.10 shows how boot camp participants might examine the biggest macropicture when measuring the U.S. equity market created paper wealth dynamic.

In this chart, you take the S&P 500 stock index, divide it by the price of WTI crude oil, and then adjust (divide again) the resultant ratio spread by the yield on the two-year U.S. Treasury note. The chart reveals the end result, which you might consider as a proxy for the true trend in equity market derived paper wealth, as affected by energy prices and interest rates.

Then you apply some basis technical indicators, and you've got a read. For sure, the deepening decline into negative territory, a rare event, is ominous in reflecting the ability, or lack thereof, of the U.S. consumer to continue taking the dual body blows being delivered by rising interest rates and rising energy prices. So, too, is that the ratio is below a declining MA, also a rare situation, implying erosion in real paper wealth.

The perspective illustrated in Figure 26.10 deserves a closer look.

Note the zoomed-in cutout of the five-year rate-of-change portion exhibited in Figure 26.11 spotlighting the proxy for macropaper

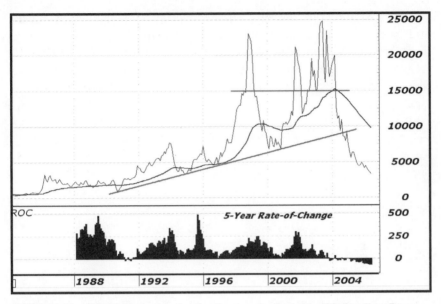

FIGURE 26.10   S&P 500 Index/crude oil ratio spread adjusted by U.S. Two-Year Treasury Note yield: monthly close

Source: Weldononline.com.

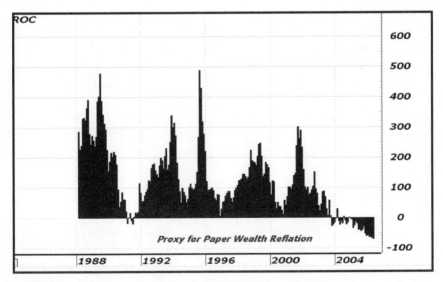

FIGURE 26.11   Five-year rate of change, S&P 500 Index/crude oil ratio spread adjusted by Two-Year Treasury Note yield: monthly plot

Source: Weldononline.com.

wealth reflation. So far, the current deflation is far more severe and sustained than that experienced during either of the two most recent official recessions, in 1990/1991 and 2000/2001. Also evident is the most recent lower low in paper wealth reflation, in line with a less sustained increase posted since the mid-1990s peak.

Global Trade

U.S. imports are nearly $120 billion per month.

In May 2006, the year-over-year growth in U.S. imports was +12.7 percent. And, while the increase in the price of imported crude oil was a major contributor, the value of the increase in imported manufactured goods was twice as much (+ $49 billion in the five-month year-to-date [YTD] period end-May versus the same period one year ago) as the increase in energy imports.

The trade balance for the first five months (YTD) of 2006 was in deficit to the tune of (–) $341 billion, an expansion of more than (–) $40 billion over the same YTD-2005 deficit.

These statistics are mind boggling, yet none of them illustrate the degree of imbalance and the magnitude of the U.S. import-driven deficit, defined by savings that have been consumed and then forward income that has been borrowed.

 On a price-adjusted basis, as evidenced in Figure 27.1, real imports are propelling toward $200 billion per month, extending an explosive acceleration related to a secular rise in place since Nixon removed the U.S. dollar (USD) from the gold standard.

Remember, everything matters.

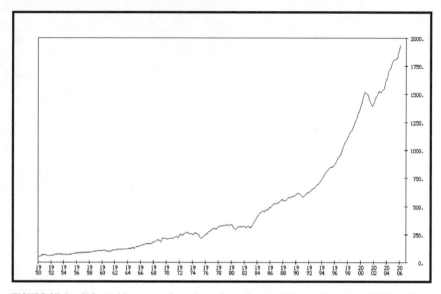

FIGURE 27.1   U.S. real imports of goods and services in billions of chained 2000 dollars: monthly since 1950

Source: Chart courtesy of Economagic, LLC. All rights reserved.

Figure 27.1 matters because it reflects why the USD is losing credibility as a reserve currency and why gold has grabbed the torch of reserve asset leadership.

Notable in Figure 27.1 is the correlation between periods of deflating U.S. imports and contracting global gross domestic product (GDP) growth. Again, this just proves the importance to the Fed of keeping the U.S. consumer "floated" to keep the USD from collapsing.

Instead of saying that the Fed should or shouldn't take a certain approach, you need to continually ask what if, what will the Fed do, if or when the imbalances are no longer sustainable and begin to snap? Aside from the effect of the 9/11 terrorist attack, Figure 27.2 reveals the actual change, in dollars, in U.S. imports on a year-over-year basis (the most recent 12-month change). You can only wonder how long the savings-devoid, income-dry, debt-loaded U.S. consumer can keep increasing imports by more than $100 billion every 12 months.

Note that each deflation in 12-month imports coincided with a contraction in global GDP. Turning things around while keeping in mind

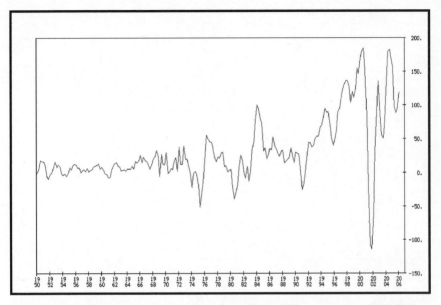

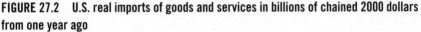

FIGURE 27.2   U.S. real imports of goods and services in billions of chained 2000 dollars from one year ago
Source: Chart courtesy of Economagic, LLC. All rights reserved.

that the Federal Reserve is constantly mentioning net exports in seeking solutions to global trade/capital/savings imbalances, note the U.S. trade situation defined by net exports, as plotted in Figure 27.3.

The boot camp inspection continues as you carve up the data to reveal the month-to-month change, at an annualized rate, plotted in Figure 27.4 on page 195. The wildly expanding volatility is pronounced as it relates to the degree of month-to-month swings, and the visible trend in such to the downside. If you have listened to the lessons of my boot camp, you should see this as a clue supporting the macro thought process. You would say the growth in the global economy is directly linked to the expansion in the U.S. consumer and, more specifically, to the growth in U.S. consumer debt.

The wild swings are predicated on expanding global trade and the parabolic growth just spotlighted in U.S. imports. The weight of the world is increasing every day. Figure 27.4 implies that some months, the weight of the world increases by more than +200 percent, annualized.

As "they" say: someday, something's gotta give.

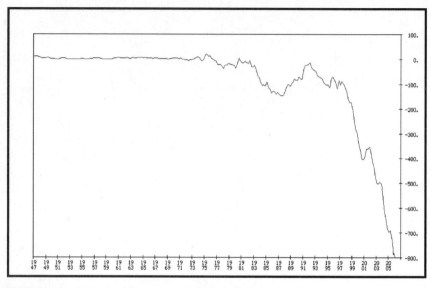

FIGURE 27.3 U.S. net exports: monthly since 1947
Source: Chart courtesy of Economagic, LLC. All rights reserved.

The Fed will do everything it can to ensure that the something is not the U.S. consumer. Thus, the weight of the world is on the Fed. Again, it's not surprising that gold continues to gain favor.

You should be asking what happens to the value of the U.S. dollar while you're looking at trade and imports. There is little doubt that as the Fed has facilitated a consumer-credit blowout situation that I'll call *bubblicious,* the impact of a perpetually expanding paper money supply becomes a policy issue reflected by the value of the USD.

For the most part, a weakening dollar indicates a soft Fed or is reflecting an unspoken Fed agenda. A weakening dollar will coincide with commodity reflation and is usually most acutely reflected by its decline in the concurrent appreciation in gold.

A strengthening USD might imply an expanding interest rate differential, usually a premium over lower yielding currencies. This was the case in the early 1980s, and the markets tried to make this the case in 2005. Or, a strengthening USD, depending on the breakdown by individual currency pair, might also suggest a liquidity contraction sparked repatriation of U.S. offshore investments.

The other side of that coin is the risk of a liquidation of reserve dollars and the ultimate repatriation of paper wealth, in which case ex-

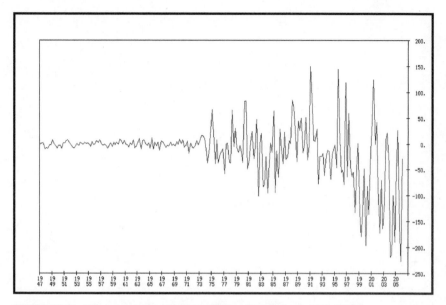

FIGURE 27.4   U.S. net exports: monthly change at annual rate since 1947
Source: Chart courtesy of Economagic, LLC. All rights reserved.

porters sell USD and hold their export receipts in something else, like gold. The problem with this thought process is that in selling their holdings of reserve dollars, exporters would be chopping off the hands that feed them, as demand for their exported goods from U.S. consumers is the driving force behind all the paper wealth reflation.

The race being run by exporting nations, particularly those in Asia, to consume more of their own output, is not likely to be run fast enough to offset a major retrenchment in U.S. consumption.

Figure 27.5 is worth studying for a specific reason: it reflects that, while overall U.S. imports have soared since 2000, the U.S. is importing less from Japan than it was at the 2001 peak.

The lack of Japanese export growth as related to U.S. imports is a direct reflection of the increased dominance of China, as a major exporter, and, as the single largest holder of reserve dollars, with more than $900 billion (as per the most recently updated data, surpassing Japan).

The most recent data reveals yet another record export figure for China, with more than $80 billion in exports reported for a single month (June 2006). Certainly there is a symbiotic relationship, as U.S. consumers benefit from final goods price disinflation amid the surge

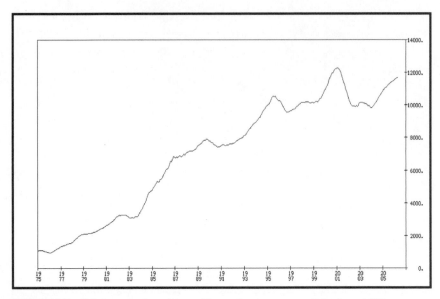

FIGURE 27.5   U.S. Imports from Japan, 12-month average: monthly since 1975
Source: Chart courtesy of Economagic, LLC. All rights reserved.

in Chinese exports, while China then receives much desired hard currency, in USD.

However, the recent boom in global excess USD liquidity has allowed a majority of debtor nations categorized by official credit ratings agencies as emerging markets to accumulate USD reserves and assets greater than their external debt. In fact, one of the most highly respected credit agencies recently reported that this circumstance now applies to three-quarters of the countries it rates as emerging market quality.

This is unprecedented since the abandonment of the gold standard and may suggest that the scales of imbalance have reached a turning point. It means that Asian central banks that now hold mountainous levels of USD paper reserves, well exceeding any amount necessary to pay down their own external debt, might seek to diversify the risk inherent in holding a majority of wealth in a single currency.

It is a well-known fact that Asian central banks—including the Bank of Japan (BOJ), the People's Bank of China (PBOC), the Central Bank of China (CBC, Taiwan), the Monetary Authority of Singapore (MAS), the Bank of Korea (BOK), and the Reserve Bank of India (RBI)—have made virtually no reserve allocations into gold.

This fact flies in the face of the high relative gold allocation, as a percentage of total official reserves, held by the European and U.S. central banks. There was an even larger discrepancy before the Swiss National Bank and the Bank of England completely cleared the vaults of their gold holdings.

Thus, going forward, if the United States comes under increasing scrutiny as a debtor nation with no savings cushion, Asian central banks might decide to allocate some of their wealth into the safety of precious metals.

And, while I may not be talking a significant percentage of total reserves, with overall Asian USD reserves now climbing to $3+ trillion, even a minimal percentage allocation relative to U.S. and European ratios would drive precious metals prices sharply higher.

The precious metals markets might not be deep enough in their own liquidity to handle such a reallocation out of paper dollars.

 You have to find the truth. Observe the evidence in offshore holdings of U.S. dollar and U.S. Treasury debt, first by noting the plot of U.S. custody holdings, or U.S. Treasury debt held on account at the Fed, for foreign official institutions (see Figure 27.6).

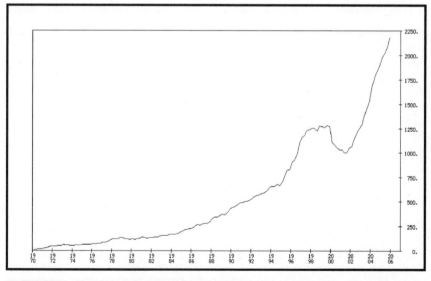

FIGURE 27.6   Total U.S. federal debt held by foreign investors in billions of dollars: monthly since 1970

Source: Chart courtesy of Economagic, LLC. All rights reserved.

Of specific interest in identifying potential risk and macro land mines is that when custody holdings (Figure 27.6) actually contracted, it was not because of any significant rise in U.S. interest rates.

Rather, it was domestically based fear amid a decline in liquidity, and was linked to the Fed's credibility in the push to record low rates against the rising tide of debt-deflation risk. It is this kind of fear that would feed into a monetary Armageddon scenario.

Of curious interest is that official foreign institutions hold far more U.S. Treasury paper than does the U.S. Federal Reserve. Figure 27.7 plots the total amount of U.S. federal debt held by the U.S. Federal Reserve Banks.

Much more ominous (not illustrated) is that the Bank of Japan and the People's Bank of China both own more U.S. Treasury paper than does the Fed. If the Fed were forced to purchase the Treasury holdings of just two foreign central banks—the People's Bank of China and the Bank of Japan—the total holdings of U.S. Treasury paper at the Fed would more than triple!

This is hard-core evidence that both Japan and China are coconspirators in the monetary misdirection and reflation of paper wealth, predicated on a permanently reflated U.S. consumer. Figure 27.8 plots the

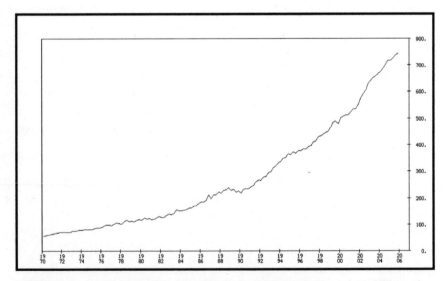

FIGURE 27.7   U.S. federal debt held by U.S. Federal Reserve banks, total in billions of dollars: monthly since 1970

Source: Chart courtesy of Economagic, LLC. All rights reserved.

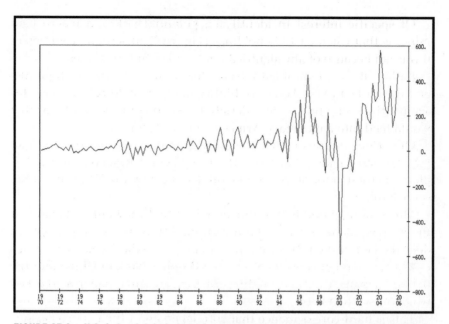

FIGURE 27.8   U.S. federal debt held by foreign investors: monthly change at annual rate since 1970

Source: Chart courtesy of Economagic, LLC. All rights reserved.

month-to-month change in foreign holdings of U.S. Treasury debt, at an annualized rate.

Can foreign central banks be expected to keep accumulating U.S. paper at a 400 percent to 600 percent annualized pace, every single month for the next 20 years? This would seem to be impossible, but markets are completely complacent about the prospects for this exact scenario. This complacency implies belief that foreign central banks will continue to accumulate U.S. paper at this astronomical pace.

Simply, something's gotta give.

As per the massive trade-import-export imbalances, and the monstrous credit-savings-income imbalances, and the egregious wealth-labor imbalances, many expect that the something that's "gotta give" is the U.S. dollar itself. Herein lies the single most bullish potential backdrop for would-be long-term macrosecular bullion bulls, a scenario where the USD gives.

You can attack the USD from the technical perspective, as noted in the long-term mega-macro-monthly in Figure 27.9, which plots the U.S. Dollar Index (USDX) all the way back to 1972.

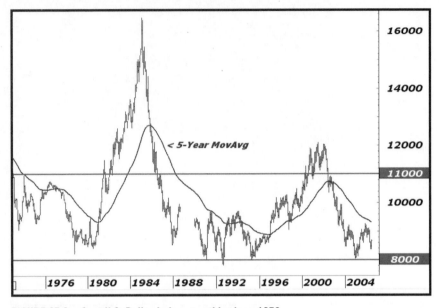

FIGURE 27.9   Spot U.S. Dollar Index: monthly since 1972
Source: Weldononline.com.

You can extrapolate this approach, and apply bands at the upper end of the longer-term USDX trading range, at 110–00, and, at the lower end, historically, at 80.00.

Observe that the lower band has held during each economic contraction and credit retrenchment, in the late 1980s, then in the early 1990s, and again in the post-2001–01 deflation-risk episode. Thus, you should be particularly troubled at the lack of recovery and the failed rally that was soundly rejected by the long-term secular moving average.

A renewed decline in the USDX, perhaps predicated on a re-reversal in Fed policy focus if disinflation risk intensifies enough to get the Fed's attention toward the lower band, would signal intensified stress, macro consumer debtwise, or intensified Fed monetary support—or, both.

But beyond that, any downside violation in the USDX below the lower band marked at 80.00 would be a whole new ball game, with the greenback tumbling into uncharted territory, probably in sync with a broader, more problematic debt liquidation scenario.

In this case, gold would likely be appreciating against all paper currencies, and all paper asset vehicles. A break of 80.00 in the USDX would have broad implications, depending on the macro-risk catalyst, and then the monetary response from the Fed.

If the Fed did not respond and interest rates spiked, the consumer would be exposed, and all asset classes might be subjected to deflation including gold. In that case, gold would simply hold its value better than other assets by declining less.

The more probable path would see the Fed respond with easier money or would see the USD breaking down as a result of a shift back toward dovish policy by the Fed.

The third scenario, again the lead into a monetary Armageddon scene, would have the Fed respond stimulatively, but with no impact on interest rates, amid wholesale dumping of dollars and full-scale retrenchment by U.S. consumers.

Trade dynamics, as they relate to the U.S. consumer and the U.S. dollar, are key considerations for bullion traders, speculators, and investors.

U.S. Fiscal Fundamentals

A credible argument can be made that there is a direct correlation between government deficit spending and growth in trade, consumption, and output.

Theoretically, government deficit spending is as effective, if not more directly effective, as money supply creation in sync with an easy monetary policy from the Fed. Deficit spending creates money representing wealth that is transferred to the consumer, usually through tax cuts or direct subsidy and social program expenditures.

In the United States, periods of expanding deficits have been associated with paper wealth reflation, rising consumption, and expanding imports.

Conversely, periods where deficits are shrinking or where surpluses are being generated by the government can be linked to times of retrenchment extending into consumers, businesses, and even into global trade.

I do not make any political statements herein, nor do I discuss the causes; I only observe the correlations as they relate to inflation and the credibility of the currency.

This is the connection to precious metals. You might simply shave it down to suggest, that all other things being equal (which they never are), rising government spending equals expanding deficits, which equals intensified underlying inflation support and a weakening currency. Thus it is bullish for bullion and vice versa, all other things being equal (which they never are).

 In your regular review of the U.S. fiscal situation, you should first examine the quarter-to-quarter change in U.S. government expenditures, plotted via the annualized rate dating back to 1950, visible in Figure 28.1.

Simply stated, U.S. government spending is soaring and reaching record heights, with the most recent quarterly pace posted above +150 percent annualized. And, the last time that U.S. government spending actually contracted on a quarter-to-quarter basis was in the mid-1960s, just prior to the escalation of the Vietnam War and the abandonment of the USD gold standard.

If the theories are correct, and if expanding deficits correlate with expanding paper wealth reflation and vice versa, then the impact of the budget balancing spearheaded by the Clinton administration was

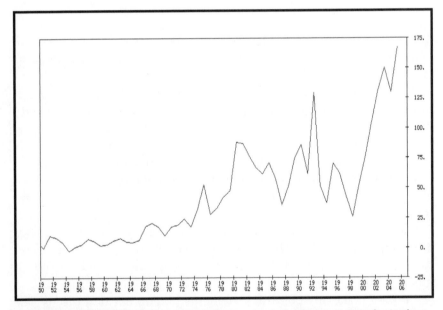

FIGURE 28.1   Federal government expenditures, quarterly change at annual rate since 1950

Source: Chart courtesy of Economagic, LLC. All rights reserved.

experienced in the post-tech-bubble period defined by intensified debt-deflation risk.

Figure 28.2 plots the "Net Total Government Savings Balance" monthly dating back to 1930. Visible is a steadily deepening U.S. fiscal deficit (declining line) from the 1970s, through the 1980s, and into the early part of the Clinton administration, much of which could be traced to Reagan's Cold War deficit spending. The trend toward larger deficits provided strong underlying support for paper wealth reflation and a perpetual expansion in U.S. consumption, and thus in global trade.

But, the sharp shift from deficit into surplus, aided by productivity gains, was primarily driven by Clinton's fiscal policies and culminated in the peak of paper equity market reflation in the year 2000.

Subsequently, the policies that the Bush administration implemented in direct response to the debt-deflation risk that resulted from the spike into a fiscal surplus have been a major reason paper wealth reflation has been sustained and a prolonged consumer-retrenchment induced recession avoided.

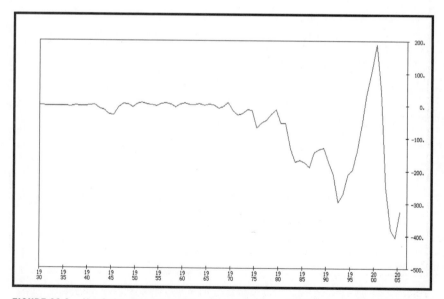

FIGURE 28.2   Net federal government savings in billions of dollars: monthly since 1930
Source: Chart courtesy of Economagic, LLC. All rights reserved.

Deepening deficits are generally considered bearish for the U.S. dollar, are reflationary in general, are thus supportive to commodities, and, are just plain bullish for gold. This is increasingly true as time goes on, and the U.S. deficit deepens past the point of a comfortable percentage of gross domestic product (GDP).

Indeed, the triple deficits—fiscal, capital, and trade—are all approaching the "event horizon" of surpassing a sustainable percentage of total GDP. This becomes, and is likely to continue becoming, an increasingly positive influence on bullion prices.

Inflation and Labor Market Fundamentals

If inflation was purely a monetary phenomenon, certainly the Consumer Price Index (CPI) and other recognized indicators of inflation such as the Personal Consumption Expenditures Price Index or the Gross Domestic Product (GDP) price deflators would be significantly higher than they are now. Many pundits pose a credible argument that inflation measures such as the CPI severely underestimate the real level of inflation.

I can only think of what my good buddy Martin Lysaght and I always say, "It is what it is."

The CPI is what it is.

The Personal Consumption Expenditures (PCE) Price Index is what it is.

The Import Price Index is what it is.

And the true level of inflation is what it is.

It's just that the true level of inflation is not necessarily determined by any of the preceding measures. The Bureau of Labor Statistics and the Commerce Department are just as transparent as the Fed, since the ways and means of statistical compilation and calculation are fully explained in the fine print.

I can fully accept these indexes, for exactly what they are telling me. Nothing more, and nothing less.

Besides, inflation is not as important as it used to be.

I am not saying this cannot change. I am merely saying that what I call the "Ladder of Inflation" is already missing a critical rung, without which inflation will have a difficult time staying inflationary.

Without wage-derived income reflation, any inflation in prices becomes more predicated on the price changes in the underlying commodities markets (something we have surely experienced), which, in turn, because of the lack of income inflation, becomes disinflationary from the macro-consumer angle.

In other words, without a concurrent push higher in U.S. wage income, a rise in the price of gasoline to, say, $4 or higher, would most certainly jack the inflation statistics higher. But just as certainly, such an event would also inhibit spending on other discretionary items by consumers, particularly in the current environment, which is defined by a savings drought.

Moreover, this upside-down thought process fits perfectly in the assessment of productivity.

Inflation pulls a phoenix by rising from the ashes of its own disinflationary impact on consumers. When the Fed realizes that since the ladder is missing a critical rung, its only other pain-avoidance choice will be to hyper-reflate, as it did in 2001/2003, to assist the consumer. In this sense, a true inflation is becoming more likely.

The alternative scenario is a nightmarish economic contraction that liquidates debt.

Again, academically, the time for solutions is long gone. Perhaps the only saving grace is the belief that global labor markets have a long time to go before the playing field has become anywhere near even, thus keeping this dominant macroinfluence overhanging the labor market. And, newer technologies down the road might even improve productivity and efficiency.

The downside to this would be an extension to the ongoing trend of core erosion in the U.S. labor market. Employment growth in this market is simply not sufficient and is running at a pace that can barely satisfy the growth in the working age population. To say that nonfarm payroll growth has been subpar during the most recent paper wealth reflation would be a significant understatement. Employment growth has been putrid on a relative basis, with very few industries experiencing tight, or even tightening, labor conditions.

The United States has outsourced labor to cheaper sources and is paying the price in line with the secular trend in productivity-driven efficiency gains at the cost of human labor input. As I have stated before, the academic answers are scant. Overall, in terms of where inflation goes from here, it is either hyper-reflation or debt-deflation—or the latter first, and the former second. Either way, both paths lead to a lower standard of living in one sense or the other.

As for precious metals, the end game is bullish, though a debt-deflation scenario that forced the Fed into a monetary Armageddon situation might entail a significant downside break and macrotrend correction in gold and silver before the Fed button-pushing drives gold to the next level.

Which inflation statistics should you monitor? There are many, and there are multiple ways to look at each one. I want to know what import and export prices look like, broken down by trading partner, as a means to identify the point of attack in price pressure. I want to determine whether price changes are commodity linked as might be indicated by rising prices of imports from Canada or within manufactured finished goods, as might be indicated by a rising Import Price Index linked to Germany or Italy.

I want to know what import prices are linked to the actions of the Organization of the Petroleum Exporting Countries (OPEC), and how they relate to the concurrent prices in the petro-patch. Rising energy prices might reflect higher Canadian (U.S.) import prices, driven by the large U.S.-CAD trade in natural gas, without being noted in OPEC-linked prices. The difference means something.

I want to know if export price increases are offsetting import price increases. I want to know what export prices are rising. Any stock market speculator should want to know this information because it could be a clue to where the industry growth dynamic is mutating most favorably.

Often with U.S. export prices, agricultural products play a key role. This data provides niche evidence to support or refute thoughts of an agricultural-led change in the overall price picture. Here, too, international trade data can be most informative, as you can dissect and determine whether China is importing more corn, and if so, you can discern what impact that might be having on U.S. export prices. From that, you can begin to gauge the potential impact on the CPI as a result of agricultural dynamics.

Global agricultural demand and trade both matter to the bullion market. Grain prices matter. Soybean and sugar prices matter to bullion traders. This might be particularly true with silver, as for some strange celestial reason, the S-commodities (soybeans, sugar, silver) often will move in conjunction with one another—sugar, soybeans. So, too, will the C-commodities often act in unison; copper and crude oil show positive correlation, and when coffee also gets going, it can be a wild-and-wooly old-time commodity contender.

In this sense, the Producer Price Index (PPI) is invaluable, since the Bureau of Labor Statistics carves up the figures into microdata that often provide keen insight.

I want to know what commodities are rising or falling in price the fastest, and which are making the biggest long-term moves.

I want to know if higher farm prices are being realized at the point of sale and if there is a positive margin for inflation.

I want to know what dairy and fruit prices are doing, and if those changes are in sync with the U.S. Department of Agriculture (USDA) supply-and-demand data that I am dissecting simultaneously. The USDA offers supply-and-demand and U.S. production data on a multitude of agricultural items such as walnuts, grapes, hops, butter, eggs, and sunseeds and chickens, many of which are also detailed within the PPI report. I want to know whether chicken prices are rising or falling. I want to know whether butter prices are rising or falling, I want to know whether the price of grapes are rising or falling.

I want to know, of course, about energy products such as propane and whether the price changes fit my assessment of the weekly American Petroleum Institute's (API) statistics.

More important within the PPI data is the breakdown between "Crude Goods and Materials" (substitute the word Raw for Crude because Crude Oil is a different/separate component group from Crude Goods and Materials) inflation, as it relates to the "Intermediate Goods" PPI and as they both relate to the "Finished Goods" PPI.

In other words, within the PPI report there is a breakdown by stage of production. Prices are tracked from the crude, or raw stage of processing, through the intermediate stage of assembly, and then into the finished stage, and the completion of the final product that will be offered to consumers.

In turn, when the sales of those finished PPI goods reach the retail level, they in turn provide the price input used to calculate the CPI.

Within the breakdown of the PPI data, it is critical to notice the interplay between the rates of change posted by Raw Materials PPI, Intermediate Goods PPI, and Finished Goods PPI.

In this sense you can also capture a feeling for producer margins, and pricing power.

Against the tide of rising raw materials prices, in light of the continued global trade competitive cost considerations, and the lack of wage income inflation supporting consumers, many producers have "eaten" the rise in inflation at the raw materials level. This has become a primary means to compete, maintain market share, and in fact, to survive.

This dynamic has been evident within the PPI data, as the pace of increase in Finished Goods PPI has been far less over the past two years than the rampant rise in Raw Materials PPI.

In a more recent troubling development, some degree of pricing power is becoming evident in the data flow. For example, in the most recent PPI report from the U.S. Labor Department covering June 2006, Crude Goods (Raw Materials) PPI rose +8.6 percent year-over-year, falling below the rate of inflation in Intermediate Goods PPI, posted at +9.3 percent.

This type of flip-flop has not been seen in some time, as rapidly rising Crude Goods PPI, in double-digit year-over-year rates of inflation, had led the entire PPI series to the upside. The subsequent reversal-crossover might be a prelude to a reversal in inflationary pressures emanating from the raw materials and commodities sectors.

Thus, this would be considered important information to bullion traders and investors, right?

Most of the time the headline numbers only tell a miniscule part of a much bigger story, and this is why you need to keep digging deeper and deeper, to find the truth.

As for the CPI, it is what it is, and the data is valuable.

I want to know how the CPI Urban Price Index is moving relative to the CPI Rural Index, or how different city CPI prices are moving, relative to the nationwide figures and relative to one another.

The Bureau of Labor Statistics also produces city indexes for most major U.S. metropolitan areas that often contain valuable nuggets of information.

I want to know how inflation in Manhattan looks relative to inflation in Minneapolis or Cleveland.

It might matter.

It might mean something, in the microsense, that should be monitored when looking for changes in leadership trends.

Of particular interest within the CPI data is the input on service sector inflation, an increasingly important source of price pressure, and one that has been steadily increasing in importance in line with the secular transition in the United States toward a more service-based output/consumption dynamic.

The BLS provides detailed breakdowns on service prices, and I want to know where the pressure, up or down, inflation-wise, is coming from. Is it education costs, health care services, or transportation services?

Putting two and two together through the city breakdown and the breakdown by services, I want to know whether public transportation service inflation is more or less significant than gasoline price inflation.

I want to know if the lower income laborer-consumer living in high-cost urban areas is paying more to take the bus to work everyday and how that relates to the midlevel income worker-consumer who drives to work.

I want to know if there are any particular cities where prices are rising and employment is falling (the BLS also provides data on unemployment for all major urban regions).

I also want to know whether the sectors/industries/goods that are exhibiting PPI price pressure, are feeding through to the same degree, in their CPI-related components.

Here, too, you can monitor pricing power in the interplay between PPI and CPI.

As usual, everything matters when dissecting the inflation data, Fed-wise, interest-rate-wise, U.S. dollar-wise, and ultimately when looking at the macro-influence on precious metals.

In the mid-to-later 1990s, gold had plunged to new post-1980 bear market lows, amid declining trading volume, shuttered bullion dealing desks, vanquished Wall Street research coverage, and liquidation/disinvestment by both private investors and official institutions. Some pundits suggested that gold, with no yield on the offer, could no longer predict inflation, and thus its appeal as an inflation hedge had vanished.

I have always said bullocks to this line of thinking. Quite the opposite is true.

In fact, gold's price decline to new lows below $300 perfectly reflected the productivity driven, secular wave of labor market disinflation that literally defined the decade.

A well-defined downtrend in the year-over-year rate of CPI and PPI inflation, along with lower lows in the Commodity Research Bureau (CRB) Index and bond yields, against a backdrop of a technology-driven reflation in equity market wealth, provided a bearish macrosetting for precious metals.

Gold reflected the lack of inflationary, or deflationary, pressure, by trading below $300, keeping its track record intact dating all the way back to the 1960s and beyond.

More recently, as the macro landscape has evolved into a rate to reflate, monetarily, gold has responded in kind, by appreciating against the USD, and by appreciating against almost all paper currencies and equity markets in the world.

Boot camp is called to attention, to look at inflation using the Consumer Price Index. The chart in Figure 29.1 is a view of the Index; note the upside breakout to new highs.

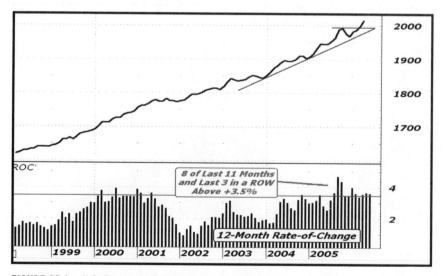

FIGURE 29.1   U.S. Consumer Price Index: monthly close
Source: WeldonFinancial@comcast.net.

More telling is the 12-month rate of change, which has probed the +4 percent level, and been above +3.5 percent in 8 of the last 18 months. See Figure 29.1.

Aside from noting that the chart appears supportive to bullion, focus on the 2000/2001 episode in which the year-over-year rate poked above +3.5 percent on several occasions. In fact, this degree of inflation in CPI was strong enough to drive the U.S. consumer into a cocoon, consumption-wise, at the first whiff of debt-liquidation-deflation risk on the rise.

In this sense, the rise in CPI exerted a deflationary influence over the U.S. consumer.

This could be highly problematic going forward if inflation spikes to levels that might otherwise be associated with the rabid, foaming-at-the-mouth appetite for credit and debt that the U.S. consumer has exhibited over the past 5-to-15 years.

As Figure 29.2 reveals in the plot of the 10-year rate of change of CPI (divide by 10 for average annual CPI), the pace of U.S. inflation (defined by CPI) has really only just begun to turn to the upside on a long-term secular basis.

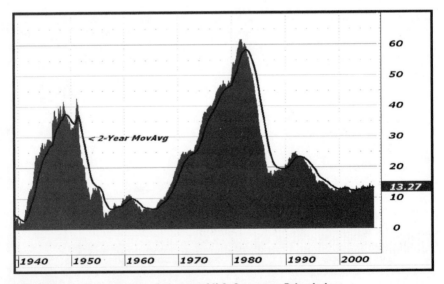

FIGURE 29.2   Ten-year rate of change of U.S. Consumer Price Index
Source: WeldonFinancial@comcast.com.

For sure, relative to the inflation of the 1970s (posted on the back of very similar price-monetary dynamics evidenced currently), inflation remains low, with a lot of upside room.

Again, this type of long-term secular evidence mandates a macro-bullish stance on bullion, all other things remaining equal (which they never are).

Boot camp attendees will be monitoring the CPI in their own way, as it will reveal the true secular trend, and that trend has just reversed to the upside, following a decade-long disinflation trend.

Also worthy of close attention going forward is the U.S. capacity utilization (Cap-U) rate, another useful gauge of inflation/disinflation pressures, as it relates to the CPI-PPI statistics.

After plummeting to multiyear depths in late 2001 on the back of the intensified deflation risk scenario playing out in paper wealth assets after the stock market peak, capacity utilization has steadily climbed back above its long-term average rate. In so doing, Cap-U data became a bullish underlying supportive feature for the bullion market, and presented the Fed with inflation-risk considerations (see Figure 29.3).

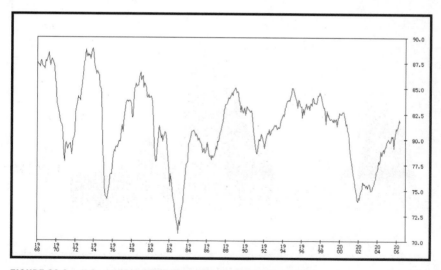

FIGURE 29.3   U.S. capacity utilization, all industries, since 1968
Source: Chart courtesy of Economagic, LLC. All rights reserved.

While an economic slowdown would quickly take the steam out of the rise in Cap-U, given the link to the domestic industrial output dynamic, any further tightening in utilization going forward would become problematic for the Fed as an indication of inflation.

Thus, it would also be potentially bullish for bullion, and perhaps the industrial metals sector as well.

The important question is whether inflation will follow suit. Figure 29.4 offers evidence provided by the long-term monthly charts of the U.S. Consumer Price Index, All Items, Urban Prices, plotted on a year-over-year basis.

From the perspective of Figure 29.4, the CPI was on the verge of a technical breakdown to new low year-over-year rates of inflation pushing zero when the most recent mini—"Monetary Armageddon" campaign was conducted by the Fed, and rates were cut to record lows.

The CPI has since recovered and is now making its first higher high, on a year-over-year calculation, since the late 1980s.

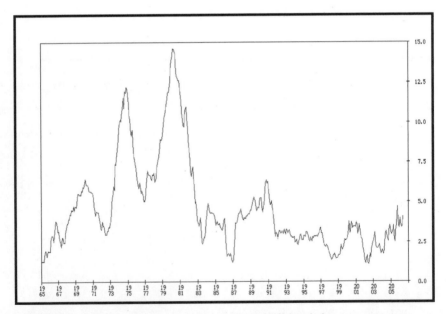

FIGURE 29.4 U.S. Consumer Price Index, all items, All-Urban Index, year-over-year percentage change since 1965

Source: Chart courtesy of Economagic, LLC. All rights reserved.

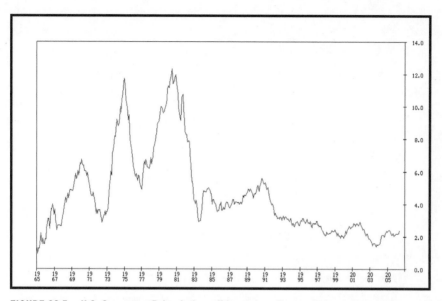

FIGURE 29.5   U.S. Consumer Price Index, all items less Energy Index, year-on-year percentage change since 1965
Source: Chart courtesy of Economagic, LLC. All rights reserved.

Hence, as seen in Figure 29.5, the more docile core CPI (excluding food and energy prices) is attempting its first upside breakout (year-on-year basis) in many moons.

However, subsequent to the missing rung, in terms of the Ladder of Inflation theory, you might take the boot camp approach to observe some nuggets extracted from the labor market data that suggest inflationary pressures are already ebbing.

The latest U.S. nonfarm payroll data reveals that retail sector jobs are declining again and that the peak in the last growth cycle was far below previous recovery growth rates exceeding 5 percent on a year-over-year basis. Evidence is in Figure 29.6, which plots the year-on-year change in retail employment.

Boot campers know a softening centered in the retail sector is a potential macrowarning sign on many fronts, from consumption, to housing, to debt, to savings, and to inflation expectations.

Thus, U.S. retail sector employment data matters to the bullion market.

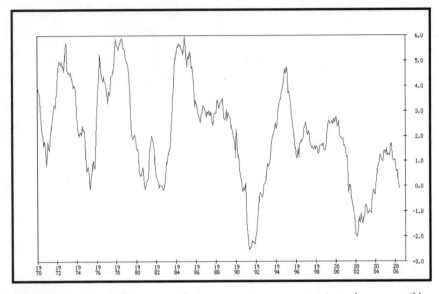

FIGURE 29.6   U.S. retail sector employment, year-on-year percentage change: monthly since 1970

Source: Chart courtesy of Economagic, LLC. All rights reserved.

Digging deeper you inspect the sentiment surveys offered by regional Federal Reserve Banks. Of specific use is the Philadelphia Fed Business Activity Survey.

Figure 29.7 plots the two-year moving average of the Philly Fed Survey's Employment Index. The long-term average has recently completed a downside reversal from levels that in the past have marked macro peaks.

This might be signaling a shift in the labor market that might be strong enough to backfire through the system and pressure final demand level prices to the downside, as income recedes at an accelerating pace (see Figure 29.8).

With that in mind, note a similar downside reversal developing in the long-term two-year moving average of the Philly Fed Survey's Prices Received Index, seen in Figure 29.8.

And finally, while I want to know all the inflation and labor market statistics from the macromonetary perspective, and as applies to the secular path going forward, any data related to housing and construction should take center stage.

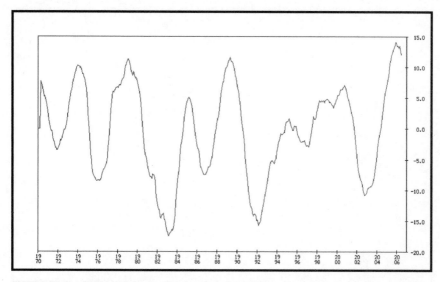

FIGURE 29.7   Philly Fed Survey Employment Index, two-year moving average: monthly since 1970

Source: Chart courtesy of Economagic, LLC. All rights reserved.

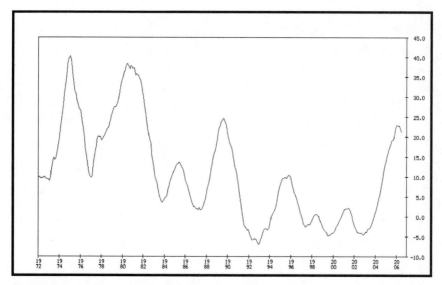

FIGURE 29.8   Philly Fed Prices Received Index, two-year moving average: monthly since 1972

Source: Chart courtesy of Economagic, LLC. All rights reserved.

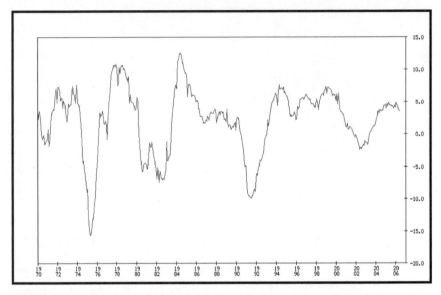

FIGURE 29.9   U.S. construction employment, year-over-year percentage change: monthly since 1970

Source: Chart courtesy of Economagic, LLC. All rights reserved.

In this case, from the labor and inflation perspective, observe the latest read for the year-over-year change in U.S. construction employment. In short, the growth rate of employment in construction has broken down (see Figure 29.9).

This reminds us of the all-telling importance of the U.S. housing sector and offers segue into Chapter 30.

U.S. Housing and the Consumer

I have already established the link between unprecedented credit and debt expansion, and the rampant paper wealth-reflation in the U.S. housing sector.

I have also discussed the macroinfluence of more than one trillion dollars in mortgage-equity withdrawal, and described how the U.S. consumer has lived high on the hog for many moons on borrowed money, and now, without permanent reflation in housing, on borrowed time, too.

A popular analogy is worthy of mention. Pundits accurately look at the pumped up and consumption-crazed U.S. consumer as being under the influence of *monetary steroids*, fed intravenously through a record low cost of money and excess available credit.

The U.S. consumer is running on *roids*. You could make a case to suggest that the U.S. consumer is addicted to this monetary steroid. Without it, reflated paper housing wealth shrivels, just as a muscle without juice will atrophy as it endures withdrawal. A consumer withdrawal would mean ridding the body of the monetary steroids, and bringing the muscle mass (debt) down to a manageable level with a sound fiscal and monetary regimen.

I doubt that achieving a soft landing is even possible, in the sense of expecting a debt-liquidation "detox" that can go smoothly for the patient (the U.S. consumer). Monetary steroid withdrawal and debt-detox are scary phrases. They portend a consumer who is forced into a consumption cocoon, where retrenchment is the catch phrase, and the word *savings* comes back into vogue.

The U.S. housing market holds the key for the consumer, the Fed, and, through decades of incestuous codependency, for the global economy as well.

No doubt then that U.S. housing dynamics are highly influential in terms of the bullion market, too.

This would suggest that it is just the United States that matters, which of course we know not to be true. In fact, housing reflation in Europe and Asia, particularly as might apply to China and India, are major considerations.

At the very least, there has been an increasingly tight positive correlation between global mortgage debt growth, property reflation rates, and the bull market in bullion priced in a variety of currencies aside from the U.S. Dollar. Nonetheless, the relationships all intersect at the U.S. housing market.

 Of all the housing-related statistics available, and there are a plethora of them, the most impressive from a macro-telltale standpoint is the series that details homes for sale, contained in the figures released by the Federal Housing Oversight Board.

You are most interested in the charts revealing the path of "homes for sale, not yet started," meaning just what it says—the number of homes for sale where construction has not yet even begun.

Observe Figure 30.1; it speaks for itself.

It shows an unprecedented increase in unsold supply at the very beginning of the supply pipeline and the speculative point of attack.

No wonder then, that other data you should monitor as reported by the National Association of Home Builders reveal plunging sentiment among builders, amid contracting interest from new buyers.

Worse yet, as noted in Figure 30.2, which plots the actual change in number of homes for sale not yet started versus the year-ago period, the buildup in the past 12 months is a record, easily surpassing all previous new unbuilt-unsold supply peaks.

The excess supply of homes not yet started already creates a problem in terms of ultimately being sold because the middle of the supply pipeline is full. Figure 30.3 on page 224 plots the total number of homes for sale under construction, dating back to 1975 on a month-to-month basis.

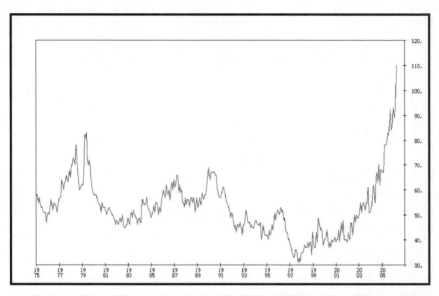

FIGURE 30.1   Homes for sale, not yet started (construction): monthly total since 1975

Source: Chart courtesy of Economagic, LLC. All rights reserved.

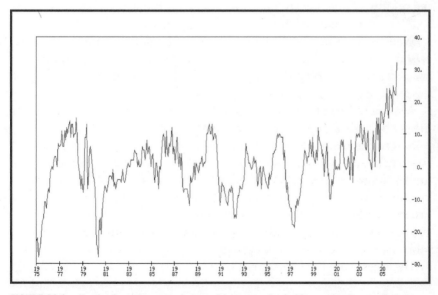

FIGURE 30.2   Homes for sale, not yet started (construction): 12-month net actual change

Source: Chart courtesy of Economagic, LLC. All rights reserved.

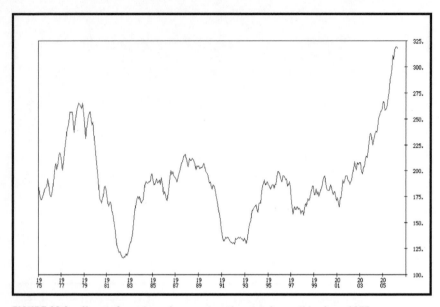

FIGURE 30.3   Homes for sale under construction, total: monthly since 1975
Source: Chart courtesy of Economagic, LLC. All rights reserved.

Again, there is a record amount of unsold supply, this time smack in the middle of the supply pipeline. Focus on the accelerated rise from 2001, thanks to the Fed and cheap credit for builders.

Even worse, there is a record number of homes for sale, completed, as shown in Figure 30.4. In other words, both ends of the supply line are packed with a record amount of unsold supply, as is the middle of the pipe.

What is the absolute worst thing that could happen right now, given the supply side setup that you have just defined?

Exactly—a decline in sales!

A decline in the sales of homes, erosion in the final demand side of this tenuous, teetering, balancing act, would be devastating. A decline in sales would lengthen the time for homes to sale, leaving the front end of the supply pipeline choking on its own exhaust fumes.

This very situation is now unfolding, as revealed in the new homes sales data and the six-month average of annualized sales, visible in Figure 30.5.

You need to keep an eye on the sales statistic, in the belief that its value to the market will increase in the midterm, as investors become more aware of the slowdown.

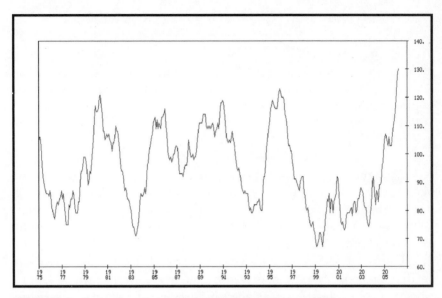

FIGURE 30.4   Homes for sale, completed, total: monthly since 1975
Source: Chart courtesy of Economagic, LLC. All rights reserved.

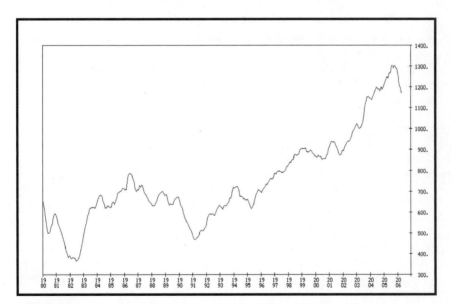

FIGURE 30.5   New single-family homes sold, six-month moving average of seasonally adjusted annual rate (SAAR)
Source: Chart courtesy of Economagic, LLC. All rights reserved.

Increasing unsold supply + Decreasing sales = Lower prices.

It's Economics 101. You can observe the end result of the excess supply and the slowdown in final sales demand—a near-term plunge in home prices. Figure 30.6 shows the median sales price of homes actually sold, plotted quarter-to-quarter, at an annualized rate. Witness an unprecedented degree of midterm price deflation in U.S. housing.

Witness also a dramatic increase in the volatility projected by this measure of home prices, a factor that mortgage holders who have extracted 100 percent (or more) of their home's equity might not have contemplated.

This might become a particularly acute problem, if they are trying to sell a home, or worse, if they need to sell a home, amid a dagger-wielding rise in debt obligation ratios.

As you dig deeper, you will find evidence to support your thought process in Figure 30.7, which shows the size of the average U.S. conventional mortgage. It seems somewhat problematic to see sales prices in decline, against a rise to a new record high in the average single-family mortgage debt obligation, now above $300,000.

Home prices are disinflating (at least), and real wage-derived income is disinflating (at least), while debt, both nominally and as measured by various consumer debt-to-obligations ratio readings, climbs

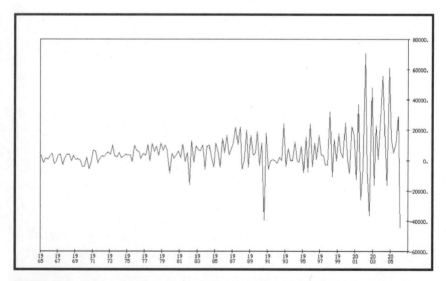

FIGURE 30.6   U.S. median home price, homes actually sold: quarterly change at annual rate

Source: Chart courtesy of Economagic, LLC. All rights reserved.

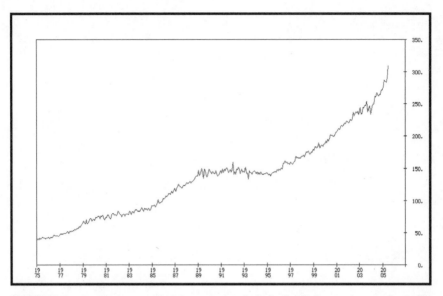

FIGURE 30.7 **Average conventional mortgage, all single-family homes (new and existing sales): monthly since 1975**

Source: Chart courtesy of Economagic, LLC. All rights reserved.

to new heights. This would seem to mean that the U.S. consumer will just draw on savings. However, this is not what happens, as you can see from Figure 30.8 plotting the U.S. personal savings rate (from the personal consumption and expenditures report) via the quarter-to-quarter annualized growth rate. U.S. savings have already disinflated, into thin air.

It becomes nearly impossible to believe that U.S. consumption growth can be sustained against the macrobackdrop offered by the U.S. housing market. More so when you observe the tremendous degree of growth that could be stripped away from the global economy, should the U.S. consumer retrench, as defined in Figure 30.9, plotting the personal consumption expenditures data, basis the year-over-year dollar change.

Again, you ask, can the U.S. consumer maintain growth of $300-$400 billion over the course of the next 12 months, and the 12 months after that, too?

The boot camp inspection continues in the same vein, reflated paper wealth in housing, with a sidebar peek at the U.S. stock market, from that same perspective.

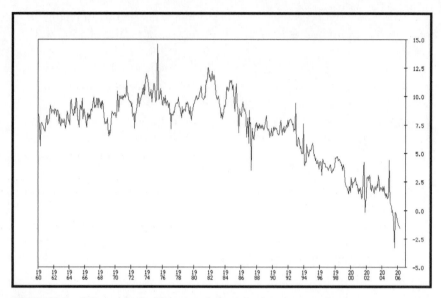

FIGURE 30.8   U.S. personal savings rate, quarterly change, annualized

Source: Chart courtesy of Economagic, LLC. All rights reserved.

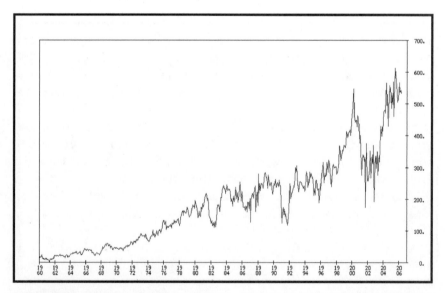

FIGURE 30.9   U.S. personal consumption expenditures, change from year ago in billions of U.S. dollars: monthly since 1960

Source: Chart courtesy of Economagic, LLC. All rights reserved.

When you consider the wealth reflation angle, the rate of change is a key determinant and offers a proxy for a rate of return. Examine this dynamic as applied to the U.S. Dow Jones Industrial Average, dating back to 1970, shown in Figure 30.10. This view offers the 12-month rate of change (year-over-year) in the Dow, plotted weekly, exposing the most recent reflation as having vanished.

Naturally, there is a debt-obligations angle here, too, as evidenced in Figure 30.11, which reveals the total margin debt at New York Stock Exchange (NYSE) member firms. Simply, a nonexistent reflation in paper wealth has been financed on credit.

The leverage machete is in play in U.S. stocks and extends into wealth reflation at risk.

Note that the bank lending data released weekly by the Fed (spotlighted earlier) recently reflected one of the largest single-month increases in borrowing against securities ever.

A downturn in the U.S. equity market would intensify an already ominous macroevolution as pertains to the sustainability of paper wealth reflation, and the life span of the U.S. consumer.

Now, it's worthwhile to look at three equity-linked charts, to exemplify a visual perspective on our macrothematic thought process.

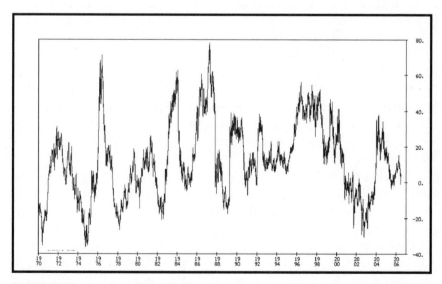

FIGURE 30.10 Dow Jones Industrial Average, year-on-year percentage change: weekly since 1970

Source: Chart courtesy of Economagic, LLC. All rights reserved.

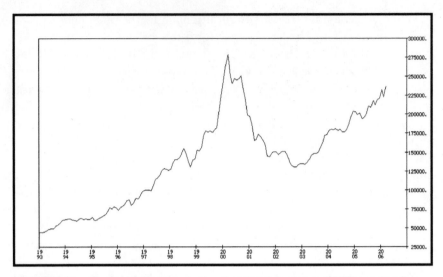

FIGURE 30.11   Margin debt balance in New York Stock Exchange (NYSE) member firm accounts, total in millions of U.S. dollars
Source: NYSE and Economagic.com. Chart courtesy of Economagic, LLC. All rights reserved.

In Figure 30.12, first observe the upside leadership exhibited by leading U.S. home builder KB Homes, as it significantly outperformed the S&P 500 Index from 2001 through the peak last year.

But now, the housing market's disinflation is acutely reflected in the breakdown and trend reversal in this type of ratio spread (we are not singling out KBH).

Putting the technical focus on the ratio spread chart seen in Figure 30.12, the downside directional reversal in the long-term two-year moving average (already violated earlier in 2006) is a significant development.

Significant is the message delivered by Figure 30.13, plotting the secular five-year moving average of the ratio spread created by comparing Wal-Mart's stock price with the broader S&P 500 index. The downturn is ominous.

Next, note the transition away from the support of an appreciation in the U.S. consumer, as defined by the Morgan Stanley Consumer Stock Index and the displayed 52-week moving average. In Figure 30.14 on page 232 we make several comparisons, overlaying the Morgan Consumer Index, and the Dow Jones Energy Index.

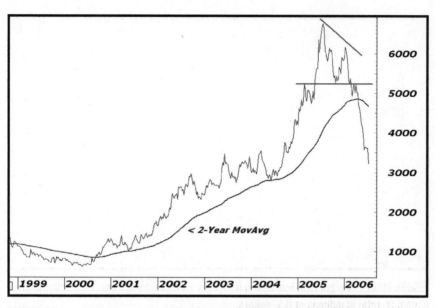

FIGURE 30.12   KB Homes versus S&P 500 Index ratio spread: weekly close

Source: Weldononline.com.

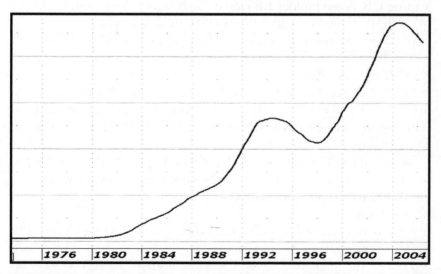

FIGURE 30.13   Five-year moving average of Wal-Mart versus S&P 500 Index ratio spread

Source: WeldonFinancial@comcast.com.

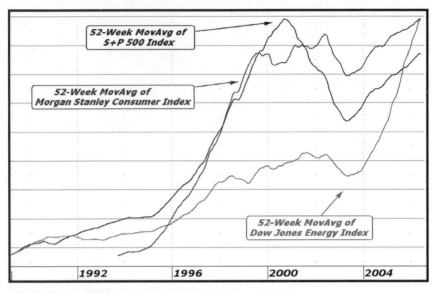

FIGURE 30.14 Overlay Rate-of-Return Comparison Chart
Source: WeldonFinancial@comcast.com.

Focus instead on the intensified contribution to the buoyancy of the overall stock market emanating from the energy sector, defined by the Dow Jones Energy Index and its 52-week moving average.

Point: U.S. consumers have not benefited as much from energy stock index reflation as they might have from a broader stock market reflation, which has been lacking.

Overall, the U.S. housing dynamic, intertwined with a similar look at paper wealth reflation in U.S. equities, suggests at the very least that the U.S. consumer should be on the alert for an increase in macroturbulence.

Again, depending on the reaction of the Fed, you would expect, that ultimately, the printing presses will be running full out again in intermediate term. Therefore, you wonder how long, and what path it takes, before the chart of gold looks more like Figure 30.15, surging to its own new all-time highs, and exceeding the 1980/1981 peak.

If the price of an acre of Texas ranch land can soar to new bull market, wealth reflation setting highs exceeding its inflation-induced peak of 1980/1981, you should expect that gold will, too.

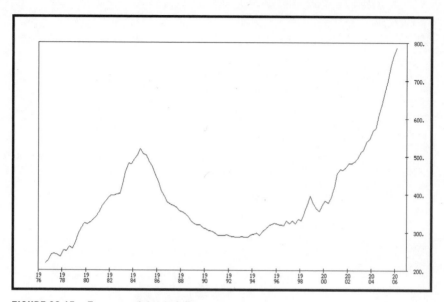

FIGURE 30.15   Texas ranch land, dollars per acre
Source: Chart courtesy of Economagic, LLC. All rights reserved.

Again, rewind to Figure 13.23 reflecting the plot of gold adjusted for the U.S. 30-year Treasury bond yield, and a price correlating with $1,200 per ounce.

As you can see from this chapter, boot campers (and serious traders) must do a lot of work to keep up with the constant deluge of data. I strongly suggest you find your own comfort zone and establish a routine that you can easily repeat so you can focus on the most pertinent information.

Indeed, the Fed itself is transparent in its shift toward greater data dependency.

Unfortunately for the Fed, for U.S. consumers, and for the global economy, dependency has already spread like a virus with no cure.

There is only a relative wealth-protecting antidote, in the form of gold.

PART SIX

Trend Identification and Momentum Trading

Why . . . Trend
Identification?

Ed Seykota, is a legendary Wall Street pioneer in systems development during the 1970s, and was a trading coach at Commodities
Corporation during my tenure there in the 1990s. According to Ed:

> Many good systems are based on following trends. Life itself is based on
> trends. Birds head south for the winter and keep on going. Companies
> track trends and alter their products accordingly. Tiny protozoa move in
> trends along chemical and luminescence gradients.

After trading and watching great traders for more than 20 years,
there is no doubt in my mind that the majority of profits have come
when markets are trending. In fact, this truism is even more evident
when a market is trending within numerous time frames. The most advantageous risk-reward dynamics exist when a market is trending on
an intraday, daily, weekly, and monthly basis.

The reality is that markets spend their least percentage of the time
trending. This is even more true today, thanks to technological ad-
vances and the global instantaneous access to news and data. The
availability of instant data and information causes shorter-term, more
violent price adjustments, meaning that markets spend less time
trending on a longer-term basis.

Nonetheless, trends remain an inherent part of market movement. "Selective aggression" becomes a catch phrase, and the catalyst for the development of a trend-momentum based investment-trading methodology.

I have been playing poker for years. I started playing in college to earn extra spending money, and more recently I have immersed myself into a serious study of the No-Limit Texas Hold 'Em Tournament play. Similar to my self-educated approach to trading and capital markets 20 years ago, I have purchased and read just about every poker book ever written.

I am fortunate (or not, depending on your perspective—I do not gamble at all, period, outside of poker tournaments) to live near Atlantic City. In 2005, I won several weekend tournaments in New Jersey, and then succeeded by "cashing" (finishing in the top ten percent of the field, and making "the money") in two World Series of Poker tournaments during the 2006 Series. What I have learned, through study and experience, is the importance of playing premium hands and being selectively aggressive.

It sounds like a cliché, but it is so true: you have to know when to hold 'em, and you gotta know when to fold 'em.

Naturally, the similarities between poker and trading should become clear at this point. In trading, it is equally if not more important to know when to hold 'em and when to fold 'em.

If you see a market that is exhibiting trending characteristics on an intraday, daily, weekly, and monthly basis, all moving in sync, with acceleration in the short-term indicators, it is akin to being dealt pocket aces or kings.

In tournament poker, folding 10, 15, or even sometimes 20 or more, hands in a row can be an integral part of a successful strategy. And while this is only half the story, there is no doubt that in poker patience is key. It is the same in trading. Wait, wait, wait, then pounce, aggressively, when you hold pocket aces or kings. Pounce when momentum is aligned in the same vein, across all time frames, to indicate a trending market.

Selectivity becomes a key factor in determining long-term success because markets rarely are truly aligned in a trending dynamic. Markets often trend for prolonged periods, and then don't trend at all for prolonged periods, sometimes agonizingly long periods, with nary a trend to trade. This is where diversity can be a key means to avoid being destroyed by directionless markets.

If I am only trading gold, then periods of directionless markets become problematic from the perspective of trying to make money with a trend-following methodology. This was the primary reason I chose to leave the trading floor back in the mid-1980s, as gold and silver prices plummeted amid the increased popularity of financial futures contracts. I did not want to be captive to one market to make a living, knowing that markets, investors, and traders perpetually evolve.

The more markets I am monitoring, the greater the odds that I can pick up pocket aces. This approach can be broken down further, even in the context of trading a single sector such as bullion. The more bullion vehicles a precious metals specific trader can monitor, then the better the odds that something will be trending.

In the precious metals complex, I hone it down as follows:

- Gold.
- Silver.
- Gold and silver mining share indexes.
- Unhedged gold mining share indexes.
- Individual gold mining shares.
- Individual silver mining shares.
- Gold and silver exchange traded funds.
- Gold and silver mutual funds.
- Gold and silver priced in foreign currencies, with a specific eye kept on the Chinese, Indian, and Russian currency dynamics.
- Gold and silver priced in the currencies of producing nations, particularly the South African rand and Australian dollar.
- Gold and silver, relative to global stock indexes, particularly versus the U.S. S&P 500 Index, the Dow Jones Industrial Average, global banking sector indexes, and the Nikkei.
- Gold and silver relative to global bond yields, particularly the U.S. and Japanese bonds.
- Gold and silver relative to global deposit rates, particularly in Switzerland, Japan, China, and the EU.
- Gold and silver relative to other commodities, particularly energy, grains, and industrial base metals.

Even if gold and silver are not trending, there are decent odds that prices are trending on a relative basis, against some other asset-investment class.

This is not to say that nontrend-following methodologies cannot be used during periods of directionless price action. The ability to identify a directionless market can be as important as identifying a trending market.

First, being able to identify periods of directionless market action leads to the application of different types of trading methodologies that do not rely on direction to generate returns. Thus, having a momentum model that identifies whether a trend exists seems eminently more valuable than having one that identifies direction.

This has become my focus in developing my proprietary algorithmic trending models. While the bulk of the profits I have generated in my career have come during the "meat" of long-term macrotrends, the fastest profits have been generated at the point of reversal and the first major correction to an exhausted major macrotrend.

Moreover, trading when markets are not trending helps smooth the volatility of returns and offers an opportunity to capture positive returns when other, slower, trend-following traders might be giving back unrealized profits. Sharp reversals and blowout corrections can be fertile ground for profitable trading, with a shorter-term focus.

My trending models have been constructed to identify periods where markets are vulnerable to these violent moves. Trend exhaustion is a pattern that can be identified and taken advantage of with trend-momentum indicators. In this way, I can also expand my possible profit opportunities in each single market, particularly if I was forced to focus on just one sector of the global markets.

I seek to profit from trends, but I also seek to profit from trend reversals.

 You want to see the momentum of the trends align with the macrotrend, as identified by our top-down analysis. Or, you want to see a trend exhaustion-reversal scenario play out in your technical readings at the same time that you observe a shift at the microlevel in the macrodata input. Such a shift that might have the same implications of an exhausted trend as the momentum signals.

All trend reversals aside, there is no doubt that taking positions when my models are in sync with (and more likely, reflecting) the macrodynamic, has produced the highest win ratio.

During my career, if I had not tried to jump the gun on a pending trend that I saw developing in microdata points—a trend that had just not yet matured as a market price breakout or breakdown—my own win ratio would have been higher.

My weakness has been a lack of patience—I try to pounce too early. My mistakes in trading have sometimes been caused by my inability to be patient while waiting for the market dynamic to deal me aces or kings. Too often, I have been overaggressive, pushing all-in with less than robust hands such as a pocket-fours instead of aces. Another mistake I have frequently made is adding to positions too late in the trend, getting overly aggressive when profits have accumulated. I begin to think that the readings are less important, and start to ignore them. I discuss this in Chapter 41.

When ego gets in the way, performance suffers. There is no doubt that part of the problem in being a discretionary, macrosystematic trader is that it opens all the doors. You try to outmaneuver the market, outrace your indicators, and outthink yourself.

Nevertheless, it is the successful call—the great trend that plays out exactly as the macroinput indicated it should—that becomes rewarding from both a cerebral perspective and financially.

It is psychological war with other market participants as well as an inner war against your own emotional crevices. My trend-momentum models offer vast potential as stand-alone allocation vehicles, in an overall portfolio application, specifically with the introduction of exchange traded funds. What is problematic is that once the trends are aligned and begin to accelerate, the risk profile begins to widen by default. If gold is going to move from $450 to $525 and I can get long at $460, risking $440, then I am exposed for $20 (plus slippage; always calculate risk using overly generous fill slippage and brokerage fees). But, if I don't buy my gold until the price gets to $480, and my stop is the same (at least initially), then my risk has doubled. Thus, timing becomes critical when you are trying to be positioned for the most advantageous trending periods.

Trend Identification Techniques— Momentum, Timing, and Trading the Trend

f Gold were to be higher today than it was 200 days ago, with the 50-day rate of change hitting a new high for the past 200 days, and the 100-day rate of change hitting a new high for the last 200 days, . . . and the 50-day rate-of-change was doing the same, . . . all while the 52-week rate of change and the 104-week rate of change indicator were both accelerating and making their own new highs, . . . I'd be more than tempted to define gold as being in an uptrend.

Digging in deeper, I draw on the groundbreaking research done by legendary author Welles Wilder to determine the trendiness of a market by defining the movements in trading ranges relative to previous trading ranges. I speak of Welles Wilder's Directional Movement Index system.

A market that gaps higher on the opening and does not close that gap throughout the day will, by definition, have a daily trading range that is outside and above the previous day's trading range. A value can then be assigned to that type of move, based on the relative price changes and ranges. This thought process can be applied over a variety of planes, from the time periods that might be compared with the definitions used to determine when an outside-the-range move actually occurs.

In its most simplistic, raw form, it would work like this:

An inside day would be given a value of zero, indicating no trend-push outside the previous day's range.

On the other side of the coin, the upside gap-day scenario (previously detailed) would be given a value of 100, for being 100 percent outside the previous day's range. The same would apply if there was a downside gap and run move.

Therefore, a day where 95 percent of the range is above the previous day's range would get a point assignment of 95.

This same calculation can be applied on an intraday and weekly basis, providing multiple series of statistics that can then be analyzed using other statistical methodologies.

To come up with a derivative indicator, you can take a range index value derived from this study and apply a rate-of-change calculation to it.

I use these examples to illustrate the starting point for trend identification, which is far from the finish line. I crossed that line as a product of endless calculating, tweaking, and back testing. My work resulted in the application of proprietary filters and add-ons. As a whole, I am talking about my Playbook Power Ranking matrix, which I discuss in detail in Chapter 34.

The bottom line does not change. Ultimately, I want to see a market that exhibits a certain degree of trend identification on a number of time frames, and basis a broad range of statistical sensitivity parameters. Still, each trader or investor must find a personal comfort zone, with a trend identification method that provides the greatest degree of individual confidence.

Using a mix of rate-of-change indicators is one method.

Using a mix of moving averages is another method.

Using some kind of directional movement system is another.

Ideally, some combination of numerous methodologies can be quantified to provide a yes or no answer to seemingly simple questions:

- Is the market trending, digesting, consolidating, correcting, topping, bottoming, or range trading while going nowhere?
- Is the market trending? In this context, you can hone a trend identification methodology to match your specific time horizon and risk tolerance.

When the answer is yes, it mandates action. Again, any short-term timing mechanism can be used as long as something signals an entry and exit price, such as a moving average, rate-of-change indicator, oscillator, parabolic indicator, point-and-figure chart, or volatility bands.

The idea behind trading a trend is to hold a core position as long as possible, if the trend remains in effect. In that context, I often employ more sensitive shorter-term timing methodologies to trade a trend more aggressively by trading around a core long-term position. I will break things down by indicator and by time frame to trade a trend with a tripronged approach, using the long-term, intermediate-term, and short-term timing indicators mentioned earlier, to become most selectively aggressive when all the time frames are exhibiting the same directional impetus and trend strength.

When the shorter-term indicators begin to roll over (or turn up following a prolonged downtrend) in the face of a longer-term uptrend, I exit the short-term portion of the position with a goal of being less exposed should a short-term trend reversal mutate into an end to a longer-term trend. This way helps me be positioned most aggressively during the meat of the move, and less so during a corrective reversal.

Moreover, I do not feel as much pressure in holding a core position against the grain of a midterm countertrend retracement, since my exposure has already been reduced and it is likely that some profits have been booked in the process.

In trading around a core position, I like to use volatility analysis to determine whether buying strength and selling weakness are warranted or vice versa. In the early, formative stages of a longer-term trend-to-be, volatility tends to be lower, usually after long periods of dormant price action that precede a breakout or breakdown.

One clue to a pending trend is an increase in volatility. As stated, one way to identify whether a market is trending is to compare volatility readings over a variety of time frames. Suppose gold is generating a rising 50-day volatility reading. And suppose that this reading has just moved numerically above a 100-day volatility reading. And further, suppose that the 100-day reading has recently changed its own "direction" (from day to day) to the upside, while both readings are pushing above a 200-day volatility reading that is, itself, in an uptrend. The market is thus exhibiting volatility-based characteristics that identify an uptrend market in the making (or, a downtrend that is coming to an end).

In either case, depending on my trend identification read, an expanding volatility dynamic suggests that strength can be bought and weakness sold. In this circumstance, using breakouts presented by point-and-figure charts can be an effective timing mechanism.

So, too, can a "band" methodology, where the market is purchased when the upper band (surrounding a baseline moving average and derived through standard deviation parameters) is touched, or the market is sold when the lower band is penetrated.

A contracting volatility dynamic might also correlate to a new trend in the making, as prices begin to slowly but surely move in one direction at a steady, nonviolent, less volatile manner. A volatility dynamic such as this, in conjunction with an expanding trend-identifying indicator, suggests that buying dips (weakness) and selling rallies (strength) would be the preferred optimum timing strategy.

This circumstance suggests the use of point and figure and Fibonacci retracement techniques, and an instrument should be purchased after a band has been touched, but the market has retraced back to the baseline on which the band is built. In Figures 32.1 on page 247 and 32.2 on page 248, I offer some examples of these techniques.

First I highlight the point-and-figure techniques for both selling strength, and selling weakness, along with buying strength and buying weakness.

Note the most recent price action, and the label "Breakdown Sale." In this example, the market is breaking down, following a somewhat soft upside breakout attempt.

These points could be used as protective sell-stops against long exposure. Further, there are multiple ways to use this method for stop-loss order placement. A stop could be placed at a price that coincides with the first downside circle breakdown point, or a stop can be placed at the next breakdown point, once the first one has been established.

I use point-and-figure methods in the context of a noncore position in a trending market or as a primary method during countertrend trading.

The first method will prevent deep retracements and minimize the "profit-give-back" that would occur on a sharp move that does not provide a second circle breakdown point as a stop-loss. Using the first method, however, is likely to result in a greater degree of trading velocity and position turnover.

Using the second method ensures that a breakdown is in fact taking place before a long position is liquidated, but using that method exacerbates the risk of experiencing a deeper, one-way reversal, which would result in smaller profits or larger losses.

I prefer the first method here (see Figure 32.1).

Another way to derive specific selling points with the point-and-figure chart shown in Figure 32.1 is to use reversals, where a three-box reversal following an extended directional run elicits the signal.

A better method is to wait for a breakdown or breakout signal, and then for the first dip or rally into which to buy or sell. An example of this can be noted in the first Buy-the-Dip signal defined on Figure 32.1. This technique also allows for a tight stop-loss, as a re-reversal through the previous pivot point will always be defined by four boxes, facilitating very accurate risk assessment.

Of course, the point-and-figure techniques can be used on their own merit, as a short-term trading tool for speculators who are involved in a

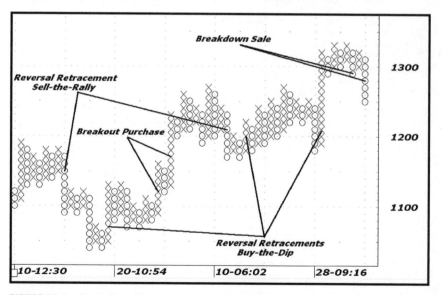

FIGURE 32.1   Spot silver 10-cent by 3 point and figure
Source: Weldononline.com.

single market, or small group of markets. A market maker might find particular value in monitoring point-and-figure charts.

By the same token, I use volatility bands on short-term intraday charts as an execution timing technique from the perspective of both position initiation and liquidation.

Depending on the overall trend definition and the volatility considerations, so-called Bollinger Bands (named after John Bollinger, the longtime technical-analysis guru) can be used to sell strength and buy weakness, or to sell weakness and buy strength.

Figure 32.2 is an execution example; examine the intraday (hourly) bar chart of spot gold, with a 50-period EXP-MA and 4 percent band.

In an accelerating trend with an expanding overall volatility backdrop, I'd likely utilize the band to buy strength. This is accomplished by buying the market when the upper band is touched, as marked in Figure 32.2.

The other method waits until after the upper or lower boundary has been touched, after which the market might trend for a period of time, before retracing back to the baseline moving average. It is this retracement to the moving average that sets up the trading signal.

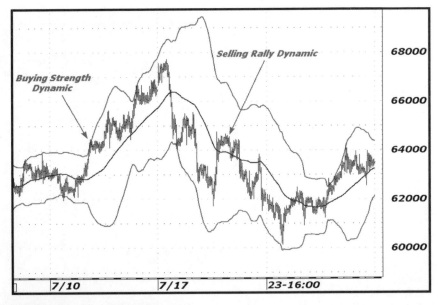

FIGURE 32.2 Spot gold: hourly
Source: Weldononline.com.

In this circumstance, I would wait for the market to retrace back through the moving average (MA); then once it penetrates the MA again back toward the direction of the trend, the signal is elected. This method also provides for tighter stops, as the opposite boundary becomes the stop level, and the MA is twice as close to each boundary as the boundaries are to one another.

One of my primary uses of these bands is to define an initial stop-loss point and to define a trailing stop-loss point once the market begins to trend and offers profits. When initiating a long position, I will use the lower band as my initial risk point. Conversely, when taking a short position, I will use the upper boundary as my stop-loss level.

Finally, this type of analysis is utilized in the creation of my upside and downside pivot points, as reflected in my TIMID matrix shown in Chapter 34.

Countertrend Trading—
Divergence, Saturation,
and Exhaustion

Trying to profit from countertrend moves is an entirely different task from riding the profit wave that a long-term directional trend can generate.

Countertrend moves tend to occur at tops and bottoms, and often occur as sharp, swift, corrective moves against the grain of a previously dominant trend.

Within any trend, there are many swings and there are numerous times that the market will ebb and flow. I am not talking about, nor am I interested in, capturing the many mini-countertrend moves that occur frequently within a longer-term trend.

I am interested in the violent trend reversal countertrend moves that most often mark significant tops and bottoms, or significant secular corrections. I am interested in being short the gold market during a setup similar to that of February 1980, when the market plummeted from above $670 to below $500 in a month.

First and foremost, taking countertrend (some might call it top or bottom picking) positions should be executed in tandem with a significantly smaller degree of risk than would be considered acceptable in a trend-following campaign. Because countertrend trading, by nature, is riskier, smaller positions should be taken. It is worth stressing that countertrend trading is just that, trading—not investing.

I would strenuously advise long-term investors avoid taking risk exposure in a countertrend scenario. Long-term investors seek to profit from a trend.

This is partly what makes the current environment in gold so exciting; as more and more investors become involved, there is a real need for investors to better diversify their macroevent risk of ruin.

As for the best setup for countertrend trading, there is no doubt that divergence in momentum becomes a key input factor in making the decision to accept risk exposure.

I want to see some kind of divergence.

And, I want to see it developing over a longer time frame, with multiple periods of divergence that get more intense on each successive occurrence.

Then I want to see some expansion in volatility in an intraday basis at first, with overhead price resistance becoming increasingly evident. Candlestick charts often offer insight in this realm, with doji and hammer patterns particularly useful in determining a move that has become exhausted.

Also, I want to know that there is lop-sided sentiment, as might be indicated by the open interest figures, or better yet, the Commitment of Traders Report from the Commodity Futures Trading Commission (CFTC).

In a countertrend campaign, it is imperative for there to be position vulnerability to provide a catalyst for a move that will be, by nature, against the grain of the dominant trend.

Certainly I love it when there is a sudden macroepiphan in conjunction with position vulnerability; I seek situations where something in the microdetails of the macrodata provides a catalyst unto itself, to drive doubt into the mind-set of the dominant sentiment.

Finally, I want to have a chart setup that can define a pertinent breakdown pivot that has the capability of touching off stop-loss orders. A breakdown pivot ultimately provides the final technical catalyst to begin a countertrend move.

I want to be in the market before that pivot is violated.

Often, this is where being a discretionary trader is most beneficial. I can bail out of a long-term, trend-following position prior to my last stop-loss order being touched. Then I can reverse on a dime to a countertrend position that seeks to benefit when others' stop orders are elected.

As for managing risk in a countertrend campaign, I use a strictly short-term mentality when entering a position, which, if not profitable by the end of the day, is liquidated.

If I see the right countertrend setup, as previously detailed, I will try (on an intraday basis) for several days in a row to catch the big impulse breakdown move.

If the downside pivot is not broken, and the trade is not successful by the end of the trading session, it is liquidated, and the whole process begins anew the next day, unless the overall conditions change.

Thus, the tightest possible stop-loss method is used in this circumstance.

Finally, the last important thing about countertrend trading is to be nimble on exiting and taking a profit.

While using the most sensitive stop-out method possible is usually not a mistake, it can be very difficult to get back into a countertrend position once an initial, highly profitable position has already been liquidated.

The "TIMID" Matrix

The initials TIMID stand for Trend Identification and Momentum Indicator Derivative. TIMID is just that, an indicator that is derived from a combination of calculations that are applied to trend index figures which are then tweaked further by using momentum indicators. From the TIMID matrix I then derive my *Power Rankings,* which are published within my research products.

The result of this proprietary process is a derivative indicator that can be defined for any and all global capital markets instruments.

Moreover, I have created the TIMID indicator so that the readings fall into certain ranges that allow for comparison between instruments, in terms of where each trend might be.

This opens up a wide range of uses for the TIMID indicators. Not only can I determine whether the market is statistically ripe for the application of trend-following methodologies, or whether a countertrend stance is desirable, but I can also compare individual instruments within the same sector, to determine which one offers the best odds of sustaining a successful trend.

Additionally, my indicators can be applied to any and all spreads in a study of mutual funds, exchange-traded funds, and individual stocks, too.

While I will not divulge the exact algorithms that I use to calculate my TIMID indicators, I am publishing my *Power Rankings* as applied to the entire universe of investment vehicles, particularly in a top-down global investment portfolio.

Since early 2006, I have been publishing my *Power Rankings* for the precious metals sector (including the spot metals markets, the mining share indexes, and individual mining companies as well) within my daily *Metal Monitor* publication (see weldononline.com).

More than trying to hawk my research product(s) and being opposed to suggesting that someone blindly follow my indicators—calculations that I am intimately familiar with, inside and out—my goal here is to provide insight into how to go about creating your own trading model.

With that in mind, this is how the TIMID matrix works.

First and foremost, I want to know if there are any trending tendencies within a market.

Thus, the first indicator to note is the TIMID Index itself, which is calculated to produce a figure that gyrates between minus (–) 400 and plus (+) 400, though it can move beyond these parameters. The index is calculated to be a whole number, and usually I attach a percentage to assist in comparisons.

The headline index is a combination of long-term (weekly) and intermediate-term (daily) input, which is multipronged on each front and is meant to determine the trend-iness of a market as a whole, both longer-term and shorter-term.

A positive reading indicates that a strong-enough trend exists for us to assume risk in the market.

Note that the TIMID indicators make no distinction between bullish and bearish price trends. My headline index is solely concerned with making a determination about the robustness of a trend. It does not attempt to define the dominant direction.

The direction of the trend should be obvious as my indicators begin to kick in. A move into positive territory by my TIMID index will most likely coincide with a breakout or breakdown of some technical magnitude that should not be difficult to discern.

It is easy to identify when my trend indicators respond positively, across the spectrum of time frames by the impulse market movement that accompanies such.

A $6 rally in gold that drives my TIMID index from –15 percent to a reading of +36 percent would indicate that a bullish trend is emerging.

Similarly but conversely, a spike lower in price that elicits the same reaction in the TIMID index would indicate a bearish price trend is taking hold.

Yes, there often is some whipsaw to this index, whereby a market will drive the indicators into a positive mode, mandating action, only to retrace back into negative territory on a failure of the market to extend the near-term trend.

Sound risk management is necessary to deal with this factor (see Part Seven).

Moreover, I want confirmation that both the long-term and intermediate-term indicators are in sync with the overall trend positive assessment provided by the headline TIMID reading. For this I break down the TIMID into two of its component indexes: the short-term ratio and the long-term ratio. For a trading and investing signal to be elected in line with a positive headline index circumstance, both of these ratios must also exhibit a positive trend reading.

Often one of the ratios will be positive and one will be negative, which indicates a lack of synchronized trend momentum and thus no trend-following trade.

This situation might mean that the trend has stalled longer term if the long-term (LT) ratio is positive but the short-term (ST) ratio has turned negative.

Also, a positive ST ratio can indicate a market that is trending in the near term, but not yet trending on a longer-term basis.

Or, such a setup could indicate a market that is beginning a countertrend move.

Once I have established that positive trend momentum exists on both a long-term and short-term basis, I can then further utilize the TIMID readings to determine how much risk I am willing to "take."

Often at the beginning of a would-be long-term sustainable trend, there are false starts. Thus, I want to be most exposed after the trend has been solidified, while being least exposed when the trend is overextended. This is something I can also determine by means of the level of the TIMID index for any given instrument.

Subsequently, I breakdown the TIMID readings into four easily defined classifications:

1. Below 0: No Trend.
2. From 0 to +100: Emerging Trend.
3. From +100 to +300: Dominant Trend.
4. Above +300: Extended Trend.

From these indictors, I simply divide by a factor of 10, to achieve my *Power Rankings*, which are then published within my research.

In this context, there are subtle hints to be gleaned from the interplay between the ST ratio and the LT ratio, which gyrate in a normal range of +1.00 to (−) 1.00, though they too can move outside these parameters during exceptionally volatile markets.

Preferably, both the ST and LT ratios are in the midrange between 0 and +1.00, and are rising together in line with a strengthening headline TIMID.

When there is a high LT ratio, it indicates that the long-term trend is mature, and when the ST ratio is low, it indicates that a new intermediate-term move within that established longer-term trend might be unfolding.

When both ratios are low, it usually means a new long-term trend might be unfolding. In this case, I would be willing to assume a greater degree of risk against a lower positive headline TIMID reading, on the belief that a major move might result, and I want to be in at favorable levels even if it means I get chopped up a little in the initial stage of the trend.

This is not the case when the LT ratio is high, and the ST ratio is just kicking into positive territory, so that the TIMID reading moves into trend mode. I am more risk adverse in this situation.

On the other hand, when there is a high ST ratio reading and a low LT ratio reading, this usually indicates an emerging trend that has accelerated rapidly and violently. In this case, I might be more predisposed to buy weakness or sell strength, thinking that a shorter-term move will be corrected so that the longer-term indicators can align properly.

The risk to this approach is that the velocity of the rise in the ST ratio is indicating a powerful move that might lessen the odds of a decent retracement, and entry opportunity.

Entry can be executed in any number of ways, either via the point-and-figure method, the Bollinger Band method, or my personal favorite: at the market when the signal is flashed and a trend has been indicated.

Previously, I covered the stop-loss procedures that I use. Most often at the initial stages of a campaign, I use the Band methodology, which offers plenty of room for noise-driven movement that might occur following the implementation of a position.

I have discovered that most often when I am stopped out of a new position by an order placed against it by the use of a band, that the TIMID reading also retraced back below zero in the process.

I have found that the standard deviation overlay within the band-stop-methodology is very complementary to the way in which the TIMID indicators are compiled.

Most of all, within the context of trading and investing in the precious metals, the TIMID index provides insight into the relative value of each precious metals investment vehicle.

Simply, a mining stock with a TIMID reading of +215 percent becomes a more desirable holding than one with a TIMID reading that is ranging between +35 percent and +90 percent when seeking capital appreciation.

Similarly, if the gold mining share index reveals a TIMID reading of +350 percent, I would be tempted to shift any exposure I had in that index, into something else less extended, with a reading of about +150 percent, to reduce risk.

Finally, here are some specific instances of how the TIMID readings look and what they imply market-wise.

First, Table 34.1 shows the latest TIMID matrix as presented in our daily (precious-metals-specific) research publication, the *Metal Monitor* (see weldononline.com for details), as of the end of trading on September 6, 2006.

Initially, peruse down the first column following the name of the precious metals vehicle, revealing the headline TIMID index reading, numbers from +274 all the way to −244.

The next two columns are marked ST and LT, for short-term and long-term trend ratio, reflective of the individual inputs that comprise the headline TIMID Index.

The last two columns (marked "Up" and "Down") provide my preferred reading as defined by Bollinger Band analysis and refer to the upside pivot point and the downside pivot point for each market.

As of the most recent readings (September 1, 2006), the highest rankings go to Kinross Gold (KGC) and to Silver Standard Resources (SSRI). These two mining shares not only boast headline readings above +250 percent, but also reflect equally strong med-term and long-term trend characteristics via the high LT and ST ratio readings (see Table 34.1).

In contrast, note the headline reading offered by AngloGold Ashanti (AU), at a −244 percent indicating that there is simply no trend to be found in this stock's price action. This is further confirmed by the fact that both the LT and ST ratio readings are negative.

Table 34.1 TIMID Matrix, June 2006

Market	TIMID (%)	ST	LT	Up	Down
Gold	−85	(0.425)	(0.229)	6660	6126
Silver	46	0.141	0.194	13806	11391
AMEX Gold Bug: HUI	20	0.323	(0.223)	38542	31684
Gold Trust ETF: GLD	−154	(0.419)	—	4902	5960
PanAm Silver: PAAS	74	0.194	0.217	2514	1981
Silver Standard Res: SSRI	254	0.936	0.747	2866	2082
Coeur dAlene: CDE	−47	(0.007)	(0.186)	620	467
Apex Silver: SIL	−69	(0.087)	(0.279)	1867	1497
Newmont: NEM	−151	(0.045)	(0.397)	5274	4984
AngloAshanti: AU	−244	(0.354)	(0.605)	4902	4421
Barrick: ABX	183	0.564	0.379	3500	3179
Freeport McMoran: FCX	29	0.458	(0.332)	6461	5346
Gold Fields: GFI	−142	(0.150)	(0.546)	2333	1791
Lihir: LIHRY	37	0.337	(0.086)	5189	4134
Rangold: GOLD	114	0.542	0.063	2672	1939
Hecla: HL	112	0.451	0.075	695	575
DRD Gold: DROOY	261	0.626	0.243	165	121
Kinross: KGC	274	0.868	0.882	1634	1193
Harmony: HMY	−96	0.156	(0.476)	1494	1312
Glamis: GLG	205	1.138	0.223	5480	0000
Bema: BGO	−117	(0.391)	(0.274)	595	477

Source: Weldon Financial Publishing. Reprinted with permission.

Figures 34.1 through 34.3 reflect the actual price action in each of the three mining shares whose TIMID readings I have just spotlighted.

First, Silver Standard Resources has accelerated to the upside, refreshing its long-term uptrend, though, with a headline TIMID reading fast approaching +300 percent—a caution flag might be waving down the road. The parabolic, explosive latest rally warrants close attention, in terms of becoming overextended.

Evidence is in the action in Kinross Gold that is associated with the TIMID readings (detailed previously) and its +274 percent headline index, which in this case reflects a strong bullish breakout and upside price appreciation trend.

As an example of the other side of the trend/nontrend coin, refer back to the examination of the TIMID readings generated by AngloGold

FIGURE 34.1   Silver standard resources SSRI: daily
Source: Weldononline.com.

FIGURE 34.2   Kinross Gold Corp. KGC: daily
Source: Weldononline.com.

FIGURE 34.3   AngloGold Ashanti Ltd.: daily
Source: Weldononline.com.

Ashanti, pegged at a −244 percent with minus signs in front of both the ST and LT ratios.

Evidence the price action in this stock that is associated with these deeply negative TIMID readings, as exhibited in Figure 34.3.

The negative readings reflect the complete lack of any trend. Observe the flat-lined moving average dynamic, and the tightening intermediate-term trading ranges.

Take a look at a time when things were different; the recent bull market was raging, and nearly all the precious metals trading/investment vehicles that I monitor were in full-blown trending mode.

Table 34.2 shows the TIMID matrix extracted from the *Metal Monitor* that was produced at the end of March 2006. There is a stark difference between the TIMID matrix displayed in Table 34.2, dating to end-March/beginning-April 2006, and the most recent matrix (see Table 34.1) dated to September 6, 2006, as the vast majority of precious metals markets were trending higher in March 2006.

The resulting *Power Rankings* for each of the precious metals investment vehicles that I regularly monitor (derived from the August 2006 TIMID readings) are listed next. It is easy to see how this method al-

Table 34.2 TIMID Matrix, August 2006

Market	TIMID (%)	ST	LT	Up	Down
Gold	116	0.325	0.695	6335	5765
Silver	288	1.089	1.404	12417	10081
AMEX Gold Bug: HUI	112	0.318	0.474	35849	31110
Gold Trust ETF: GLD	98	0.078	—	5695	5521
PanAm Silver: PAAS	193	(0.099)	1.302	2744	2427
Silver Standard Res: SSRI	207	0.379	0.990	2183	1960
Coeur dAlene: CDE	214	0.022	1.154	692	612
Apex Silver: SIL	202	0.158	1.651	2539	2280
Newmont: NEM	−205	(0.676)	(0.479)	5447	4897
AngloAshanti: AU	11	(0.145)	0.217	5695	4930
Barrick: ABX	−148	(0.575)	(0.126)	2925	2529
Freeport McMoran: FCX	9	(0.005)	0.060	6544	5528
Gold Fields: GFI	36	(0.053)	0.331	2420	1939
Lihir: LIHRY	170	0.633	0.585	4154	3245
Rangold: GOLD	175	0.670	0.300	2068	1561
Hecla: HL	147	0.630	0.196	699	603
DRD Gold: DROOY	−140	(0.337)	(0.241)	168	129
Kinross: KGC	169	0.237	0.829	1161	989
Harmony: HMY	−58	(0.279)	(0.058)	1721	1479
Glamis: GLG	124	0.543	0.470	3644	2816
Bema: BGO	94	(0.317)	0.983	470	422

Source: Weldon Financial Publishing.

lows for a quick comparison, in terms of which investments are exhibiting the most robust "trending" dynamic:

- Gold: +11
- Silver: +29
- HUI: +11
- GLD: +10
- PAAS: +19
- SSRI: +21
- CDE: +21
- SIL: +20
- NEM: (−) 20

- AU: +1
- ABX: (–) 15
- FCX: zero
- GFI: +4
- LIHRY: +17
- GOLD: +18
- HL: +15
- DROOY: (–) 14
- KGC: +17
- HMY: (–) 6
- GLG: +12
- BGO: +9

Hence, I would view Silver itself, with a TIMID of 288 percent, and a subsequent *Power Ranking* of +29, as the precious metals market that exhibited the most advantageous trend-trading characteristics, of any precious metals market investment, as of August 2006.

Indeed, within the operation of my new mutual fund (scheduled to open in January of 2007) I will be using my *Power Ranking* methodology to select the Exchange Traded Funds that are outperforming the broader market, as the fund seeks to provide superior returns by focusing its investment in the best performing market sectors. In addition to the precious metals markets, the commodities markets, the forex market, the fixed income market, and the global stock index arena, I also monitor *Power Rankings* for the entire universe of Exchange Traded Funds. This includes U.S. industry sector funds, emerging market funds, commodity funds, currency funds, fixed-income funds, and international stock index funds.

In short, the TIMID readings and my *Power Rankings* can be utilized in any market.

Referencing the March 2006 matrix, gold had a positive trend indicator of +116 percent, with both the LT and ST ratios into positive territory, a situation generated by the upside breakout relative to the pattern highlighted in March 2006, as seen in Figure 34.4.

Compare the readings and subsequent price action in the spring of 2006 with the readings exhibited in the earlier matrix dated to the present, early September 2006.

FIGURE 34.4   Spot gold: daily
Source: Weldononline.com.

The current readings for gold are decidedly negative, implying that there has been no trend to trade, a thought that is fully confirmed by the sideways, range-bound, directionless price movement generated by the market.

Oddly enough, in the current situation, silver looks good, trend wise, during periods of strength in the complex; whereas gold looks bad, bearish-trend potential wise, when the complex has come under selling pressure of late. In this case, I have been bullish on silver, but fearful that the most recent upside breakout is a head fake and potential bear trap, to be sprung if gold were to violate its recent lows at the $605 area.

By now, readers should immediately spot the technical vulnerabilities exhibited by the most recent gold chart, as defined by a reverse launching pad pattern that implies an intensified chance of a crash landing in the shorter term. In this case, the trend momentum suggests that a breakdown in gold could lead to a more significant, sustained move to the downside.

The same indicators, however, suggest that silver is about to resume a primary bull market, in line with weakness in the gold-to-silver ratio, which has recently violated long-term uptrend lines and key underlying support.

In fact, even the macrobackdrop is somewhat polarized with the focus in Europe, Japan, and China being on rising inflation rates; overheated capital spending; and rapid growth in exports, money supply growth, and credit. There is a chance that the central banks attached to these three areas will intensify their monetary policy hawkishness by raising rates more aggressively.

Meanwhile, the focus in the United States has already shifted to the potential fallout, final-demand-wise, of a deepening disinflation that has begun to paralyze the U.S. housing market along with the odds that the Fed eventually will need to address the situation with easier monetary policy.

Right now, the market is going nowhere fast amid a lack of clarity in the macroscene that is reflected by the heavy weighting toward current nontrending readings emanating from the TIMID matrix.

PART SEVEN

Defining and Managing Risk

Defining
Overall Risk

There are many ways to examine risk along with a variety of methods to manage it. A top-down portfolio risk overlay is critical in maintaining balance and a proper degree of diversity, which helps limit your total risk.

I like to look at risk across a broad spectrum so that I'm considering different measures of risk related to individual positions within a certain sector and positions within an overall portfolio.

Because this book is focused on trading the bullion markets from my personal perspective, a discussion of risk analysis must begin at the top-down portfolio level.

Let's break it down.

Diversity

Assuming that you're not investing 100 percent of your trading stake, or personal portfolio, in gold, and you're involved in other markets and investment vehicles as well, I can proceed from the top-down perspective.

First, I break down the portfolio by class, assigning the following major categories:

- Foreign Exchange.
- Fixed Income.
- Stocks.
- Metals.
- Energy.
- Agricultural Commodities.

And then, separately, in a brand-new universe, I also classify exchange traded funds.

There is cross-pollination as the stocks category can overlap with the bullion mining shares. To reconcile this, I categorize all the petroleum and metals equities within their respective class (energy and metals), and thus outside the stocks classification.

As for the exchange traded funds (ETFs) arena, I am excited about the prospects for continued growth and expansion in the application of these products. The ETFs offer average investors the opportunity to diversify and become far more selectively aggressive while maintaining a low volatility, return-seeking, portfolio approach.

An investor can effectively buy or sell gold as a stock market transaction, through the gold (and silver) exchange traded funds, of which there are already several choices.

It is important to understand that not all exchange traded funds can be redeemed physically for the underlying metal, despite the claim that ETFs are all backed by the raw material. They are not all backed by metal that is transactionable. In some cases, a metal ETF is merely another paper claim on gold that cannot be exchanged for gold. These are definitely not minor issues, and you should research them prior to the commitment of risk capital.

What excites me the most about the growth of exchange traded funds is that it gives me, and every individual investor, the opportunity to bring a commodity-trading niche-mentality, to the global equity market universe.

I can now hone my view down to specific sectors of the global equity market in a single investment fund. Now, I can cover a far wider range of potential trading-investment vehicles, opening up a universe that encompasses industrial and service economy sectors as well as all types of commodities and currencies—fixed-income funds that can be honed by maturity and credit-risk genre. Not to mention global stock indexes, along with emerging market stocks and bonds.

I have been told on many occasions that the proliferation of ETF vehicles in so many tangents will diminish interest in gold bullion generally, as a hedge for geopolitical tension, monetary debasement, and inflation.

I could not disagree more.

Being able to specify gold as a single commodity that has a singular role as a monetary metal, during an era defined by the ongoing monetary debasement of all paper currencies opens the door to an increasing number of potential participants. This is particularly true for the individual investor.

In the past, the individual investor was essentially, structurally forced to carry a Paul Bunyon sized axe when making decisions and executing investment strategies. Stocks, bonds, cash, real estate . . . what percentage . . . small-cap, big-cap, growth, income . . . yada yada yada.

Today, all investors can wield a scalpel when making decisions with their money and paper wealth. We've come a long way, baby, from

Bunyon's axe to a surgeon's scalpel, and the proliferation of ETF products is likely to provide an ongoing scalpel-sharpening influence.

Still, I am only talking about diversity as a tool to manage risk.

First risk must be defined initially, from the top-down. I break risk-analysis into three categories, all of which I want to monitor on a constant basis.

First, I look at *position leverage.*

Second, I look at *trade risk.*

And third, I examine *correlated risk.*

Position Leverage

Starting with leverage, I use two calculations to assist with measuring the degree of leverage I might be carrying, and, I can break that down further by individual position, sector, and overall portfolio.

For example, I want to manage my risk by capping my leverage in any individual position, at, say, 200 percent.

I might, depending on the input offered by the other risk measurements, consider a 200 percent position in gold to be a maximum degree of leverage.

In that case, I simply take the nominal value of one gold futures contract, which at $600 per ounce would be $60,000 ($600 times 100 ounces per contract). Hence, for an account size of $60,000 I would hold a two-contract maximum at any given time when my indicators and macro overview were at their most bullish (or bearish, short two-contract maximum).

For a $1,000,000 account, carrying 200 percent leverage in gold would mean 1,000,000 divided by 60,000, times 2 (200 percent leverage). At $600 per ounce, a 200 percent leveraged position would equal 33 contracts of gold. Likewise, a 100 percent leveraged position, which means $1,000,000 worth of gold held for each $1,000,000 in capital, would equate to 16 contracts of COMEX gold futures, whereas a 50 percent leveraged position for a $1,000,000 account would be 8 contracts.

For a long-term investor then, who wants the minimum margin, not the maximum margin sought by the most aggressive (and nimble) trader/speculator types a 5 percent allocation of wealth into gold would mean holding just under one contract of COMEX gold, or about 84 ounces:

$$5 \text{ percent of } \$1 \text{ million} = \$50{,}000 \div \$600 \text{ per ounce cost}$$
$$= 83.33 \text{ ounces}$$

Taking it deeper, say I want a 100 percent leveraged position in precious metals, but I want to diversify that between gold and silver. To arrive at the desired position size, I can break down the calculations in any percentage terms I choose. I might want 50 percent in each, and since silver is 5,000 ounces per contract at a current price of, say (for ease) $10 per ounce, then each silver contract is worth $50,000.

To achieve a balanced 100 percent overall leveraged position in precious metals, I would assume the risk on 10 silver contracts and 8 contracts of gold, for a 50 percent split leveraged position.

This simple analysis can offer a unique and valuable way to assess the overall risk in any portfolio.

Another way to measure degrees of leverage is to use the margin-to-equity ratio, whereby the down payment that an exchange or brokerage house charges a trader to hold a position in any given commodity or financial futures contract can be used within the leverage calculation. Moreover, the programs used by the exchanges and brokerage houses reflect the recent tech-driven revolution in software and now incorporate risk modeling in the determination of the margin requirement.

Thus, I might use the margin figure to arrive at a comparative leveraged position that is more in line with what might be considered basic portfolio theory. From this perspective, I am looking at the actual amount of money that is being put into the markets at risk with the exchange (or broker, as the case may be). The end result is a closer approximation to the actual amount of capital at risk, giving us yet another angle on the degree of leverage being deployed.

On this basis, the leverage calculation looks different and ends up as a risk measurement that will be significantly smaller than the nominal value leverage figure, but one that I still consider to measure my degree of leverage.

For example, a 5 percent leveraged position defined by margin-to-equity ratio calculation might equate to a 100 percent leveraged position basis the nominal value of the position. In fact, a 5 percent leveraged position on a $1,000,000 account with gold at $600 per ounce, basis a $3,500 margin requirement, would equal 14 contracts. It is not far removed from the 16-contract position size indicated by a 100 percent leveraged position, as defined by nominal value.

Thus, I have two ways to look at my leverage, basis whatever size position I may choose. This is just another relative means to measure and examine risk within a trading portfolio. Again, I want to look at things from as many angles as possible, to get the most comprehensive perspective.

Once I have established some continuity, I can use leverage to adjust position sizes based on my technical and fundamental readings and outlook.

Using a black-box approach, I could say that a Power Ranking (see Chapter 34) between zero and +10 indicates that I employ 50 percent leverage (nominal value). Meanwhile, a reading in excess of +10 and up to +30 mandates full 100 percent leverage; whereas when the risk and volatility are higher, as is likely when my Power Ranking exceeds +40, I might look to scale back to 50 percent leverage.

It is not that I use any particular hard-and-fast rules, though I most certainly could. Instead, I prefer to look at my risk from several angles and apply those that are most desirable relative to the rest of the circumstances.

Trade Risk

My next risk-assessment category is *trade risk,* which is identified on a variety of planes, each of which represents a possible scenario where the market moves against my position.

I want to measure my trade risk in terms of my downside possibilities. I want to envision my exposure in a situation where all my protective stops are elected on the same day (meaning every position is moving against me by the maximum amount).

And, I want to get a read on what my worst-case scenario exposure is. I want to look at several angles that pertain to a situation where the market is gapping against me on the opening, exhibiting wild price gyrations, wide bid-ask spreads, and buying-selling vacuums. In these extreme circumstances, my investment capital exposure can be significantly skewed to the upside.

I begin by determining my individual position risk. I start with my pretrade risk assessment, which is derived from a determination of a stop-loss price level prior to the implementation of a position.

For an initial stop, I use a point-and-figure chart derived stop, or a Bollinger Band derived stop, usually dependent on which one creates the largest spread, relative to my trade initiation point.

Once I have determined my stop-loss price, I can then easily identify my dollars at risk for each contract I might buy or sell. In gold, if I purchase 100 ounces at $600, and predetermine a stop loss via point-and-figure analysis at $588, I would be risking $12 per ounce, or $1200.

In a $1,000,000 account, I might risk from one-tenth of one percent to as much as three-tenths of one percent, on any individual position, depending on where in a secular trend the market is, or whether I am taking a countertrend position.

As stated earlier, I like to have a core position, around which I can trade secondary positions. That might mean having 0.10 percent of capital at risk in a core position, with one or two other 0.10 percent risk tranches available for play.

If I am bullish on gold (with my $1 million account) and looking to take on 0.10 percent of risk, I am willing to risk $10,000. Since I have already established an initial $12 stop-loss via my technical analysis, I can trade 833 ounces of gold and adhere to my risk parameters:

$$\$10,000 \text{ risk unit} \div \$1,200 \text{ risk per } 100 \text{ ounces} = 8.33 \text{ contracts} $$
$$\text{of } 100 \text{ ounces, or } 833 \text{ ounces outright}$$

Aha, eight COMEX equivalent contracts of gold fits my trade risk parameter, which then gives me a position leverage of 50 percent, for a $1,000,000 account.

This move should remind you of the discussion of leverage. You should see how leverage and continuity work together.

At my maximum 0.30 percent trade risk parameter in gold, with a $12 stop-loss, my position leverage in gold would be 150 percent.

If I am buying gold, I am risking 0.30 percent of capital on a position that is leveraged 150 percent long.

Conversely, if I am bearish and taking the same action on the sell side, I am risking 0.30 percent of capital on a position that is leveraged 150 percent short.

I plug in my trade risk as defined by my dollars at risk, nominally, and as a percentage of total capital, to my stop-loss point. Then, as the market begins to move, I monitor the changes in this calculation, whether that change is a widening of the risk that occurs as a bullish position experiences profit. Until the initial stop-loss order is moved, all unrealized paper profits become risk.

As per the example I have been using, if I am long gold at $600, risking $12 to my $588 sell stop, and gold rallies to $610 on the first day, on day two my risk has expanded to $22, from $610 down to $588.

Thus, my initial 0.10 percent of capital trade risk on my 50 percent leveraged, eight 100-ounce contract position will jump to 0.176 percent:

22 risk = $2,200 × 8 = $17,600, or 0.176 percent of $1,000,000

Of course, my account value will have risen by $8,000 at the same time, thus reducing that risk back down to 0.174 percent, as the $17,600 in risk is calculated against our new account value of $1,008,000.

My original risk has not changed, but I insist on resetting all statistical categories at the end of each U.S. trading session, so I can begin fresh every morning.

Yesterday does not matter, only today, when it comes to risk. Profits are at risk until they are booked.

One of two things could happen.

First, I could be stopped out and take my original $12 loss.

Or, my point and figure, or Bollinger Band stop levels might begin to rise, as the market rallies, and my unrealized profits start to build.

When I move my stop up (assuming our long gold example) (or down, when short) the numbers all change and the risk begins to narrow.

Say gold rallies to $635, and I am long from $600 with my $588 stop-loss sell point. As the technical indicators play catch-up, I might be prompted by my stop methodology to move my stop order up to $620.

As such, my trade risk will be whittled down from $47 ($635 minus $588) to $15 ($635 minus $620).

I keep constant tabs on these figures, for every trade and position. There are other things to be gleaned from a discretionary perusal of the trade risk calculations. Specifically, when the trade risk appears bloated, often it can exceed 1 full percent of total equity; it is symptomatic, by definition, of large unrealized profits.

Say gold spiked to $680, on a geopolitical event, then our trade risk will blow out to the upside and will reflect that all our profits are at risk, without implying that our total initial risk has changed one iota.

In fact, our initial risk has not changed at all, nor has our position leverage calculation. This is why I want to assess risk from a multitude of angles and perspectives. Moreover, at some point, the accumulation of profits feeds into the timing of adding to a position, or trading more aggressively around the initial core position. Depending on the specific circumstance, I will either buy strength or buy weakness (in our long gold example), and then I will incorporate those trades into the position leverage and trade risk calculations.

Again, I do this mostly by feel, though the short-term macroeconomic input and the short-term technical developments are critical in making a timing determination.

There is still much more to consider under trade risk.

I look at two other measurements of trade risk as applied to every trade, investment, or position.

I calculate an average true range (ATR) as a shorter-term measure of the probable range in which my risk might fluctuate on a day-to-day basis.

I prefer a 21-day average true range, which covers about one month of trading sessions (four weeks times five days of trading per week), since it will more readily incorporate any most recent expansion in volatility as defined in a widening average daily trading range.

Say the average true range in gold over the past 21 days is $16, which equals $1,600 for every 100 ounces of gold. Assuming I hold my 50 percent leveraged, 0.10 percent risk, position of eight contracts via my theoretical $1,000,000 account size, my ATR calculation will be $12,800, or .128 percent.

This figure will change, every day, sometimes by a little, other times by a significant degree, dependent on the market's volatility.

While I do not use this measure except to provide another perspective on my potential day-to-day risk in any given position, in conjunction with the ATR calculation for all my open positions, I can get a specific vantage point on my risk that other calculations do not offer.

Moreover, this methodology allows me to slow down and pull back by reducing my overall position sizes in the event of a blowout to the upside in volatility that takes place across the board, market sector wise.

More importantly, I also calculate a standard deviation figure for each market to measure the worst-case scenario variance in the market's probability curve for whatever time frame I choose to incorporate.

According to probability and statistics theory, 95 percent of values in a population having a normal distribution are within two standard deviations of the mean.

I might use a 2.5 or 3.0 standard deviation measurement calculated over a long-term time frame to gauge the possible worst-case scenario collapse or spike that might take in any given market, on any given day.

I want to know what might happen to each individual position if a worst case scenario were to render my stop-loss orders moot.

If the 2.5 standard deviation of gold for the past 250 days (approximately one year of trading days) is $60 per 100 ounces of gold, then I calculate my worst case scenario risk exposure based on a move of that magnitude, against my position.

Hence, with a position of 800 ounces of gold in a $1,000,000 account, my ATR risk is 0.128 percent, my risk to stop (initial) is 0.10 percent, my leverage is 50 percent, my margin-equity risk is 0.28 percent, and my standard deviation risk is $48,000, or 4.8 percent.

Thus, in a disaster scenario where my standing stop-loss order is not enabled (executed by the broker) for whatever reason, I might be at risk for as much as 4.8 percent of my capital in this position.

Naturally this seems high, and it is. Such a scenario would only occur under the guise of a major risk-event, such as the breakout of war or a major announcement of a concerted shift in global macroeconomic policies by several countries at the same time.

These things do happen. And most likely, even in the event that a major risk event does unfold, I can exit any of my positions in a timely manner that does not cause me to suffer a two standard deviation move.

Still, it can be invaluable to know how risk stacks up in a disastrous worst-case scenario and what might be the potential for the risk of ruin to come into play. This would be particularly true if the risk of such an event can be discerned as it develops and before it explodes.

Specifically, I might keep an eye on my standard deviation risk measurement while adjusting my overall portfolio, when I deduce that global macroevent risk is on the rise.

That brings me to my third measurement—correlated risk.

Correlated Risk

Perhaps the toughest challenge to any trader, speculator, or investor is to quantify correlated risk.

Correlated risk is defined by the degree to which individual positions will move in sync to provide either simultaneous profits or losses.

A perfect example would be if I were long gold futures contracts, and long several gold mining companies, and long call options on silver.

I might be tempted to take the viewpoint of having three separate positions. Basing my risk analysis on this thought process could be disastrous if the precious metals complex plummets.

For sure, silver, gold, and gold mining shares move in a positively correlated manner. The most popular way to actually gauge the degree of positive or negative correlation between any two given markets or sectors is to conduct an R-squared regression study.

In my research work, I make great use of correlation studies; the resultant overlay charts compare two markets, providing a unique and most often valuable perspective. However, in my trading and fund management, I have always tended to rely on feel as much as anything.

Nonetheless, I look at a run of correlation figures every day that are reflected in a matrix that provides R-squared calculations in a broad grid of major market sectors. From the perspective of a precious metals trader, it would certainly be important to know if gold's correlation with the equity market, bond market, and U.S. dollar is trending toward a more, or less, positive or negative reading.

As with everything else I have discussed, the most powerful market moves tend to come on the back of highly correlated trends taking place in a wide range of market sectors.

In other words, all things should be in alignment, correlation-wise, too.

Consider a situation where the U.S. dollar is under pressure against a broad range of currencies that are moving in an increasingly positive correlated manner. At the same time, the Commodity Research Bureau (CRB) Index of prices is accelerating higher, and the energy complex is making new multimonth price highs. I would certainly expect gold and silver to be rallying in this situation, purely on their positive correlation with each and every other market movement in the background, particularly if the intermarket correlations are intensifying.

Correlation studies can offer insight beyond the risk management arena. But, when it comes to observing correlated market activity, it is critical to understand that correlations can change in an instant.

In fact, often a change in correlation can signal a pending turn in the broader market. In the precious metals markets, imagine if gold bullion were making a new multimonth price high and the gold mining share indexes were not, and the R-squared calculation between the two was becoming less positive. I would take notice of this for sure, from the perspective of evolving divergence between two normally correlated vehicles.

I would take notice from the perspective of becoming more cautious on bullion, if I were long. Overall, the regulatory buzz words "past performance is not indicative of future results" apply specifically to correlations that are exhibited at any given time between market sectors.

While I am fully aware of the changing R-squared readings among the universe of markets and market sectors, I prefer to handle my correlated risk in the context of my breakdown by sector, within the overall portfolio.

Sector and Portfolio Risk

I begin with the assumption that there is a high degree of positive correlation in many of the markets I trade, particularly in the currency and commodity arena.

As laid out in Chapter 36, I break my portfolio down into metals, petroleum, commodities, currencies, fixed income, and stock indexes (again, the entire exchange traded funds [ETF] breakdown is considered as a separate universe, with a different portfolio structure).

Then I break down each sector into the following subsectors:

■ *Fixed Income:* Asia, European-Nordic, Anglo (United States, Canada, United Kingdom, Australia, New Zealand), Asian emerging markets, Eastern European emerging markets, and South American emerging markets.

■ *Foreign Exchange:* U.S. dollar versus Asia, U.S. dollar versus Europe, U.S. dollar versus commodity producers, U.S. dollar versus emerging market currencies, Japanese yen versus global currencies, Eurocurrency versus Eastern European, Nordic, and Asian currencies.

■ *Stock Indexes:* Asia, Europe, Anglo, emerging markets.

■ *Metals:* Precious metals, platinum group metals, industrial base metals, specialty metals (rhodium, titanium), mining shares.

- *Petroleum:* Crude oil and petroleum products, natural gas, energy shares.
- *Agricultural commodities:* Oilseeds sector (soybean complex, vegetable-palm oils), grains (corn, wheat, rice, oats), livestock, tropicals (coffee, cocoa, sugar, orange juice), cotton, rubber.

In the precious metals sector, the breakdown is:

- Gold.
- Silver.
- Gold mining shares.
- Silver mining shares.
- Gold mining share indexes.
- Gold ETF.
- Silver ETF.
- Gold-Silver ratio.
- Platinum-Gold spread.
- Platinum-Palladium spread.
- Gold calendar spread.
- Silver calendar spread.
- Gold swaps and lease rates.
- Silver swaps and lease rates.
- Platinum swaps and lease rates.
- Gold options.
- Silver options.
- Gold versus S&P 500.
- Gold versus bonds.
- Gold versus CRB Index.
- Gold in foreign currencies (all, from G-7 to emerging FX).
- Gold in producer currencies (rand, Canadian, Australian).
- Gold in consumer currencies (Chinese, Indian).

It becomes easy to see how managing sector risk is important, as I want to hone down my view to the subsector vehicle that gives me the best chance to benefit from the macroenvironment and the technical trend.

In each of the major sectors, I assign a risk allocation, which is usually (depending on the dominant macromarket circumstance), about one percentage point (though this can be higher). This means that in each major sector of the market, I am willing to commit up to one percent of total capital to individual trade risk defined by my risk-to-stop calculation. I will then distribute my risk allocation in each sector to the subsectors I desire to trade or invest in.

I might have one percent allocated to fixed income and one percent allocated to precious metals, and one percent allocated to energy, based on the dominant macrodynamic and my trend-momentum readings.

From there, I might allocate 0.3 percent of risk (a full position based on trade risk tranches of 0.10 percent per trade) to U.S. bonds, 0.3 percent to Japanese government bonds, and then 0.2 percent allocation to a short-term interest rate spread that is positively correlated to the bond position.

In that context, I have 0.8 percent trade risk (risk-to-stop) in the fixed-income sector, à la my exposure to the Anglo-U.S. and Asian fixed-income subsectors.

In the precious metals subsector, this might mean that during the most dynamic trend setup, I could have 0.2 percent exposure in gold, and 0.2 percent exposure in silver, capping my total subsector exposure at 0.4 percent.

It would be rare for me to carry a maximum individual trade risk in gold and silver at the same time.

Another thing that becomes evident is that the precious metals subsector cannot handle as large a risk allocation as can the fixed-income market.

I know this. I do not need any statistical studies to understand the need to properly weight my risk allocation within each sector.

But, this is not to say that I cannot have 0.30 percent exposure in copper at the same time, either correlated or not correlated. Often within a major sector, I use spread positions to minimize my risk exposure and to facilitate greater diversity.

If I look and see a bearish macrotechnical trend scenario in copper and a bullish scenario evolving in gold, I will immediately examine the spread relationship and the correlation figures. If I can be short copper and long gold, with each getting its own risk allocation, but in sync with what would be a separate spread trade, it makes me comfortable holding a more significant position.

To rewind, this is where correlation studies can provide insight beyond the risk management perspective.

I assess my sector risk on all the same levels as I do my trade risk and position leverage.

I also calculate combined figures for the leverage calculation, the average true range risk calculations, the margin-equity exposure, and the worst-case scenario, as defined by the standard deviation reading, for each sector.

In the preceding example, I am holding 0.4 percent risk-to-stop exposure in gold and silver. This then becomes my sector risk-to-stop measure. Then I add the 100 percent leverage held in gold (2 times 50 percent leverage on the theoretical $1,000,000 account, à la the 0.2 percent trade risk) to the leverage in silver, at 100 percent, to come up with a reading that says I am 200 percent long the precious metals sector.

From this perspective, I can more easily see that I should not carry a maximum position in both gold and silver at the same time, which would push my sector risk to an unacceptably high level of 300 percent or more. This is how I can read my sector risk figures, and use them to hone my overall risk by individual position. Also, by combining the readings provided by my worst-case scenario standard deviation calculation for each subsector and then for each major sector, I can define the risk of ruin as applies to my entire portfolio.

For example, my combined standard deviation figure for the fixed-income and precious metals positions might put my portfolio risk at somewhere north of 10 percent.

Occasionally, the figures appear exaggerated, and in the case of something like U.S. Eurodollar futures (which have a nominal face value of $1,000,000 each), we need to make adjustments to reflect the actual risk.

Helping exaggerate the final figures, particularly as they apply to the standard deviation risk in the entire portfolio and the total leverage suggested by the combined figures, is that these final numbers are not adjusted for negative correlation.

Without being adjusted for the likelihood that not every position would move in a positively correlated manner to the maximum standard deviation loss; without a single stop-loss order being executed; or without pre-stop-loss intervention by me, the end result is that my actual risk will be significantly less than the portfolio figures imply.

My goal is not to attach hard-and-fast rules (though I do precisely that with my ETF Model Portfolio approach). My goal is to gain insight into how much risk I am carrying in my portfolio, and where that risk originates. With these insights, I am better prepared to make changes, liquidate positions, or move my stop-loss orders, as the environment dictates, using a scalpel rather than an axe.

And as always, each individual trader, investor, or speculator needs to define his or her own risk profile, and apply the most comforting risk overlay on a highly personal level.

Although personal comfort is such an understated factor, it is perhaps the most critical one in pursuing long-term trading or investing success.

Psychological Risk

The single most important thing I can relate in this book is simple to understand, but difficult to define. It becomes the crux of the matter, the point-of-attack, in taking the path toward becoming a long-term success in the trading-investing arena.

Comfort.

You need to be comfortable in your methodology. You need to have confidence in it so that you can apply your methodology without hesitation, in the heat of the battle. It is important to have a methodology, no matter what it is, so that when the markets are at their most intense price change volatility, you can act without overthinking.

This is one reason I love to "scenario-ize," whereby I discuss myriad possible scenarios that might play out in the macroeconomic or geopolitical spheres, or even in terms of sentiment, lop-sided speculative exposure, and technical vulnerabilities.

Armed with a confidence-inspiring methodology, and having visualized a wide range of potential changes to the trading environment or market circumstance, it becomes far easier to implement a strategy when the heat is turned up.

In this chapter, I discuss psychological factors I have encountered, and grappled with during my career. What makes the psychological risk dynamic so interesting is that even the most experienced traders and investors can make rookie mistakes, and can make them over and over and over.

I have had to learn many trading lessons the hard way. I have incurred plenty of losses to go along with my successes. Most of those losses and my worst drawdowns have been the result of making the same set of mistakes.

I have had to relearn the same lessons multiple times. This is the nature of the beast, and a constant self-examination is required to keep these factors from leading to failure. I have always said my mind is my best asset, and my worst enemy.

With that thought, we begin.

Overtrading

Patience is key, as I have repeatedly highlighted. Overtrading or investing is almost always a function of the three primary psychological (emotional) influences—fear, hope, and greed.

It might sound cliché, but it is cliché for a reason—it is true.

Overtrading can occur following a particularly large loss, when the mind-set becomes "recover as quickly as possible."

I have seen a single, large but manageable losing position (provided it was liquidated) drive traders into a frenzy of activity as they try to recapture the loss before it becomes realized.

I have seen the mind-set develop in traders who have suffered sizable losses, so that risk aversion dissipates and they pass the point of no return. This happens simply because taking an even bigger loss is not likely to have any worse end result than the loss already incurred.

For me, this type of overtrading is not a factor. Instead, my overtrading risk emanates from periods of somnambulant market activity, when low and contracting volatility is pervasive across a wide range of market subsectors, but the macrofundamental situation compellingly points to the potential for a new price trend to emerge.

My overtrading mistakes have occurred in this circumstance, mostly when my TIMID trend readings indicate no trend is currently in force, but that the technical foundation is being laid for one to emerge. In this situation, I have often tried to force trades that just were not there, trying to jump the gun and catch the very beginning move in a budding new trend.

This has meant that my overtrading often subjects me to unnecessary whipsaws, where I will plunge into a market, sometimes with more risk than is dictated at the early stage of a trend (0.10 percent per trade risk at first). I am swinging for the fences and trying to hit the ball out of the park on the first pitch of the game.

This rarely works and more often than not results in a strikeout.

Worse is when I might attempt to jump the gun twice, maybe three times, unsuccessfully, dumping 0.3 percent of risk allocation into the garbage playing less than premium hands. At that point, I stop; and then the readings kick in and the market moves without me being properly positioned.

This exact mind-set is dangerous and might allow me to make even more overtrading mistakes if I continue to swing based on the fear that I will miss the move if I do not swing.

While timing is important, mostly from a standpoint of entering the market with the least amount of risk, long-term macrotrends can take months to develop and can last for years. There is almost always an opportunity to get involved. I am tempted to say, without sarcasm, that the markets are open every day. There are always opportunities for those who wait for them.

Whether that applies to me, overtrading as I attempt to get in early and jump the gun on my technical-trend readings, or to the traders who have just suffered a sizable loss, the best action is to retrench and rewind, rather than to push forward without regard to risk.

From this perspective, fear is a positive element that can prevent pursuing self-destructive behavior while wearing "risk blinders."

Paralysis

While patience is required, so too is action.

A good trader or investor must be willing to commit capital to risk, in an instant, without hesitation, in a bold, decisive, calculated manner without any second-guessing.

One-time Commodity Corporation Trading Mentor Randy Rose once told me something that I will never forget: "You can take an aggressive overly risky trader and tone him down, and rein him in. But, it is much more difficult to induce or teach an overly risk-adverse trader to become more aggressive. Show me a guy willing to put it all on the line, willing to live on the edge, and I will show you someone who has what it takes to be successful."

In other words, you either have it, or you don't, and if you are not willing to take the risk through decisive action, than you are likely to be an underachiever in the investment world.

Paralysis also applies to undercapitalized traders who are assuming risk that they cannot afford to take. Letting a position ride against you to the stop-loss becomes significantly more problematic, psychologically, if the trader does not have the capital to lose in the first place.

An extreme example would be the person who is considering risking his rent money. The knowledge that he cannot afford to lose that money can cause paralysis, undertrading, whipsaw trading without conviction, overtrading, second-guessing, and ultimately self-destructive failure.

You must be able to afford the losses.

Of course, you do everything you can to avoid them, but you must take them.

Consider the conflict—you cannot be afraid, but you should be!

We talk about this conflict later in this chapter.

Slow Motion

Have you ever watched Wayne Gretzky or Mark Messier in action? What amazes me about watching these two legends play hockey, which, outside of NASCAR, is arguably the fastest sport on earth, is how they can slow the game down to a speed that suits them.

Wayne Gretzky often seemed to be moving in slow motion, as he captured and controlled the puck in a mega-deliberate fashion, while staying focused on seeing the entire playing field (ice). He would hold the puck on his stick for what seemed like forever, waiting for opponents to react to lulling activity, and then boom, he would spring into action, and a goal was most often the result.

Magic Johnson and Larry Bird did the same thing while dribbling the basketball up the court, leading a fast break with a deliberateness that gave them the maximum time and space into which to make the great play or complete the perfect pass.

All the other players appeared to race past Bird, Magic, Gretzky, and Messier, leaving them seemingly all alone to finish the play.

I like to try to do the same thing with trading the markets, specifically when chaos appears to be breaking out, when volatility spikes amid the release of key economic data, or on the back of an important policy announcement.

I try to slow things down, and let the other market participants pass me by, reacting to the new stimulus without pausing for thought or to examine the actual news, or the potential longer-term implications for any given market.

I try to visualize everything taking place in slow motion.

I pause, take a deep breath, and deliberately run down whatever checklist I need to contemplate, comprehensively dissecting the new input prior to acting. I have already scenario-ized and visualized the events that are then suddenly unfolding in real time. If I know what I want to do in any given situation, it also helps me calmly assess the scene, and then confidently and deliberately take action as dictated by the individual circumstance.

The line from Rudyard Kipling's well-known poem advises, *If you can keep your head when all about you/Are losing theirs . . .*

This is a particularly useful thought process, in the trading/investment world.

Ego versus Confidence

Consider the following thought process that creeps into my mind all too frequently:

I know more than my indicators can tell me.

Danger—Danger—Danger.

At this point, when my mind begins to suggest that I am smarter than my input, or the market itself, my ego has taken over, and I am in danger.

I have always said, *the market will mess with the most people as possible.*

Usually that happens following a prolonged trend, when participants have been lulled into complacency, and begin to think that they have outsmarted the market with their profits and prescience.

When ego gets in the way, the technical indicators become less of a focal point, and even macrofundamental data that should be signaling a shift is often ignored by traders who think they know more than the marketplace.

The market is always right, even when it is wrong.

I know this is a psychological risk that applies to me in the sense that following a prolonged profitable run, I tend to get sloppy. I cannot allow success to breed complacency, ego-inflation, and ultimately sloppiness.

When I am the most profitable, it means I need to be even more vigilant in trade selection and overall leverage than when I am suffering a drawdown. This is simply because a drawdown forces me to become more careful by default.

But, the ego risk does not apply to me in the sense of refusing to take losses, or refusing to admit that I am wrong.

Indeed, I am wrong more often than I am right. That is a statistical fact.

That is not to mean I cannot be profitable.

Aha, quite the contrary—to become profitable, I need to admit I am wrong more often than I need to realize that I am right.

Take the simple example of a baseball designated hitter. By definition, he is assured of failing more often than he succeeds. Indeed, a .350 batting average is considered outstanding, yet this also means the player is failing to get a hit during two-thirds of his at bats. So, failing 65 percent of the time can lead to overall success.

It is the same in trading, though it is less critical as pertains to longer-term investing.

Throughout the world, and particularly in the United States, children are raised in the belief that winning is a determinant of personal success. Win at all costs is a mantra that has invaded and pervaded our society and is exemplified by the increasing frequency of sports-parent rage, whereby a parent storms the children's playing field in an often-violent display of anger.

From our earliest experiences as children, we are conditioned to view winning as strength and losing as weakness. Great traders and investors must relearn these lessons and must recondition themselves to accept the necessity of losing and avoid allowing it to define their self worth.

For sure, it would be easy to feel like a loser, when losing two-thirds of the time, but this mentality is perverse. As stated earlier, in poker folding a losing hand can be the strongest move possible. The same is true in trading; taking a loss can be the strongest move, and does not at all reflect weakness.

I need to lose, so I can win—it becomes that simple.

And with that simple realization and the proper conditioning, this can become a new way of life and can pave a path to trading or investing success.

Conversely, I must not allow myself to be tempted to take a profit, just because it is a profit. I need my profits to be their maximum size to offset all the smaller losses. One missed megaprofit can magnify a dozen small acceptable losses by not offsetting them.

Exiting a profitable position too early can be just as devastating to overall performance as letting a loss become larger than it should have been. And yes, while exiting a profitable position too early has likely never been the direct cause of a trader going bust, it can become a major contributing factor if it is done often enough.

Again, having confidence in a methodology serves to bridge these conflicts. I am comfortable taking a loss with the knowledge that it is a necessary part of a bigger-picture strategy. I can separate my self-worth as a person from my trading performance, on a day-to-day and month-to-month basis. This is not to suggest that this is easy to do; it takes work, constant self-reinforcement, and an open mind-set.

Understanding yourself is key. Keeping ego out of the way becomes a constant and critically necessary task, just as much as does maintaining the proper conditioning when it comes to taking a loss and letting a profit ride.

Ego presents a risk that must be managed.

Gambling

If I am willing to be right only 35 percent of the time, then I must be gambling.

Well, that may be true in poker, but it is not true in trading or investing since, supposedly, my profits exceed my losses by a magnitude that statistically ensures long-term profitability. I seek to do in trading what I do in poker: skew the odds in my favor and avoid playing to the "house's odds."

While I do play poker, I do not gamble.

This means that while there is a gambling and luck element inherent in playing poker, I can pursue a strategy that skews the gambling odds to favor my success over the long haul, and often, those odds can become skewed heavily in the short term.

In trading and investing, my strategic approach incorporates a blend of macro top-down fundamental analysis, psychology, a technically based statistical overlay, and a staunch risk management protocol. With these tools, I can skew the odds to favor my success.

I want to eliminate the gambling mentality by playing only when the odds are in my favor. I conclude with something I blurted out once while trying to explain psychological risk to a layperson; it is something I have said repeatedly ever since:

> Gambling is the creation of risk for risk's sake. Investing is the assumption of risk that already exists, and would anyway, whether I am involved, or not.

I trade and invest on a strategic basis. I do not gamble.

PART EIGHT
Putting It All Together

Using What You Know When Making Decisions

How can you determine your trading theme and then figure out what research you need to make your moves? You need to define the long-term secular macroeconomic environment, and in this context, label a dominant trading theme.

You need to define the macroenvironment on a short-term basis, as it evolves on a constant, minute-to-minute basis. If you're not an investment professional, you need to review the pertinent macroeconomic data and geopolitical developments each morning and evening.

Decide whether the short-term environment fits with, enhances, or supports the current dominant macrotrading theme. Or, do the short-term developments conflict with the dominant theme? Then, consider whether this suggests that the dominant macrotrading theme is intensifying, diminishing, or reversing.

Do the long-term technicals support the dominant macrotheme? If so, do the intermediate term technicals support the long-term technical stance, and does the short-term dynamic support the intermediate-term technical conclusions? If all the macro and technical factors are aligned, then the assumption of capital risk becomes an option, and a trade or investment is warranted.

Next, you need to asses the risk level as it applies to the individual trade or investment as well as the existing risk already present within the overall trading or investing portfolio.

Thereafter, you will be monitoring the position, adjusting the stop on a regular basis as required, and staying on top of all the macro-to-micro data input for any signs of a potential shift in the fundamental backdrop.

Anyone can do it who is willing to invest the required time and effort. The information is readily available, and the markets are easily accessible to any investor.

Global Supply-and-Demand Fundamentals: The Mining Industry, Gold Consumption, Gold Holdings, and Central Banks

There is a great deal of material that I could not include in this book. Perhaps the most pertinent would be a discussion of the global mining fundamentals, particularly as they apply to producer hedging practices. Also, I have not provided a full examination of the specifics related to central bank sales. These are critical factors in any fundamental assessment of the precious metals sector. In this chapter, I provide a brief overview and urge you to do more research into global supply-and-demand statistics for gold. This information is available from the World Gold Council (www.gold.org), the International Monetary Fund, and Gold Fields Mineral Service (GFMS).

According to data provided by the World Gold Council (WGC) and by GFMS Ltd., global producers of gold include:

South Africa	12 percent (196 tonnes in 2005)
Australia	10 percent (263 tonnes in 2005)
United States	10 percent (262 tonnes in 2005)
Latin America (ex-Peru)	10 percent
Africa (ex S.A.)	9 percent
China	9 percent
Peru	8 percent
Russia	7 percent
Asia (ex-Indonesia)	7 percent
Indonesia	7 percent
Canada	5 percent
CIS (ex-Russia)	5 percent
Others	1 percent

According to the World Gold Council (WGC), 155,500 tonnes (metric tons) of gold have been mined over the course of history, two-thirds of that total since 1950.

Globalization of output has meant diversity in geopolitical risk. In fact, South Africa's percentage of total global annual output has collapsed, from over 70 percent in 1970, to just 12 percent currently.

Peru, where output was only 18 tonnes of gold in 1992, is pegged by the WGC at 207 tonnes for 2005, due primarily to the presence of Yanacocha, the second largest gold mine in the world. Figure 43.1 maps out the global mine output dynamic by region.

Also important when considering mining output fundamentals, specifically when picking individual gold mining shares to own, is the output cost, which can vary widely by mine and by company. According to GFMS, the average cost, globally, to mine an ounce of gold is $269 (though exploration costs, depreciation, and amortization, and mine closure costs boost the adjusted "cash-cost" figure to $339 per mined ounce).

You also need to consider scrap supply, which has been steadily rising with the price of late. It had been flat at about 600 tonnes per year through the 1990s and then began to slide in 2001. As of 2005, according to GFMS Ltd., scrap supply had risen to nearly 900 tonnes.

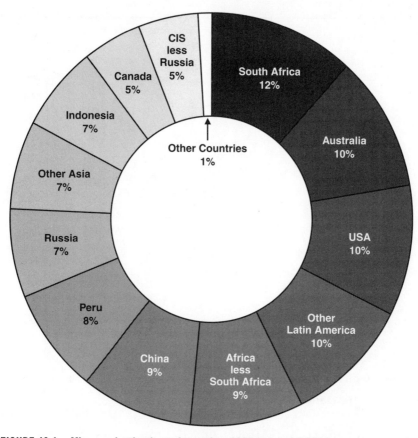

FIGURE 43.1   Mine production by major region, 2005 (total of 2,518 tonnes)
Source: Gold Fields Mineral Service (gfms.co.uk) and the World Gold Council (wgc.org).

Observe the positive correlation between a rising price, and an increase in supply that is extracted from the hands of those who might be hoarding physical gold shown in Figure 43.2.

And central banks hold approximately one-fifth of all above-ground supply of gold. For years, sales of gold by central banks have made up an annual supply-and-demand shortfall. Moreover, producers are active sellers on a forward basis, as they hedge their expected output, often several years in advance.

Hedged sales of gold by Australian producers in the early to-mid 1990s were believed to have exceeded any realistic forecast for future production, and led to a short-covering rally by several producers in the late 1990s.

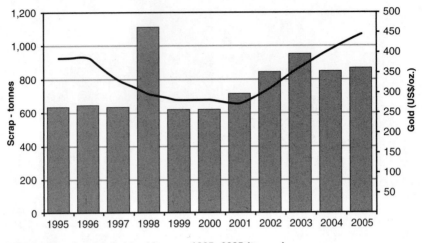

FIGURE 43.2   Supply of old gold scrap, 1995–2005 (tonnes)
Source: Gold Fields Mineral Service (gfms.co.uk) and the World Gold Council (wgc.org).

Demand for gold is broken down into three primary categories:

1. Industrial Demand.
2. Jewelry Demand.
3. Investment Demand.

According to the World Gold Council, Investment demand in 2005 was pegged at approximately 600 tonnes, having nearly doubled since 1996 when it was marked at less than 300 tonnes.

Hoarding of gold bars makes up the largest percentage slice of investment demand, pegged by the WGC at more than 250 tonnes that is socked away in basements, safes, mattresses, and vaults.

Official sales of gold coins define another 100 tonnes' worth of annual demand, while investment in exchange traded funds (ETFs) and related products is by far the fastest growing source of gold demand, having reached more than 100 tonnes in 2005. Figure 43.3 defines the identifiable investment demand.

Still, it is jewelry demand that defines the largest source of gold consumption, with about $40 billion in global sales, making up almost 70 percent of all final demand for the yellow metal. The World Gold Council lists the following countries as the largest gold-jewelry consumers (in order per 2005 demand):

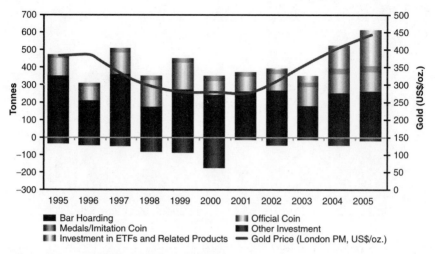

FIGURE 43.3   Identifiable investment demand
Source: Gold Fields Mineral Service (gfms.co.uk) and the World Gold Council (wgc.org).

- India.
- United States.
- China.
- Saudi Arabia.
- Turkey.
- United Arab Emirates.
- Egypt.
- Indonesia.
- Italy.
- United Kingdom.
- Japan.
- Taiwan.
- Vietnam.
- Hong Kong.

This list might seem surprising to the average gold investor, as defined by the connection to India (consumed a massive 590 tonnes in 2005) and China, neither of which holds any significant amount of reserve gold. Look at the presence of petroleum producers as large buyers of gold, amid the shift of global paper wealth (see Figure 43.4).

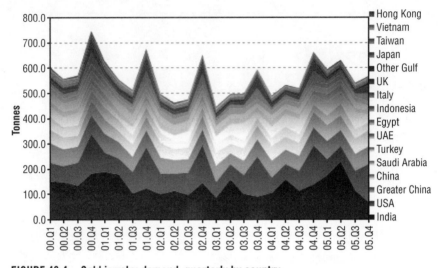

FIGURE 43.4   Gold jewelry demand: quarterly by country

Source: Gold Fields Mineral Service (gfms.co.uk) and the World Gold Council (wgc.org).

Also of interest is the number of emerging Asian countries on the list, as the shift in global paper wealth from the U.S. consumer to Asian exporting nations is perhaps nowhere more pronounced, than in this list.

Industrial demand is less of a factor, accounting for only 11 percent of all global demand for gold. In addition to a noticeable demand for gold from the dental industry (2 percent of total demand, or 18 percent of Industrial demand), most of the demand (7 percent of total, or 64 percent of Industrial demand) comes from the use of gold in electronic components.

In this respect, again, Asia is a key, as companies relocate output to this region of the world.

The World Gold Council and the Gold Fields Mineral Service offer excellent data on fundamental supply-and-demand statistics as they relate to gold.

Finally, the major holders of gold, both on an official basis (i.e., central banks) and a demand basis are shown in the following list, based on data from the International Monetary Fund on World Gold Holdings (see Figure 43.5):

United States	26 percent
Euro-area	39 percent

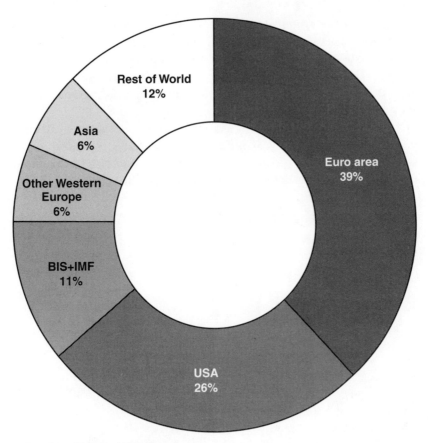

FIGURE 43.5 World gold holdings
Source: Gold Fields Mineral Service (gfms.co.uk) and the World Gold Council (wgc.org).

Bank of International Standards and the IMF	11 percent
Western Europe (ex-Euro-area)	6 percent
Asia	6 percent
Rest of World	12 percent

As discussed throughout this book, Asia remains heavily under-invested in gold, compared with its vast and rapidly expanding holdings of reserve U.S.-denominated paper currency and debt. Someone recently said: "It's a perfect relationship, Asia gets the jobs, and the United States gets the profits." That someone was way wrong: Asia gets both the jobs and the profits, while the United States gets the finished goods and the debt required to pay for them. The United States exports its monetary paper wealth reflation, and Asia exports their labor market disinflation. In the end, the gold holdings are heavily skewed toward the United States as a debtor nation. I can envision a day when Asian central banks offer to swap their massive holdings of U.S. currency and debt, for U.S.-held gold.

China has gone from holding virtually no U.S. dollars to holding almost one trillion in reserve. China will not keep accumulating just one asset at this pace. The global macro supply-and-demand fundamentals are wildly bullish for gold, on a long-term secular basis, over the next decade or more.

Chart Library

In closing, I offer the following reference library of long-term charts (Figures 44.1 through 44.21). They reflect the modern trading era of the precious metals on an outright basis and relative to other asset classes, and gold denominated in global currencies.

Every chart has the same stock technical studies applied allowing for a more accurate comparison, with the following pair of indicators repeatedly visible:

1. Five-Year Exponentially-Weighted Moving Average (60 months).
2. Two-Year Rate of Change (24 months).

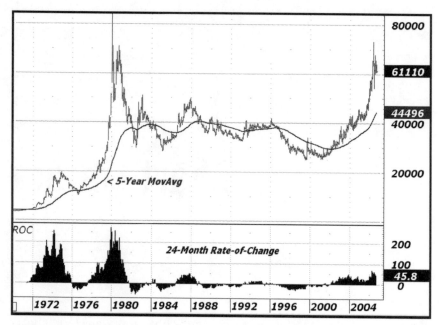

FIGURE 44.1   Spot gold (in U.S. dollars): monthly since June 1969

Source: Weldononline.com.

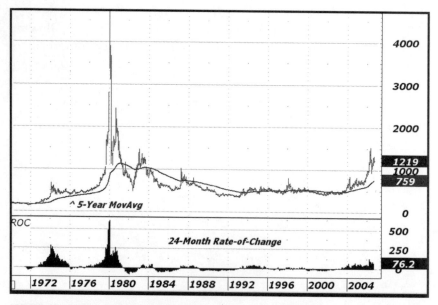

FIGURE 44.2   Spot silver (in U.S. dollars): monthly since June 1969

Source: Weldononline.com.

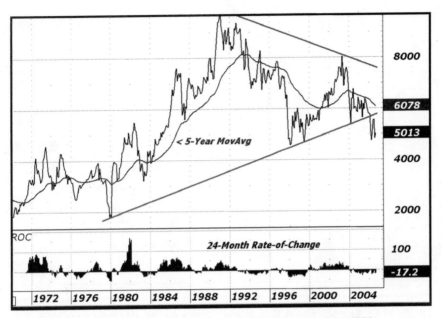

FIGURE 44.3 Gold-silver ratio spread (spot): monthly close since June 1969

Source: Weldononline.com.

FIGURE 44.4 Platinum minus gold price spread: monthly close since July 1985

Source: Weldononline.com.

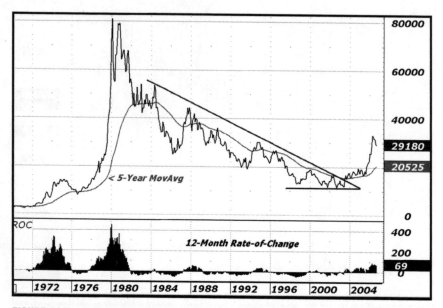

FIGURE 44.5   Gold adjusted by U.S. 10-year T-note yield: monthly close since 1969

Source: Weldononline.com.

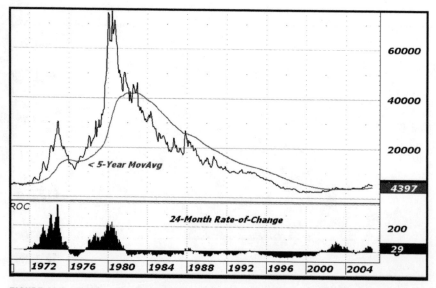

FIGURE 44.6   Gold versus Dow Jones Industrial Average ratio spread: monthly close since June 1969

Source: Weldononline.com.

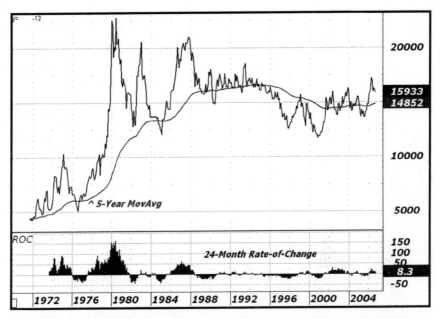

FIGURE 44.7   Gold versus Commodity Research Bureau Index ratio spread: monthly close since September 1971

Source: Weldononline.com.

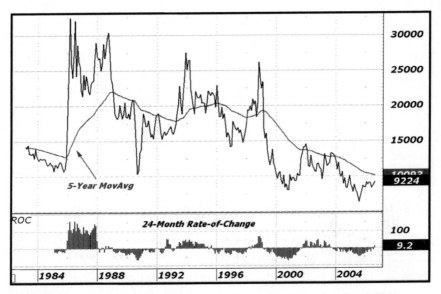

FIGURE 44.8   Gold versus crude oil ratio spread: monthly close since March 1983

Source: Weldononline.com.

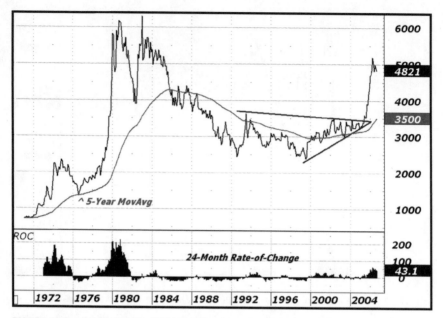

FIGURE 44.9   Gold priced in EUR: monthly close since January 1971

Source: Weldononline.com.

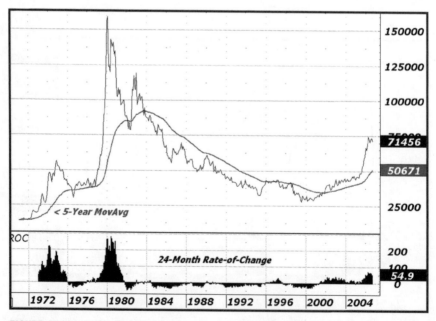

FIGURE 44.10   Gold priced in Japanese yen: monthly close since January 1971

Source: Weldononline.com.

318

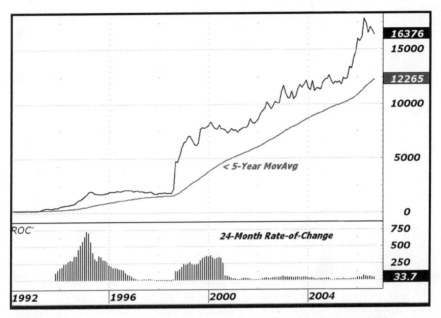

FIGURE 44.11   Gold priced in Russian rubles: monthly close since January 1992

Source: Weldononline.com.

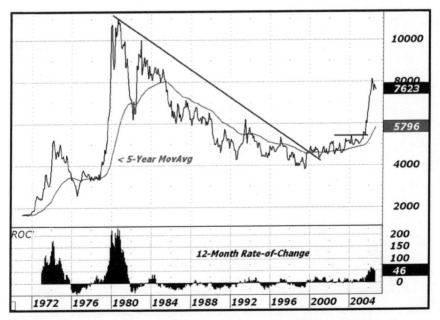

FIGURE 44.12   Gold priced in Swiss francs: monthly close since January 1971

Source: Weldononline.com.

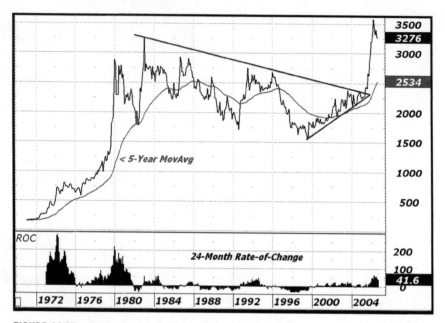

FIGURE 44.13   Gold priced in British pounds: monthly close since January 1971
Source: Weldononline.com.

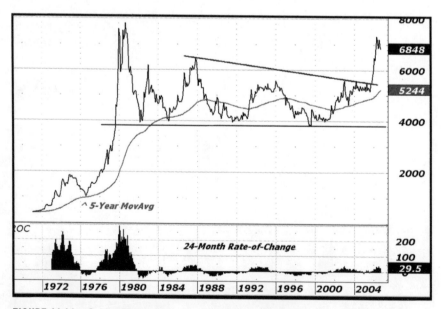

FIGURE 44.14   Gold priced in Canadian dollars: monthly close since January 1971
Source: Weldononline.com.

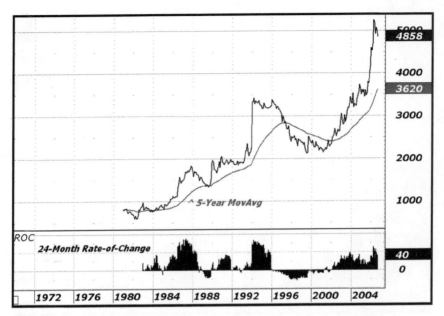

FIGURE 44.15   Gold priced in Chinese yuan: monthly close since January 1981

Source: Weldononline.com.

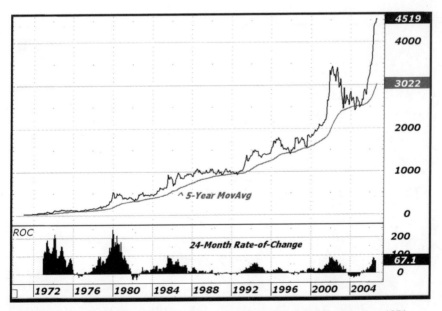

FIGURE 44.16   Gold priced in South African rand: monthly close since January 1971

Source: Weldononline.com.

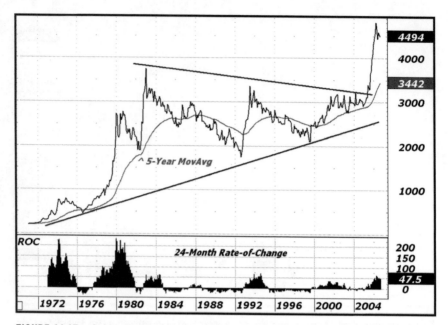

FIGURE 44.17   Gold priced in Swedish krona: monthly close since January 1971
Source: Weldononline.com.

FIGURE 44.18   Gold priced in Aussie dollars: monthly close since January 1971
Source: Weldononline.com.

322

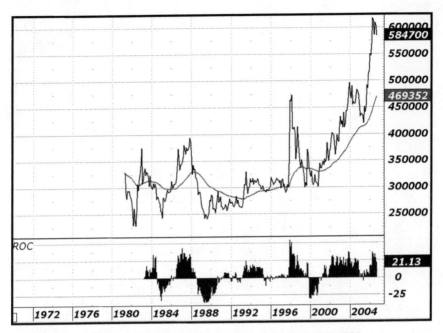

FIGURE 44.19   Gold priced in Korean won: monthly close since April 1982

Source: Weldononline.com.

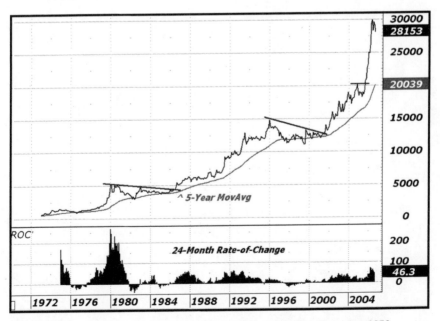

FIGURE 44.20   Gold priced in Indian rupee: monthly close since December 1972

Source: Weldononline.com.

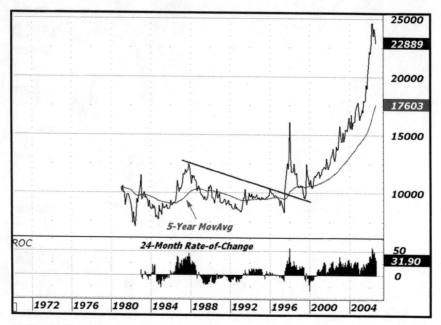

FIGURE 44.21   Gold priced in Thai baht: monthly close since January 1981

Source: Weldononline.com.

Precious Metals: A Secular-Macro Overview

The following is a reproduction of a Power Point presentation made by the author in August 2006.

Global capital, savings, income, labor, and wealth imbalances have been intensifying for DECADES, at least since Nixon removed the USD from the Gold Standard, amid widening U.S. deficits. The global economy has become incestuously codependent on the U.S. consumer.

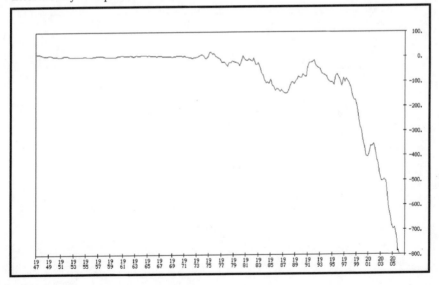

U.S. net exports: monthly since 1947

Source: Chart courtesy of Economagic, LLC. All rights reserved.

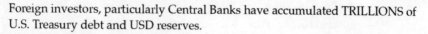

Foreign investors, particularly Central Banks have accumulated TRILLIONS of
U.S. Treasury debt and USD reserves.

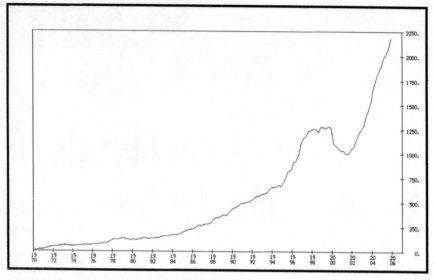

Total U.S. federal debt held by foreign investors in billions of dollars: monthly since 1970

Fiscal "reflation" has been an integral part of the "debasement" of the dollar,
as rabid government spending has resulted in historic fiscal deficits.

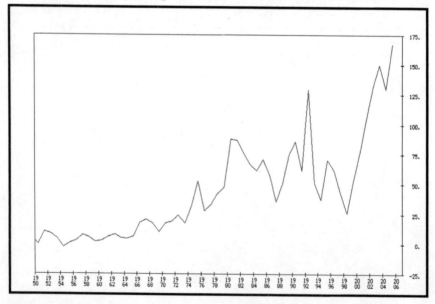

Federal government expenditures: quarterly change at annual rate since 1950

The U.S. Federal Reserve has been complicit in the dollar's debasement, by expanding their own balance sheet at an historic pace. Still, the Fed holds LESS Treasury debt than either the PBOC or the BOJ.

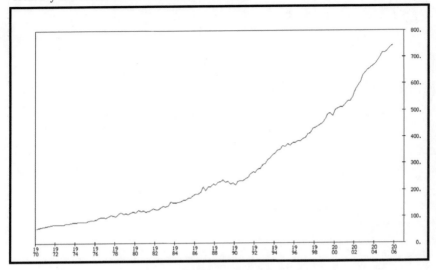

U.S. debt held by U.S. Federal Reserve Banks, total in billions of dollars: monthly since 1970

Source: Chart courtesy of Economagic, LLC. All rights reserved.

Indeed, the Fed has allowed the U.S. monetary base to EXPLODE, with the bulk of the expansion taking place once the Gold Standard was abandoned. This "printing-press-policy" has been a key reason why ALL assets have begun to inflate on a correlated basis, from paper to gold.

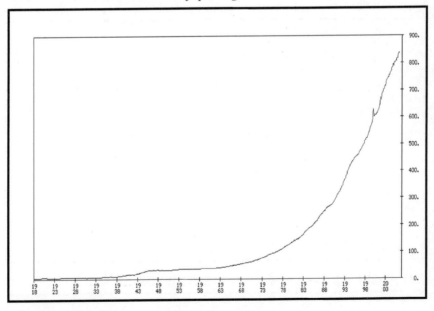

U.S. monetary base total since 1918

Source: Chart courtesy of Economagic, LLC. All rights reserved.

Ever-cheaper credit via the Fed's printing-press-policy has facilitated a housing boom in the United States. Mortgage loans have exploded, with U.S. commercial banks now holding more than $3 TRILLION in real estate loans.

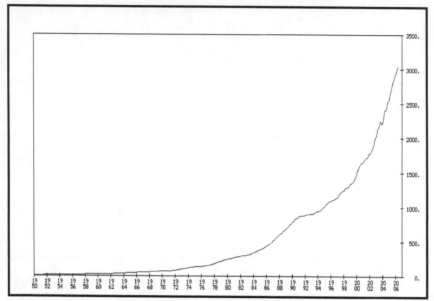

Real estate loans at all commercial banks in billions of dollars since 1950
Source: Chart courtesy of Economagic, LLC. All rights reserved.

It takes a perpetual increase in lending to sustain consumption based on credit creation, as households have now extracted nearly ALL of their paper wealth from housing. If this were an EKG of the consumer, it might suggest a Heart Attack!

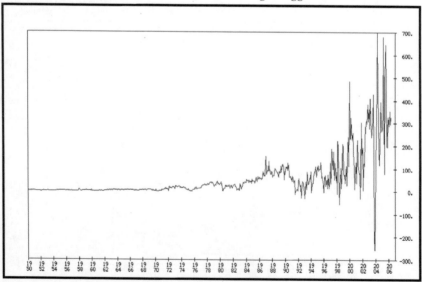

Real estate loans at all commercial banks: weekly change at annualized rate
Source: Chart courtesy of Economagic, LLC. All rights reserved.

Cheap credit has also resulted in a BOOM in new home building, amid a RECORD supply of unsold homes, a supply which is now also rising when measured against (declining) sales. The number of new homes for sale, not yet started has exploded to new record highs.

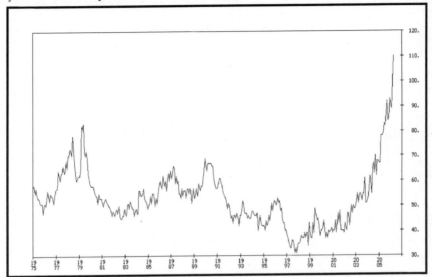

Homes for sale, not yet started (construction): monthly total since 1975
Source: Chart courtesy of Economagic, LLC. All rights reserved.

Sales of new homes has broken down and is violating its secular up trend, in place since the last recession in 1991. With supply on the rise, and sales on the decline, deflation in home prices is becoming an increasingly tangible and dangerous macro-risk.

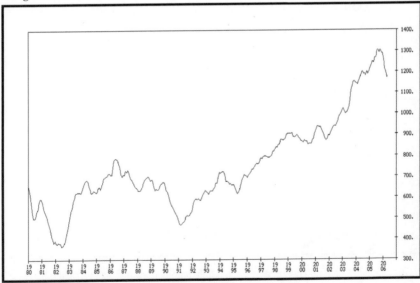

New single-family homes sold: 6-month moving average of SAAR
Source: Chart courtesy of Economagic, LLC. All rights reserved.

Thus, thanks to RECORD supply of unsold homes, and PLUNGING buyer-traffic and sales ... U.S. home prices are disinflating, and, in the near-term have experienced a RECORD degree of price DEFLATION. This is another EKG that points to a consumer Heart Attack evolving.

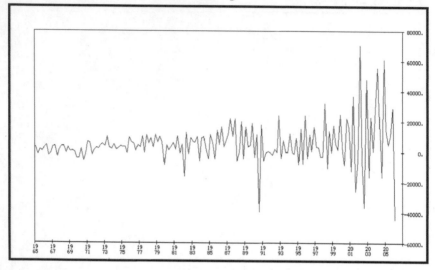

U.S. median home price, homes actually sold: quarterly change at annual rate
Source: Chart courtesy of Economagic, LLC. All rights reserved.

The average debt load being carried by the U.S. consumer/household has also exploded, as home-owners have extracted the majority of their paper wealth reflation via home equity loans. The average single-family mortgage debt has spiked to more than $300,000.

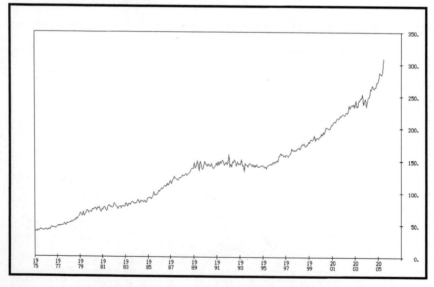

Average conventional mortgage, all single-family homes (new and existing sales): monthly since 1975
Source: Chart courtesy of Economagic, LLC. All rights reserved.

Consumers have expanded their borrowing via direct lending by commercial banks. However, while consumer borrowing has spiked to new heights, there have only been three instances of year-over-year debt pay down since the 1970s, and NONE since 1998/1999.

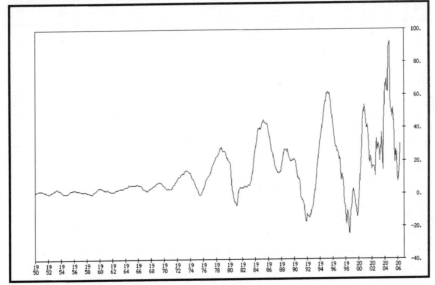

U.S. consumer loans at all commercial banks: actual change in dollars from year-ago
Source: Chart courtesy of Economagic, LLC. All rights reserved.

Subsequently, the Fed-calculated Household Debt Obligations/Disposable Income Ratio has soared to a new all-time high, implying that without perma-paper-wealth-reflation the U.S. consumer is destined to experience some significant macro-turbulence, when debt liquidation begins.

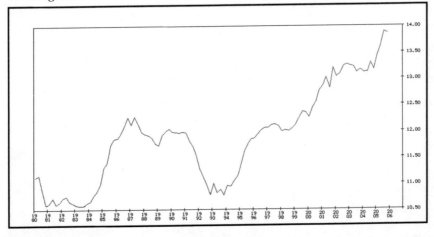

Household debt payments as percent of disposable personal income: quarterly since 1980
Source: Chart courtesy of Economagic, LLC. All rights reserved.

Technologically driven gains in productivity and output efficiency, combined with the globalization of labor markets, has kept wage-induced income gains subdued, creating a missing link in terms of a sustained reflation in wealth AND income. The U.S. labor market is now turning down, implying that the odds of a consumer retrenchment are rising.

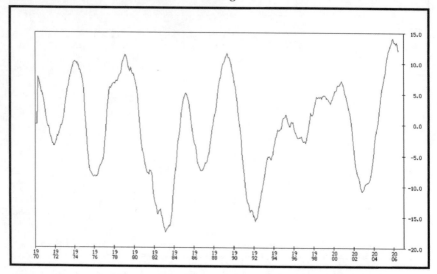

Philly Fed Survey Employment Index, 2-year moving average: monthly since 1970
Source: Chart courtesy of Economagic, LLC. All rights reserved.

Bottom line: the U.S. consumer has NO savings, NO wage-income reflation, NO more paper wealth reflation in housing, and NO more support from fiscal reflation … leaving only TONS of debt.

U.S. personal savings rate: quarterly change, annualized
Source: Chart courtesy of Economagic, LLC. All rights reserved.

Even the paper equity market's recent reflation has been driven by CREDIT expansion, in a way that is eerily similar to the tech-stock bubble of 1997–2000. However, on a longer-term basis, the rate-of-reflation in U.S. stocks has been severely diminished; prices are NOT significantly higher than they were at their 2000–2001, and in some cases, are lower.

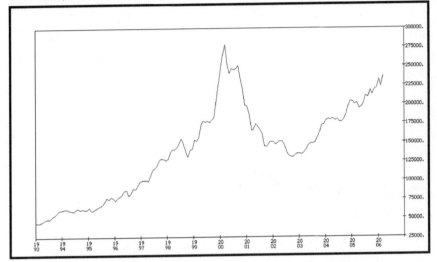

Margin debt balance in NYSE member firm accounts, total in millions of USD
Source: Chart courtesy of Economagic, LLC.

Thanks to EASY money conditions in Europe, a credit BOOM has also evolved in the European Union and United Kingdom, with nominal credit hitting a new all-time high, in line with new highs in the pace of growth, particularly as relates to the European housing market.

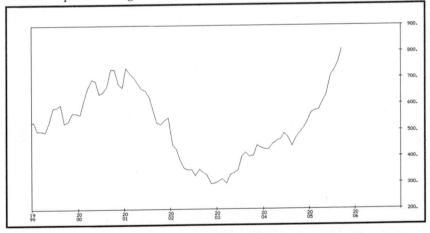

European credit outstanding to area residents, change in EUR from year-ago: monthly since 1999
Source: Chart courtesy of Economagic, LLC.

In August 2005, Gold in EUR was at 360 (EUR per ounce). Since then, amid the explosion of European credit, Gold has rallied more than 50 percent versus the European currency, with a rabid rate-of-change.

Gold priced in EUR: weekly close since 1985
Source: Weldononline.com.

The Chinese currency has appreciated by 30 big figures since it was de-linked from the USD last summer, but the pace is slow relative to the fundamental imbalances. The Chinese currency will be KEY to Gold going forward, as will the actions of the PBOC, as per their reserves.

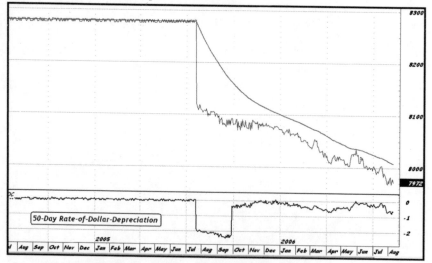

U.S. dollar versus Chinese yuan: daily w/100-day EXP-MA
Source: Weldononline.com.

As reported in August of 2006, Japanese Bank Lending and credit growth have begun expanding again, after YEARS of post-bubble contraction and Gold priced in Japanese Yen has broken out to the upside.

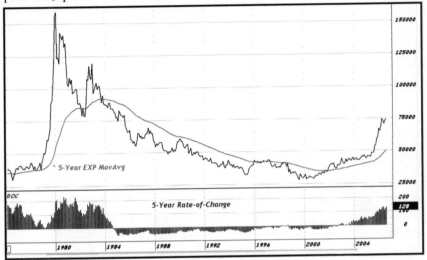

Gold priced in Japanese yen: monthly close since 1975
Source: Weldononline.com.

Many Emerging Market Central Banks have become BUYERS of Gold, rather than USD debt, as paper wealth reflation, commodity reflation, and cheap credit conditions have sparked a BOOM in Emerging Market debt, currencies, and stock indexes.

MSCI Emerging Market Index iShare EEM: daily since 2003
Source: Weldononline.com.

Relative to Fed monetary policy, Gold not only experienced a bull market, but also exploded to new all-time highs above $2,500 per ounce on an equivalent basis. Now, a cessation of Fed tightening might provide the catalyst for a fresh upside breakout.

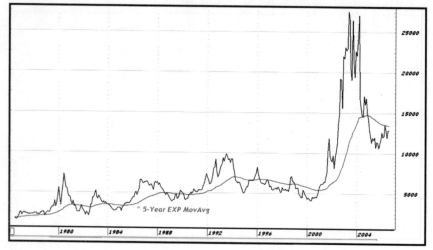

Gold adjusted by U.S. 2-Year T-Note yield: monthly close since 1975
Source: Weldononline.com.

Relative to (still) LOW long-term interest rates, Gold remains near a new all-time high above $1,300 on a relative basis, nearly TWICE the adjusted price seen at the 1980/1981 high—most accurately reflecting the 25-year expansion in money supply, credit, and global capital imbalances.

Gold adjusted by 30-Year T-Note yield: monthly close since 1976
Source: Weldononline.com.

Silver has broken out to the upside relative to Gold, providing bullish-confirmation on a long-term technical basis for the entire complex.

Silver versus gold ratio spread: monthly close

Source: Weldononline.com.

The unhedged gold stocks as defined by the AMEX Gold Bug Index (HUI) have been the stellar performer within the complex and maintain a bullish long-term trend, technically and fundamentally.

AMEX Gold Bug Index (HUI): weekly close since 3Q 1999

Source: Weldononline.com.

At the bottom line, Gold is seen as the ultimate storage vehicle for wealth, and as such, we look for a long-term secular bull market in bullion versus paper equities to extend and intensify. This is a KEY chart.

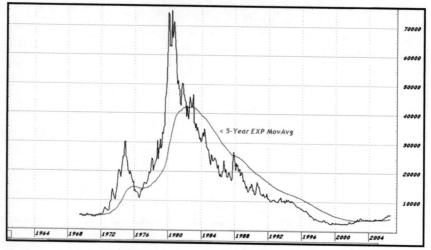

Gold versus Dow Jones Industrial Average ratio spread: monthly close since 1971
Source: Weldononline.com.

Since August of 2005, Gold has FAR out performed the U.S. stock market and has broken out to the upside on a relative basis in the process.

Gold versus Dow Jones Industrial Average ratio spread: weekly close since 3Q 1999
Source: Weldononline.com.

Ultimately, the fate of the U.S. currency hangs in the balance, amid the monetary debasement of the dollar. A breakdown in the U.S. Dollar Index below its secular support line defined just below 80.00 would be very bullish for bullion. Such a move is looking increasingly likely, and thus we remain long-term secular bulls on bullion.

Cash U.S. Dollar Index: monthly since 1977
Source: Weldononline.com.

INDEX